YOUR RIGHTS IN A CLASS ACTION SUIT

by
Margaret C. Jasper

Oceana's Legal Almanac Series:
Law for the Layperson

2005
Oceana Publications, Inc.
Dobbs Ferry, New York

Information contained in this work has been obtained by Oceana Publications from sources believed to be reliable. However, neither the Publisher nor its authors guarantee the accuracy or completeness of any information published herein, and neither Oceana nor its authors shall be responsible for any errors, omissions or damages arising from the use of this information. This work is published with the understanding that Oceana and its authors are supplying information, but are not attempting to render legal or other professional services. If such services are required, the assistance of an appropriate professional should be sought.

Library of Congress Control Number: 2004114433

ISBN 0-379-11388-0

Oceana's Legal Almanac Series: Law for the Layperson
ISSN 1075-7376

Manufactured in the United States of America on acid-free paper.

To My Husband Chris

Your love and support
are my motivation and inspiration

-and-

In memory of my son, Jimmy

Table of Contents

CHAPTER 3:
CERTIFICATION OF THE CLASS

CHAPTER 4:
NOTICE OF CLASS ACTION

CHAPTER 5:
SETTLEMENT

CHAPTER 6:
TYPES OF CLASS ACTION CLAIMS

APPENDICES

ABOUT THE AUTHOR

MARGARET C. JASPER is an attorney engaged in the general practice of law in South Salem, New York, concentrating in the areas of personal injury and entertainment law. Ms. Jasper holds a Juris Doctor degree from Pace University School of Law, White Plains, New York, is a member of the New York and Connecticut bars, and is certified to practice before the United States District Courts for the Southern and Eastern Districts of New York, the United States Court of Appeals for the Second Circuit, and the United States Supreme Court.

Ms. Jasper has been appointed to the panel of arbitrators of the American Arbitration Association and the law guardian panel for the Family Court of the State of New York, is a member of the Association of Trial Lawyers of America, and is a New York State licensed real estate broker and member of the Westchester County Board of Realtors, operating as Jasper Real Estate, in South Salem, New York. Margaret Jasper maintains a website at http://www.JasperLawOffice.com.

Ms. Jasper is the author and general editor of the following legal almanacs: AIDS Law; The Americans with Disabilities Act; Animal Rights Law; The Law of Attachment and Garnishment; Bankruptcy Law for the Individual Debtor; Individual Bankruptcy and Restructuring; Banks and their Customers; Buying and Selling Your Home; The Law of Buying and Selling; The Law of Capital Punishment; The Law of Child Custody; Your Rights in a Class Action Suit; Commercial Law; Consumer Rights Law; The Law of Contracts; Copyright Law; Credit Cards and the Law; The Law of Debt Collection; Dictionary of Selected Legal Terms; The Law of Dispute Resolution; The Law of Drunk Driving; DWI, DUI and the Law; Education Law; Elder Law; Employee Rights in the Workplace; Employment Discrimination Under Title VII; Environmental Law; Estate Planning; Everyday Legal Forms; Executors and Personal Representatives: Rights and Responsibilities; Harassment in the Workplace; Health Care and Your Rights. Home Mortgage Law Primer;

Hospital Liability Law; Identity Theft and How To Protect Yourself; Insurance Law; The Law of Immigration; International Adoption; Juvenile Justice and Children's Law; Labor Law; Landlord-Tenant Law; The Law of Libel and Slander; Living Together: Practical Legal Issues; Marriage and Divorce; The Law of Medical Malpractice; Motor Vehicle Law; The Law of No-Fault Insurance; Nursing Home Negligence; The Law of Obscenity and Pornography; Patent Law; The Law of Personal Injury; Prescription Drugs; Privacy and the Internet: Your Rights and Expectations Under the Law; Probate Law; The Law of Product Liability; Real Estate Law for the Homeowner and Broker; Religion and the Law; Retirement Planning; The Right to Die; Rights of Single Parents; Law for the Small Business Owner; Small Claims Courts; Social Security Law; Special Education Law; The Law of Speech and the First Amendment; Teenagers and Substance Abuse; Trademark Law; Victim's Rights Law; The Law of Violence Against Women; Welfare: Your Rights and the Law; What if it Happened to You: Violent Crimes and Victims' Rights; What if the Product Doesn't Work: Warranties & Guarantees; Workers' Compensation Law; and Your Child's Legal Rights: An Overview.

INTRODUCTION

The class action represents one of the most important developments in contemporary civil litigation in this nation. The modern class action was established in 1966 by a major revision of Rule 23 of the Federal Rules of Civil Procedure, due in large part to the social revolution of the 1960s. During this time period, there were movements which established civil rights and equal protection; addressed environmental issues, including health and safety concerns; gained rights for the consumer; and expanded due process rights.

Along with the creation of these new rights came the problem of enforcing those rights. It was obvious that an individual would not have the financial ability to prosecute a lawsuit against a large corporation who violated his or her rights, nor was it economically feasible for a lawyer to take on such a lawsuit. The advent of the class action allowed individuals with similar complaints to band together, and pool their resources and efforts in order to bring one large action against the more powerful defendant.

This almanac discusses the historical background and purpose of the class action, and explores the necessary prerequisites for bringing a class action in federal and state court. The procedures for initiating the class action, including the requirement of notice, are also explained, as well as the steps one must take when they are notified that they may be a member to a pending class action.

The Appendix provides sample forms, and other pertinent information and data. The Glossary contains definitions of many of the terms used throughout the almanac.

CHAPTER 1:
OVERVIEW OF THE CLASS ACTION

HISTORICAL BACKGROUND

The modern class action has its roots in the English court of chancery during medieval times—a procedure called the bill of peace. The bill of peace permitted individuals who had similar claims and interests to band together in order to enforce their equitable rights, which if left unaddressed would confer immunity on the wrongdoer.

In order to proceed with the bill of peace, the plaintiff had to show that the group of aggrieved individuals had the same interest in the issue to be litigated, and that the parties who were named in the suit would adequately represent all of those individuals' interests. The final judgment rendered by the court would then be binding on the entire group, even if they were not named parties to the suit.

Early American law recognized the availability of a class action to enforce equitable rights, however, when the states began to develop their own codes in the nineteenth century, class actions were expanded to address actions at law in addition to equitable actions.

In 1938, the federal system made law and equity class actions available in the federal courts, and Rule 23 of the Federal Rules of Civil Procedure was established in order to promote the class action device. However, this early version of Rule 23 had a number of drawbacks, and led to arbitrary results because the classes that were formed contained not only common issues but allowed for numerous and substantial individual issues. These problems defeated the goal of judicial economy and a binding resolution on the class, thus a plan to overhaul Rule 23 was initiated.

As more fully discussed in this almanac, in 1966, a completely revised Rule 23 went into effect, focusing on the proper determination of the "class," and its functionality. Many states have since modeled their own class action laws after the revised version of Rule 23.

The text of Rule 23 of the Federal Rules of Civil Procedure is set forth at Appendix 1.

PURPOSE

A class action is a civil lawsuit by or against large numbers of individuals or organizations who have common interests. Permitting a class action is a more efficient procedure designed to adjudicate the rights or liabilities of these individuals or organizations in one large civil action rather than in multiple individual lawsuits. Class actions are used to obtain monetary damages and other relief from the responsible parties.

The class action combines a number of complaints, which have common issues and allege similar facts, into one large, inclusive action. The class action is more expeditious, less costly, and provides certainty in the outcome. It allows one judge to adjudicate all of the claims at the same time instead of having numerous individual complaints filed in different jurisdictions, with different judges and different outcomes.

For example, if thousands of individuals throughout the United States suffered injury as a result of the same defective product, the common issue would be whether that product caused the injuries. Insofar as the principal issue is the same for all of the plaintiffs, it is a much more efficient use of the judicial system to try that issue before one judge in one lawsuit.

Class actions may involve a variety of legal claims, and have been used to bring racial and sexual discrimination cases, toxic tort cases, product liability actions, prescription drug claims, environmental suits, and to address securities and antitrust matters, among other claims.

A list of pending and proposed class actions is set forth at Appendix 2.

ADVANTAGES OF A CLASS ACTION

As set forth above, if individual plaintiffs are required to file separate complaints when their allegations are similar both in law and fact, this is a waste of judicial resources, costly, and risks a variety of outcomes to essentially the same claim. Literally thousands, and possibly millions, of individual actions could overwhelm and paralyze the nation's courts. The class action permits the plaintiffs to file one complaint on behalf of the entire class, and reach one binding resolution on behalf of all.

In many cases, the damages suffered by the individual are too small to justify hiring a lawyer and bringing an individual lawsuit, and an illegal or dangerous business practice would continue unchallenged.

However, when a company's business practices cause the same type of injury to numerous individuals, the damages add up, and suing as a class in order to stop the bad business practices is justified, and encourages the corporate defendant to act in a more responsible manner.

In addition, class actions carry much more weight than individual actions. Class action lawyers are familiar with the process, highly experienced, and bring resources an individual would not be able to match. When faced with a class action, the defendant knows that it has a formidable adversary, making it more likely the business will change its practices. Arguably, this benefits not only the class of plaintiffs, but society as a whole.

> **Example**: John Doe is a small-time dabbler in online stock investments. He purchased 100 shares of stock in an Initial Public Offering (IPO) by ABC Corporation based on a favorable prospectus he read on the company website. He paid $20 per share for a total cost of $2000.
>
> Shortly after John purchased the stock, he learned that ABC Corporation was under investigation for making false statements in its prospectus, and the stock plummeted to $10 per share in a matter of hours. John had relied on the fraudulent prospectus and lost $1000.

If John were to initiate his own action against ABC Corporation to recover his losses, it would cost him far greater than the $1000 he lost. If neither John nor any other stockholders with the same grievance take action, ABC Corporation gets away with defrauding its stockholders without any incentive to change the way it does business.

The class action provides an alternative. Insofar as John is one of many stockholders who suffered similar relatively small losses, combining their claims in a class action strengthens their position and forces ABC Corporation to settle their claims and change its business practices.

DISADVANTAGES OF A CLASS ACTION

The class action has been the source of much controversy, particularly considering the increase in nationwide and multi-district products liability and consumer fraud class actions. Class actions are complex and expensive to prosecute. For example, there are costly and time-consuming pre-certification steps that must be undertaken before there is any guarantee that the class action can go forward.

Corporate America views the class action as a device for lawyers to gather together individual class members with trivial claims and use them as pawns in order to extort settlements. It is argued that the lawyers get paid large legal fees from the settlements for handling the case, but the majority of the aggrieved plaintiffs who make up the class receive nominal damages as part of the settlement. These nominal settlements may be in the form of rebate checks, or discount coupons towards future purchases.

For example, in one class action suit involving disposable contact lenses, the class members received the following nominal settlement:

> **A. COMPENSATION TO CLASS MEMBERS**
>
> 1. Upon presentation of an appropriate proof of claim, for every box of Acuvue® contact lenses purchased between January 1, 1995 and July 31, 2001, each Class Member will receive:
>
> (a) Three dollars ($3.00) in cash;
>
> (b) Three dollars ($3.00) credit towards purchases after July 31, 2001. . .
>
> (c) One dollar ($1.00) cash for the otherwise unreimburseable (i.e. through insurance or other third-party payment) portion of the cost of an examination by a qualified eye care professional. . .

By comparison, the attorneys who prosecuted the same class action received the following compensation:

> **F. ATTORNEYS' FEES, COSTS AND EXPENSES**
>
> Class Counsel have been aggressively prosecuting this case on behalf of the Class since its inception on a contingency basis, without charge to the Class. In addition to the settlement amounts described above, Defendants have also agreed to pay to Class Counsel attorneys' fees and expenses up to $20 million (which includes approximately $3 million in expenses), subject to Court approval of the fees and the Settlement. Such attorneys' fees and expenses as may be awarded by the Court will not reduce the class benefits in any way.

The full text of the above-referenced Notice of Pendency of Class Action, Proposed Class Action Settlement and Settlement Hearing is set forth at Appendix 3.

Another major criticism of the class action is that these suits are often "lawyer driven" without any real clients directing or having substantial input during the litigation phase of the action. Insofar as the "class" is generally not identified until the remedy phase of the action, there is no real "client" to whom the class lawyer must answer during much of the procedure. Although the lead plaintiff is named in the lawsuit, he or she is not usually involved in the prosecution of the class action, which is often left to the lawyers to pursue on behalf of numerous, but yet unknown, class members.

Critics of the class action also argue that class actions permit big businesses to get off without paying enough of a penalty to deter bad business practices, and without having to expend large sums of money in defending numerous individual lawsuits.

CHAPTER 2: CLASS ACTION PREREQUISITES

FEDERAL CLASS ACTIONS

In the 1960's, in order to address the inefficient use of judicial resources in hearing numerous cases based upon the same issues of law and/or fact, the Federal Rules of Civil Procedure were amended and Rule 23 of the Federal Rules which permitted class actions was completely revised. The Federal Rules of Civil Procedure is the body of procedural rules which govern all civil actions in U.S. District Courts and after which most of the states have modeled their own rules of procedure.

The full text of Rule 23 of the Federal Rules of Civil Procedure governing class actions is set forth at Appendix 1.

A major advantage in bringing a federal class action is that it can be brought on behalf of parties who live in different states. Cases pending in different districts can be consolidated and transferred to the Multidistrict Litigation Panel provided the cases involve similar defendants or common liability questions. Multidistrict Litigation is discussed more fully below.

Prerequisites

In order to determine whether a particular case qualifies for federal class action status, it must first be determined whether several procedural prerequisites have been satisfied. Pursuant to Rule 23(a), as further discussed below, the class action must have certain definite characteristics:

1. There must be numerosity—i.e., there must be an adequate number of plaintiffs such that joinder of all members is impracticable;

2. There must be common legal issues and the class members must have sustained common damages;

3. The claims or defenses of the representative parties must be typical of the claims or defenses of the class; and

4. The representative plaintiff must be able to adequately protect and represent the interests of the entire class, and the attorneys representing the plaintiffs must have adequate financial resources to prosecute the class action.

The party seeking to use the class action device has the burden of demonstrating that all of these requirements have been met. Although the judge has broad discretion in determining whether the requirements have been satisfied, if any of these prerequisites are not met, the case cannot proceed as a class action.

Numerosity

The class must be so large that joinder of the claims would be impracticable. Insofar as one of the major reasons for class actions is to preserve judicial resources, it is essential that forming the class will avoid numerous individual lawsuits involving the same claims.

Common Issues of Law or Fact

It is essential that common questions of law or fact exist which connect all of the class members, although all questions of law or fact need not be common in order to proceed. It will suffice if it can be shown that a pattern of activity existed which affected the class members, even if they were affected in different ways.

Typicality

In addition, the claims of the representatives must be typical of the claims of all class members, i.e., they must rely on the same events or legal theory. If the representative's claims are radically different from the class members, this requirement would not be satisfied.

Adequate Representation

At least one of the representatives must be a member of the class. The representative class member is referred to as the "named plaintiff," or the "lead plaintiff." The requirement that there be a named plaintiff reflects the concept that a representative who has a personal interest in the outcome of the litigation will vigorously prosecute the case, and protect the interests of all class members, including absent class members.

If the rights of absent class members are not adequately represented, an individual absent class member can attack the procedure and avoid being bound by the judgment. This would defeat the purpose of the class action device in reducing litigation.

In determining whether there was adequate representation, the court will look at the competence and quality of the representatives and their legal counsel. The lawyer's experience in the particular field of litigation involved in the suit will be examined, as well as the quality of the lawyer's submissions to the court. The representative's motive for bringing the case, as well as their ability to fund the litigation costs, will also be considered. A class action usually requires sufficient financial resources in order to prosecute the claim.

For example, the public must be notified through complex notice requirements, e.g. a notice of class action in order to locate all potential class members; a notice to advise class members of their rights to "opt out" of the class; a notice of settlement of the claim, etc. In a large class action, the notice requirements alone may be so costly that the action cannot be financed.

Maintainable Class Actions

In addition to satisfying the Rule 23(a) prerequisites set forth above, in order to proceed in federal court, the class action must fall within the definition of one of the permissible types of class actions set forth in Rule 23(b):

(1) the prosecution of separate actions by or against individual members of the class would create a risk of:

(A) inconsistent or varying adjudications with respect to individual members of the class which would establish incompatible standards of conduct for the party opposing the class, or

(B) adjudications with respect to individual members of the class which would as a practical matter be dispositive of the interests of the other members not parties to the adjudications or substantially impair or impede their ability to protect their interests; or

(2) the party opposing the class has acted or refused to act on grounds generally applicable to the class, thereby making appropriate final injunctive relief or corresponding declaratory relief with respect to the class as a whole; or

(3) the court finds that the questions of law or fact common to the members of the class predominate over any questions affecting only individual members, and that a class action is superior to other available methods for the fair and efficient adjudication of the controversy. The matters pertinent to the findings include:

(A) the interest of members of the class in individually controlling the prosecution or defense of separate actions;

(B) the extent and nature of any litigation concerning the controversy already commenced by or against members of the class;

(C) the desirability or undesirability of concentrating the litigation of the claims in the particular forum; and

(D) the difficulties likely to be encountered in the management of a class action.

Jurisdiction

A class action may be brought in either Federal or State court. The court must have both subject matter and personal jurisdiction in order to hear the complaint. If the claim involves a federal question or if the parties are located in different states, the plaintiff's attorney may decide to file in Federal court, if the jurisdictional requirements are met, as set forth below.

Federal Question Jurisdiction

In order to bring an action in Federal court based on federal question jurisdiction, the case must arise under the Constitution or federal law. There must be a substantial federal issue raised in the plaintiff's complaint or the complaint will be dismissed. For example, the Federal court would have jurisdiction over class actions alleging federal antritrust violations.

Diversity of Citizenship Jurisdiction

Federal courts also have jurisdiction over cases in which there is diversity of citizenship. Diversity of citizenship exists if:

(1) the plaintiff(s) and defendant(s) are citizens of different states; and

(2) the amount in controversy exceeds the jurisdictional monetary amount—presently $75,000.

There must be complete diversity of citizenship between the parties. For example, in multiparty litigation, the presence of any plaintiff, who is a citizen of the same state as any one of the defendants, will destroy diversity and the case cannot be heard in Federal court.

These rules have raised issues concerning the application of federal subject matter jurisdiction to class actions under Rule 23. It has been held that only the citizenship of the named class representatives should be considered when determining whether there is diversity of the parties. Otherwise, given the number of potential out-of-state class members who may reside in the same state as a defendant, it is likely that many class actions would be rejected on jurisdictional grounds.

Another issue is whether the individual class members must satisfy the jurisdictional amount in controversy requirement, or whether the total amount in controversy claimed by all class members can be pooled together to meet this requirement. According to the most recent decisions of the U.S. Supreme Court, each class member must have a claim that satisfies the jurisdictional amount, unless the class members have a common, undivided interest. This is known as the "no aggregation rule."

The problem with this rule is that individuals with small claims that are not joint or common are unable to proceed with a federal class action even though the totality of the damages suffered by all class members is substantial. Some federal courts have permitted such class actions to proceed based on the concept of supplemental jurisdiction, provided at least one of the class representatives has a claim which satisfies the jurisdictional amount.

STATE CLASS ACTIONS

Governing Law

Following the federal model, many states have amended their laws to permit class actions in state court, and have adopted the same or similar provisions as set forth in the federal rules. Nevertheless, the exact requirements for maintaining a class action varies from state to state, thus the reader is advised to check with the law of his or her own jurisdiction in this regard.

A disadvantage of bringing a class action in state court is that it is difficult to venue a large national class action claim in one state without facing due process problems concerning absent class members. Further, state court judges do not have the experience in handling such complex litigation.

Types of Statutes

Class action statutes differ considerably from state to state. Those states that have modeled their class action statute after the 1966 version of Federal Rule 23 commonly follow the federal requirements for maintaining a class action. Many states provide that those requirements are binding. For example, the following prerequisites for maintaining a class action in New York are nearly identical to the Federal requirements:

1. The class must be so numerous that joinder of all members, whether otherwise required or permitted, is impracticable;

2. There must be questions of law or fact common to the class which predominate over any questions affecting only individual members;

3. The claims or defenses of the representative parties must be typical of the claims or defenses of the class;

4. The representative parties must fairly and adequately protect the interests of the class; and

5. The class action must be superior to other available methods for the fair and efficient adjudication of the controversy.

The text of the law governing class actions in New York is set forth at Appendix 3.

Some states merely set forth a general requirement for the maintenance of a class action:

(1) That the issue is one of common interest of many individuals; and

(2) When the parties are numerous and it is impracticable to join them all before the court, one or more may sue for the benefit of all.

Nevertheless, in both situations, as in the federal requirements, there must be an identifiable class—i.e., although it is not necessary to identify every member of the class specifically in order to proceed, the class must be defined sufficiently enough so that the court is able to easily determine whether an individual qualifies as a member of the class.

Jurisdiction

Due to the limited jurisdiction of Federal court, many class actions must be filed in state courts. Because there are usually numerous absent class plaintiffs from a variety of states, there are due process concerns among state courts that any resulting judgment would not be binding on the absent, out-of-state plaintiffs. There has been an attempt to remedy this problem by instituting procedural protections which give out-of-state class members notice and the opportunity to "opt out" of any binding judgments.

MULTIDISTRICT LITIGATION

When civil actions involving one or more common, and often complex, questions of fact are pending in several different federal district courts, such actions may be transferred by the Judicial panel on Multidistrict Litigation to any one federal district court for coordinated and consolidated management and trial under a single judge pursuant to 28 U.S.C.A. §1407.

The types of cases in which multidistrict litigation is frequently employed include civil antritrust actions; common disaster actions; product liability actions, including pharmaceutical and medical device claims; and securities law violation actions.

Multidistrict litigation is governed by the Manual for Complex Litigation; the Rules of Procedure of the Judicial Panel on Multidistrict Litigation; the Federal Rules of Civil Procedure; and any local rules of the District Court in which the action is transferred.

The Judicial Panel on Multidistrict Litigation

The Judicial Panel on Multidistrict Litigation consists of seven federal judges designated by the Chief Justice of the United States. The Panel is responsible for determining which cases qualify for multidistrict litigation treatment, and where to transfer these cases for consolidation. If the Panel decides that the transfer of cases will be convenient for the parties and witnesses, and will promote judicial expediency and fairness, it will transfer the cases.

All papers filed must be submitted to the Panel at the following address:

Judicial Panel on Multidistrict Litigation
Thurgood Marshall Federal Judiciary Building
One Columbus Circle, N.E., Room G-255, North Lobby
Washington, D.C. 20002-8004
Attn: Clerk of the Panel

Transfers

The Panel may make the decision to transfer cases on its own initiative, or may do so upon a motion by a party in any action in which transfer may be appropriate. However, before transfer can take place, the panel must hold a hearing. All parties are notified of the time and place of the hearing, at which time evidence may be introduced that would assist the Panel in deciding whether transfer is appropriate.

Once a transfer is deemed appropriate, it becomes effective when the Panel files a transfer order in the clerks' office of the designated transferee court. All future submissions related to the case are made in the transferee court. In addition, the attorneys who handled the case in the original court are automatically permitted to continue handling the case in the transferee court without having to obtain local counsel.

Advantages of Multidistrict Litigation

As with a typical class action, multidistrict litigation promotes judicial economy and cuts costs and expenses by consolidating similar cases which may be pending in numerous courts throughout the country. Multidistrict litigation ensures that there will not be conflicting orders or evidentiary standards among jurisdictions concerning the same or similar issues. In addition, discovery can be coordinated more efficiently in multidistrict litigation. For example, witnesses who are common to more than one case need only be deposed one time. Thus, the pre-trial phase of the litigation is more uniform and consistent.

CHAPTER 3: CERTIFICATION OF THE CLASS

FORMING AND IDENTIFYING THE CLASS

A class action starts with one or more plaintiffs who represent an entire class of individuals who have similar complaints, involving similar facts and issues. Before the class action will be allowed to go forward, the class must be identified. It is not necessary that every member of the class be specifically identified in order to proceed with the litigation, however, the class must be defined sufficiently enough so that the court is able to easily determine whether an individual qualifies as a member of the class.

For example, in the class action notice involving disposable contact lenses, previously discussed in Chapter 1, the class was defined as follows:

> [A]ll persons who are residents and domiciliaries of the United States who, between 1993 and the present, purchased disposable contact lenses marketed under the name Acuvue®."

The full text of the above-referenced Notice of Pendency of Class Action, Proposed Class Action Settlement and Settlement Hearing is set forth at Appendix 4.

Obviously, the class must be discernable in order to send out proper notices to all potential class members, and to distribute proceeds of any settlement or judgment. Further, without being able to ascertain whether an individual is a class member or not would make it difficult to determine whether a particular individual is bound by the judgment entered in the action. This could create problems, such as additional litigation of the same or similar claims.

LEAD PLAINTIFF

The class representative who is named in the lawsuit on behalf of the class is known as the "named plaintiff" or "lead plaintiff." In some cases, there may be more than one lead plaintiff. The lead plaintiff, through his or her attorney, makes decisions on how to proceed with the litigation.

The lead plaintiff's claims must be typical of the entire class because he or she is proceeding on behalf of all others "similarly situated" as well as on his or her own behalf. The court generally appoints the lead plaintiff and must determine, as previously discussed, that the lead plaintiff will adequately represent the interests of all class members. Serving as lead plaintiff does not involve a lot of time as the class attorneys are responsible for handling the litigation. Nevertheless, the lead plaintiff usually receives a larger settlement than other class members in return for acting in that capacity.

For example, in the class action notice involving disposable contact lenses, previously discussed in Chapter 1, the lead plaintiffs received the following compensation:

> **G. COMPENSATION TO REPRESENTATIVE PLAINTIFFS**
>
> Defendants will make a cash payment in the amount of $15,000 to each Representative Plaintiff. This amount is over and above the settlement amount to be paid to Class Members and will not reduce the class benefits in any way.

The full text of the above-referenced Notice of Pendency of Class Action, Proposed Class Action Settlement and Settlement Hearing is set forth at Appendix 4.

If a class member wants to participate in the class action as a named party, they must hire an attorney to represent them and intervene in the litigation.

CERTIFICATION PROCEDURE

When the summons and complaint is filed, or shortly thereafter, the plaintiff in a class action usually brings a motion to have the class "certified." The defendant generally opposes the motion to try and stop the class from being certified. If neither party seeks such a determination, the court may do so on its own initiative. It is the court's obligation to make sure that a lawsuit can be maintained as a class action and, pursuant to Federal Rule 23, the court must make the decision whether to certify the action as a class action "at an early practicable time."

In making its decision whether to certify the class action, the court will consider all of the facts and circumstances surrounding the case. Such considerations may include whether there are any pending or related lawsuits. For example, in a securities class action, an underlying investigation by the Securities and Exchange Commission (SEC) may delay certification.

In addition, the court must determine whether all of the class action prerequisites discussed in Chapter 2 have been satisfied. If money damages are being sought, the court will consider whether the common questions of law or fact predominate over individual claims, and whether the class action would impinge upon the individual member's rights to protect their own interests.

The court will also examine the complexity of the case and consider whether the size of the class would make it difficult to manage. If there has already been litigation involving class members, the court will determine whether the action is in an appropriate forum to litigate all of the claims. Finally, the court will consider whether the expected recovery for individual class members if the action is successful justifies the time and expense of administering a class action.

The court has wide discretion on whether to certify a class action, and to decide how the action will proceed. Due to the complexities of class action litigation, the Federal rules contain a list of types of orders that a judge presiding over a class action may issue in order to control and manage the suit. For example, an order certifying a class action must define the class and the class claims, issues, or defenses, and must appoint class counsel under Federal Rule 23(g).

In addition, the judge may order counsel to provide notice to all class members at any step in the litigation, of any issue the court considers important to afford absent class members due process. Further, if the court deems proper, it can issue an order revoking the class action status of the suit and ordering it to proceed as an individual action.

A sample Class Certification Order is set forth at Appendix 5.

CHAPTER 4:
NOTICE OF CLASS ACTION

DUE PROCESS CONCERNS

In the ordinary course of civil litigation, a court does not have jurisdiction over a nonparty, and a judgment cannot be entered either for or against the nonparty. To permit otherwise would be a violation of the nonparty's constitutional right to due process. The essential elements of due process of law are the individual's right to notice and opportunity to be heard and to defend oneself, and the guarantee that every individual has their day in court to do so. Thus, in order for a court to exercise jurisdiction, the person must be a party to the action and must have been properly served with a summons to appear.

The class action, however, is an exception to this general rule because it allows a court to extend jurisdiction over a nonparty without violating that person's right to due process. The class action allows a lawsuit to go forward when there are so many interested persons that it would not be possible to join them all in the suit.

The class attorney and lead plaintiff are primarily responsible for prosecuting the action, and any judgment or settlement is binding on all class members, whether or not they appear or have any involvement in the proceedings or negotiations. Thus, notice of the pending class action litigation and a chance to opt out or otherwise be heard are extremely important to provide some measure of due process to the absent class members.

MANNER AND FORM OF NOTICE

As set forth above, notice is an essential requirement for maintaining a class action. Adequate notice ensures that any resolution of the litigation—e.g., by settlement or judgment—will be binding on all class members. The manner and form of notice, however, is within the court's discretion. For example, notice may be made in writing, by publication, by telephone, or by radio, depending on the facts of the case. The goal is to use a method that will reach as many class members as possible.

A sample Notice of Class Action is set forth at Appendix 6.

MANDATORY NOTICE

Under the federal rules, if an action seeks damages, the mandatory notice provision found in Federal Rule 23 (c)(2) controls. The class members in these types of actions usually have claims that have common issues of law or fact, but the individuals may have different interests in the outcome of the litigation.

Thus, there is concern by the courts as to whether the lead plaintiff's interests and objectives are compatible with the individual absent class members. Notice affords the individual the opportunity to hire an attorney to represent their interests, and/or to exclude themselves from the class so that they are not bound by any settlement or judgment that may not be in their best interest.

The mandatory notice provision set forth in Federal Rule 23 (c)(2) requires "the best notice practicable under the circumstances, including individual notice to all members who can be identified through reasonable effort." The "best notice practicable" does not require that all class members be formally served, but is determined on a case by case basis.

Rule 23 further provides that notice in such cases must concisely and clearly state in plain, easily understood language:

1. The nature of the action;
2. The definition of the class certified;
3. The class claims, issues, or defenses;
4. That a class member may enter an appearance through counsel if the member so desires;
5. That the court will exclude from the class any member who requests exclusion, stating when and how members may elect to be excluded; and
6. The binding effect of a class judgment on class members under Rule 23(c)(3).

Notice may be made by ordinary mail to all identifiable class members, and by publication for class members who cannot be identified through reasonable effort. However, the chosen method of notice must be likely to reach the absent class members. If there is any reasonable way to identify potential class members, individual notice must be given.

For example, if the class action involves securities litigation, all known stockholders must receive individual notification of the class action. Likewise, if the class action involves an overcharge of credit card fees, all credit card holders must receive individual notification of the class action.

When a class is large, the cost of providing individual notice to all identifiable class members may be so expensive as to preclude maintaining a class action. Nevertheless, the Supreme Court has held that this requirement must be followed, and all identifiable class members must receive individual notice.

DISCRETIONARY NOTICE

Under the federal rules, if an action seeks injunctive or declaratory relief, the discretionary notice provision found in Federal Rule 23 (d)(2) controls. Insofar as there are fewer issues that would affect an individual class member in such cases, and it is likely that the lead plaintiff's claim will have the effect of protecting the interests of all class members, the court is less concerned about an individual receiving notice and an opportunity to be heard.

The discretionary notice provision set forth in Federal Rule 23 (d)(2) requires that "notice be given in such manner as the court may direct to some or all of the members of any step in the action, or of the proposed extent of the judgment, or of the opportunity of members to signify whether they consider the representation fair and adequate, to intervene and present claims or defenses, or otherwise to come into the action."

Nevertheless, as a practical matter, whether notice is deemed mandatory or discretionary, some type of notice is usually given to assure that the interests of absent class members are protected.

THE FEDERAL JUDICIAL CENTER (FJC) INITIATIVE ON PLAIN LANGUAGE NOTICES

At the request of the Subcommittee on Class Actions of the U.S. Judicial Branch's Advisory Committee on the Federal Rules of Civil Procedure, the Federal Judicial Center (FJC) developed illustrative notices of proposed class action certification and settlement. The notices were designed to comply with the requirement that class action notices "must concisely and clearly state in plain, easily understood language" specific information about the nature and terms of a class action and how it might affect potential class members' rights.

In order to devise notices that satisfied the requirement, the FJC tested several notices from closed class actions by presenting them to nonlawyers, asking them to point out any unclear terms, and testing their comprehension of various subjects. Through this process, the FJC was able to identify terms that confused nonlawyers, such as "class" and "class action."

The FJC then drafted preliminary illustrative class action notices and forms and tested them before focus groups composed of ordinary citizens from diverse backgrounds. The important challenge is to get potential class members to actually open, read and follow through with any instructions contained in a class action notice.

The testing explored the participants' willingness to open and read a notice as well as their ability to comprehend and follow the information contained in the notice. They found that most focus group participants displayed a very general knowledge of class action lawsuits but were relatively unfamiliar with class action notices. Their expectations were that the notices would be full of "legalese," and difficult to understand. Their impressions towards reading such a document were generally negative and they likened it to "junk mail."

The focus group offered some suggestions that would increase their willingness to open and read a class action notice, such as providing a professional-looking package with a postage stamp rather than a meter mail stamp; a return address from the District Court rather than an attorney's office; and an imprint on the envelope reading "Notice of Proposed Class Action Settlement."

The FJC then conducted a survey comparing the FJC's plain language illustrative notices with comparable notices from closed class action cases. Their finding was that participants who received the FJC's plain language notices exhibited significantly higher comprehension than participants who received the other notices.

The FJC determined that the following elements in a class action notice made it much more likely that a potential class member would read the notice and follow through with the instructions:

1. Non-legal, plain language throughout;
2. Concise opening page making specific points;
3. Detailed table of contents;
4. Question-and-answer format;
5. Summary chart of important information;

6. Color-coded response forms; and

7. Information regarding a contact person, telephone number, and Internet site in the notice's opening page.

As a result of this endeavor, the FJC has posted the newly-revised plain language class action notices on their website for attorneys and judges to use in drafting clear, simple, plain language class action notices. In drafting the illustrative notices, the FJC used three hypothetical cases: (1) a securities case; (2) a products liability case; and (3) an employment discrimination case.

A sample long form full notice, and a sample summary legal publication notice, in a securities class action are set forth at Appendix 7 and 8 respectively.

A sample long form full notice, and a sample summary legal publication notice, in a product liability class action are set forth at Appendix 9 and 10 respectively.

A sample long form full notice and a sample summary legal publication notice, in a employment discrimination class action, are set forth at Appendix 11 and 12 respectively.

WHAT TO DO IF YOU RECEIVE NOTICE OF A CLASS ACTION

Once you receive a notice that you are a potential class member in a pending class action, you generally do not need to do anything to "join" the class. Occasionally, a notice may require a potential class member to file a claim form to "opt in" to the class. It is more likely, however, that you are automatically a member of the class unless you "opt out." If you wish to exclude yourself from the class, the notice provides information on how you can opt out of the class action, as more fully discussed below.

You will not incur any legal fees or expenses by remaining in a class action. The plaintiff's attorney works on a contingency basis and is paid from the proceeds of any settlement or judgment should they prevail. You will share in any such settlement or judgment simply by participating in the class action, and you will also be bound by the results of the litigation.

OPTING OUT

Before the 1966 amendments to Federal Rule 23, it was unclear whether a potential class member had to affirmatively "opt in" to avoid being excluded from a pending class action litigation, or whether potential class members were automatically included in the class unless they "opted out." An "opt in" requirement obviously worked to the disadvantage of numerous potential class members who never received notice of the action and simply may not have known they were entitled to any compensation until it was too late.

In addition, under the old system, one could wait and see whether the outcome was favorable before they decided to participate and, if not, could still bring their own individual action if the statute of limitations had not yet expired. The 1966 amendments to Rule 23 addressed these concerns and clarified the ambiguity by permitting binding judgments on all class members except those who affirmatively "opt out." Therefore, if you receive a class action notice, and you do not want to be part of the litigation, you must opt out by a certain date as described in the notice.

A significant number of class actions involve a large number of small claims that would not be worth the time and expense of litigating individually. For example, a class action may seek recovery of credit card overcharges that amount to less than $100 per individual but, in the aggregate, may add up to a substantial amount of money damages.

Thus, there is really no upside to "opting out" of a class action unless you have a substantial interest in the litigation-e.g., significant damages-and wish to hire an attorney and proceed as a named party in order to protect those interests. You may also wish to opt out if you believe your interests are significantly different from the class, and you do not feel that the lead plaintiffs can adequately represent those interests.

If you have a substantial interest in a class action, it is wise to consult an experienced class action attorney to determine whether opting out of the class would be in your best interests. You should do so as early in the litigation as possible to avoid any statute of limitations problems which would preclude you from filing an action on your behalf.

If you do not "opt out" of the action, and the outcome of the action is favorable, absent class members will still have to identify themselves and present whatever proofs are required to demonstrate that they are entitled to share in any settlement or judgment. Therefore, the problem of identifying and providing notice to all potential class members still presents a hurdle, as shown by the low response rates from absent class members in successful class actions.

WHAT TO DO IF YOU DON'T RECEIVE NOTICE OF A CLASS ACTION

There are literally thousands of class actions pending in the United States against a variety of companies, but many potential class members are not aware that they may be entitled to money or some other type of compensation. It is quite possible that you may be an absent class member without ever receiving any type of notice. As a result, you may not be able to share in any recovery because the class administrator does not know that you exist.

Many class actions are published in the legal notices section of the newspaper, or are broadcast on the radio and television. It is important to be able to recognize these advertisements so you do not forego your fair share of a class action settlement or judgment in which you were entitled to participate. You may discover that a class action in which you may have a claim is either in progress or has already been resolved.

There are also a number of internet-based companies that collect information on class actions and post them to the website on a regular basis. For example, "BigClassAction.com" publishes an alphabetical listing of class actions that are proposed or pending, eligibility requirements, and proposed settlement provisions. They also provide a way for an individual who has a similar complaint to join the class action if they so desire.

In addition, if there is no class action pending or proposed, the website permits the individual to register their complaint on the website to find out if there are other potential plaintiffs who may have the same claim. The information gathered on the website is passed on to law firms who specialize in class actions and offer free evaluations of claims that are registered on the website. The website also provides a list of class action verdicts and settlements.

A list of class action verdicts and settlements involving well-known defendants is set forth at Appendix 13.

CHAPTER 5: SETTLEMENT

COURT APPROVAL

In order to protect the interests of absent class members, any settlement or dismissal of a class action requires court approval. The judge presiding over the class action must approve the fairness and appropriateness of the proposed settlement of the claim. The judge, however, does not engage in the actual settlement negotiations. Once negotiations have been completed, and a settlement agreement has been reached and presented to the court, the judge determines whether the terms of the agreement are fair and in the best interests of the class members.

In making this determination, the judge will consider certain factors including:

1. Whether the class would have ultimately succeeded in the litigation, and the amount the class could have recovered if successful compared to the amount of the settlement;

2. Whether there has been adequate notice of the proposed settlement to absent class members and whether there are any objections to the proposed settlement;

3. The complexity of the litigation and the costs that would be required to proceed; and

4. The proposed plan to distribute the settlement and the likelihood the plan will be successful.

Notice of the proposed settlement must be given to the class members, who are then entitled to object to the settlement if they disagree with the terms. Some class actions settle within 1 year of being initiated, however, most take considerably longer.

BINDING EFFECT

The disposition of the class action, either by settlement or judgment, binds both the lead plaintiffs and all other individuals who were included in the class, provided all of the requirements for maintaining the class action have been met. An absent class member will not be bound by the decree, however, if he or she can show that there was insufficient notice or that representation was inadequate. In addition, the disposition does not bind any individual plaintiff who "opted out" of the class, as discussed in Chapter 4 of this almanac.

PAYMENT OF LEGAL FEES

Attorneys representing class action plaintiffs are paid on a contingency basis, meaning they do not receive a fee unless the case is successful. Considering the complexities of class action litigation, and the enormous costs associated with prosecuting a class action, the lawyer often risks a lot of money in bringing such a claim. Nevertheless, as discussed below, class action legal fees are the subject of much criticism given the explosion of class action filings over the last decade.

Generally, the attorney submits a fee petition to the court, which sets forth details of all of the work undertaken in connection with handling the class action. The class members are afforded an opportunity to comment on the proposed fee award. The court must then approve the legal fee, which must be fair and equitable considering all of the facts and circumstances.

In deciding whether a proposed fee is fair and equitable, the court will consider certain factors including:

1. The number of hours spent working on the case;
2. The complexity of the case;
3. The quality of the attorney's work; and
4. The risk involved in taking the case and the result achieved.

Once the court is satisfied that the legal fee is fair and equitable, it will enter an order awarding the attorney his or her legal fees. If the class action does not seek money damages, but involves injunctive or declaratory relief, the lawyers may be paid by the plaintiff that hired them or by the defendant, if the plaintiff prevails.

THE ROLE OF THE FEDERAL TRADE COMMISSION

The Federal Trade Commission (FTC) has an interest in class action issues. The FTC shares antitrust jurisdiction with the Department of Justice and has primary responsibility for enforcing federal laws prohibiting false and defective practices. The FTC's enforcement undertakings are supplemented by an extensive consumer education program to assist it in its efforts to compensate injured consumers and punish or deter wrongful conduct.

Insofar as the FTC is responsible for consumer protection, it recognizes the value of private litigation, including class actions, in compensating injured consumers. However, it is also concerned with class action settlements that do not adequately compensate injured consumers, e.g., by providing class members with worthless coupons while the class action lawyers receive substantial monetary compensation.

In addition, the FTC has an interest in making sure that the recoveries are fair and adequate, and that the consumer does not ultimately bear the burden for "overdeterrence" in the form of unfairly large verdicts or settlements. On one hand, companies that engage in bad business practices must be deterred. On the other hand, class action settlements that are too large increase the cost of doing business, a cost that is ultimately passed on to the consumer.

Thus, the FTC has expressed its views in class actions generally, and in specific class action settlements, in a variety of ways. They have issued informal comments in interviews, speeches and consumer education pamphlets, and more formal comments in submissions to the Judicial Conference, Congress, and in amicus briefs submitted in judicial proceedings.

The FTC's comments to the Judicial Conference support amendments to Rule 23, and endorse a proposal that would provide a more competitive process for selection of class counsel. They also support "mutual notification," so that a class action court would be aware of the FTC's involvement in a similar matter, and vice-versa. The comments also caution that courts should review coupon settlements with particular care to ensure that the coupons are properly valued when calculating attorney fees; that they are not unreasonably difficult to use; and that they do not simply create bonus sales for the defendant that will undermine the deterrent aspect of the settlement.

The FTC's amicus briefs to the courts in class action suits routinely address two problems in particular concerning specific class actions: (1) excessive awards of attorney fees; and (2) non-monetary settlements, e.g. coupon settlements. On a case-by-case basis, they argue whether the proposed compensation is of any real value to the consumer, and whether excessive legal fees directly diminish the total compensation available for injured consumers.

COLLUSIVE SETTLEMENTS

There is much concern that class actions are "lawyer driven," as discussed in Chapter 1 of this almanac. The fact that there are no actual plaintiffs during the litigation phase of the class action encourages collusive settlements between class counsel and defendant's counsel. There is concern that the injured class members do not receive anything of real value in many of the settlements, while the lawyers receive excessive fees.

This, in turn, provides an incentive for more and more class actions being brought by lawyers whose real interest is in obtaining large fee awards rather than in obtaining redress for the injured class members. In addition, when response rates to class action notices are low, and thus actual payouts are expected to be low, there is the potential for a substantial pool of unclaimed funds which can be split between plaintiffs' lawyers and the defendants.

COUPON SETTLEMENTS

As discussed above, the use of coupons as compensation to injured consumers in class actions has been criticized. A coupon settlement is one in which the class member receives a discount on future purchases from the defendant instead of a cash award. Critics of coupon settlements argue that these types of settlements are being overused in class actions, and the only ones who really benefit are the defendants and the plaintiffs' lawyer.

For example, a defendant may agree to offer discount coupons as compensation because they expect a low payout;—a small percentage of the coupons will actually be redeemed. In addition, those coupons that are used will generate future sales for the defendant. Thus, the defendant's net loss is low and the deterrent factor is minimal. Plaintiffs' lawyers may agree to settle for coupons that offer very little compensation to the class members provided the coupons appear valuable enough on their face to garner large fee awards for the attorneys.

CHAPTER 6:
TYPES OF CLASS ACTION CLAIMS

IN GENERAL

The list of pending and proposed class actions set forth at Appendix 2 demonstrates the variety of claims that are brought in the context of a class action. Claims include but are not limited to defective products; toxic torts; discrimination; price-fixing; employee wage and benefit claims; prescription drug and medical device claims; unfair business practices; credit card overcharges; overbilling; deceptive advertising; environmental claims, and numerous other types of complaints brought on behalf of classes of individuals who have been similarly affected.

Class actions seek all types of relief, including compensatory money damages; punitive damages; lost wages; injunctive relief; as well as attorneys' fees and litigation costs. This chapter discusses several common types of class action lawsuits.

SECURITIES CLASS ACTIONS

In General

A securities class action is a lawsuit which is brought on behalf of a group of investors who have suffered economic damages as a result of stock fraud or a violation of securities laws. For example, if a group of investors purchase stock in a company as a result of the company's fraudulent press release that causes the stock to rise, and the falsity of the press release comes to light causing the stock to drop, those investors have suffered economic damages. Of course, the amount of damages suffered by each individual stockholder depends on the number of shares he or she purchased.

A copy of the securities class action complaint against Critical Path, Inc. is set forth at Appendix 14.

The Lead Plaintiff in a Securities Case

A securities class action is brought by one or more named plaintiffs—referred to as the lead plaintiffs—on behalf of the rest of the class members who have suffered financial losses as a result of the fraud or other violation. According to the Private Securities Litigation Reform Act of 1995, the most adequate Lead Plaintiff is the person or group of persons who the court determines, has the "largest financial interest" in the relief sought by the class. For example, this may be the individual who has lost the most money as a result of the alleged violation.

There is a deadline, known as the "Lead Plaintiff Deadline," during which applications for Lead Plaintiff must be filed. In a securities class action, the Lead Plaintiff Deadline is the sixty-day period after the securities class action has been filed. Thus, anyone wishing to serve as Lead Plaintiff in a securities case should contact the class lawyer early on in the litigation.

The Class Period

The "class period" refers to the time period during which it is alleged that the fraud or securities violation caused the price of the stock to be artificially inflated. In the above example, it would be the period between the time the press release was announced that caused the stock price to rise, and when the fraud was discovered, causing the price to drop.

Only those investors who purchased the stock during that time period are included in the class action. Also, it is not necessary for the investor to have retained the stock after the class period ended in order to be a member of the class action.

Pending Litigation

Class members other than the Lead Plaintiff generally do not receive regular reports concerning the pending litigation. However, all class members receive notification of any significant developments that take place during the course of the litigation.

Recovery of Damages

It takes approximately two to three years to resolve a securities class action. A favorable outcome would be in the form of a settlement or judgment. If the class action does not succeed, the claims will be dismissed. A settlement generally consists of the payment of cash and/or stock. The settlement is pooled into a common fund, and is then distributed to the class members proportionately depending on how much they lost.

After the case is settled, the class members will receive a notice from the class administrator requesting proof of the number of shares of stock they purchased. Class members can submit the confirmation slips provided at the time of purchase, or copies of their brokerage statements, as proof of ownership.

Legal Fees

As with any class action, the attorneys in a securities class action are generally paid pursuant to a court order provided they prevail in the action. The attorneys submit a fee petition setting forth all of the work they performed in the litigation. The court reviews the fee petition and enters an order establishing a percentage of the gross settlement as the legal fee, e.g. 25 to 30%.

The Securities Litigation Reform Act of 1995

In 1995, Congress passed The Securities Litigation Reform Act. The Act was designed to deter frivolous and abusive "lawyer driven" class actions and create uniformity in the way courts handle securities fraud claims. The Act was intended to reduce the cost of settling frivolous claims by encouraging the courts to dismiss such cases in the early stages of litigation. For example, the complaint must meet a "heightened pleading standard." In addition, discovery cannot proceed while a motion to dismiss the action based on an inadequate complaint is pending.

The heightened pleading standard requires that the complaint "state with particularity facts giving rise to a strong inference that the defendant acted with the required state of mind." Courts have interpreted this standard in different ways. Some courts have ruled that there must be evidence of intent, i.e.,—deliberate reckless or conscious misconduct. Other courts have upheld complaints that merely plead that the defendant had "motive and opportunity."

The text of the Securities Litigation Reform Act is set forth at Appendix 15.

DISCRIMINATION

Class actions are often brought on behalf of groups of individuals who allege that they have suffered discrimination in violation of state and/or federal law. Such actions may be brought in Federal court, which would have subject matter jurisdiction over cases involving violations of Title VII of the Civil Rights Act of 1964 which, along with other Federal laws, prohibits discrimination on the basis of race, national origin, gender, age and disability.

Wal-Mart Litigation

In 2001, a gender discrimination class action was filed in a California Federal District Court against Wal-Mart Stores by six female Wal-Mart employees "on behalf of themselves and all other similarly situated." The complaint alleges that the named plaintiffs, and over 700 potential class members, have been the subject of gender discrimination in that Wal-Mart (1) advances male employees much more quickly than female employees; (2) denies female employees equal job assignments, promotions, training and compensation; and (3) retaliates against those who oppose the illegal practices.

The complaint details specific allegations of discrimination suffered by the named plaintiffs. Damages sought include compensatory money damages; punitive damages; lost wages and benefits; reinstatement and promotion; injunctive relief; and attorneys' fees and litigation costs.

A copy of the employment discrimination class action complaint against Wal-Mart is set forth at Appendix 16.

BREACH OF CONTRACT ACTIONS

A class action may also be brought to enforce a right under a contract. For example, in a class action brought against State Farm Insurance Company, the complaint alleges that individuals insured by State Farm paid for and received policies providing that, in case of an accident, vehicles would be restored to their pre-loss condition using parts of "like kind and quality." The complaint further alleges that, contrary to this policy provision, wrecked vehicles were being repaired using inferior, substandard imitation crash parts.

The class representatives were individuals whose vehicles were wrecked and repaired using the inferior parts. It was alleged that it was common practice for State Farm to require the use of inferior parts, therefore, the plaintiffs sought to have a class action certified, on behalf of all policyholders nationwide. The class was defined as follows:

> "All persons in the United States, except those residing in Arkansas and Tennessee, who (1) were insured by a vehicle casualty insurance policy issued by Defendant State Farm; and (2) made a claim for vehicle repairs pursuant to their policy and had imitation, that is, non-factory-authorized and/or non-OEM parts installed in their vehicles or else received monetary compensation determined in relation to the cost of imitation parts."

The plaintiffs requested an order certifying the class and appointing plaintiffs and their attorney to represent the class. They further sought an award of compensatory damages and monetary relief; a declaratory judgment of the rights of the class and obligations under the State

Farm policies; injunctive relief preventing State Farm from using inferior parts to repair wrecked vehicles; and attorneys fees and costs.

A copy of the breach of contract class action complaint against State Farm is set forth at Appendix 17.

PHARMACEUTICAL AND MEDICAL DEVICE CASES

The class action device is often utilized in pharmaceutical drug and medical device litigation. Class actions have been brought against the manufacturers of medical devices such as hip replacements; contraceptive intrauterine devices (IUDs); penile implants; heart valves; silicone breast implants, etc.

Many more class actions have been filed by classes of persons alleging injuries from prescription drugs, such as the Phen Phen diet drugs; Rezulin; and Paxil, among others. In addition, class actions have also been filed against the manufacturers of certain non-prescription drugs.

Certification Issues

The courts are particularly careful when certifying a class action in a pharmaceutical or medical device case because such cases attract thousands of potential claimants who may not be able to demonstrate that they have suffered any injury from the particular drug or device. Their only claim to recovery may be an emotional distress claim over fear of future injury, or a claim for medical monitoring for future injuries. Plaintiffs who have serious injuries may be better advised to bring individual actions so as to avoid their claims from being weakened within the context of the class action.

The Court must carefully scrutinize the defined "class" in a pharmaceutical or medical device case. If it is defined as including all persons who have been prescribed and have used a particular drug or medical device, then it may include large numbers of people who have suffered no injury whatsoever. If the class is defined as including all persons who have been injured by the drug or device, it may be very difficult to identify the class prior to certification. If the class members cannot be identified, a class action cannot go forward because it fails to satisfy the "numerosity" requirement for certification.

Critics of these class actions argue that the result of certification could be catastrophic for drug companies because any verdict involving so many plaintiffs would likely far outweigh the actual merit of the claims. In addition, the certification of the class, and the notice requirements which follow, would most certainly have a negative impact on the defendant company and its product, even before there has been any finding of wrongdoing by the company.

Further, it may turn out that the Court will decide to decertify the class at some future point if it finds that the class allegations were improperly presented. Unfortunately, by that time it is likely too late to undo the damage caused by the publicity of the initial filing.

Paxil Litigation

A class action filed in 2001 against Glaxosmithkline, a large pharmaceutical manufacturer, is representative of a prescription drug class action complaint. The Glaxosmithkline Complaint alleged causes of action for (1) fraud and deceit; (2) negligence; (3) strict liability; (4) breach of express warranty; and (5) breach of implied warranty. There were approximately 35 named plaintiffs who sued Glaxosmithkline "on behalf of themselves and all other persons similarly situated."

The class action was brought in California State court based on the defendant's activities in the State of California. The class was defined as "all former or present Paxil patients who, after December 29, 1992, suffered or continue to suffer from withdrawal reactions following reduction or termination of their Paxil dosage."

In order to satisfy the numerosity requirement for class certification, as discussed above, the class attorney stated that, in addition to the named plaintiffs, over 1000 persons had registered drug withdrawal complaints to Glaxosmithkline on the internet, providing their contact information and detailed commentary, and at least 500 individuals contacted the class attorneys with similar allegations.

Damages sought include compensatory money damages; punitive damages; injunctive relief; and attorneys' fees and litigation costs.

A copy of the pharmaceutical class action complaint against Glaxosmithkline is set forth at Appendix 18.

MASS TORT LITIGATION

In General

A mass tort refers to a tort claim involving multiple parties. The "tort" may involve, for example, personal injuries suffered by numerous plaintiffs as a result of a defective product, or a mass disaster in which there were many injured persons, such as an airplane crash. Due to the sheer number of injured plaintiffs, such mass torts are often certified as class actions provided they meet all of the prerequisites discussed in Chapter 2 of this almanac.

History of Mass Tort Litigation

Forty years ago, courts were more reluctant to certify mass tort cases as class actions due, in large part, to the individual nature of the injuries. In the 1980s, federal courts began to certify mass tort class actions out of necessity, particularly insofar as there were thousands of asbestos-related lawsuits pending at that time. The courts could not reasonably accommodate that many individual lawsuits, which would be introducing the same witnesses and evidence over and over. Thus, it was determined that the class action was clearly the more superior and expeditious means to resolving the asbestos claims.

The asbestos cases began a trend in certifying class actions in mass tort litigation. Soon after, the court certified a class of soldiers and their families who suffered injuries as a result of exposure to the herbicide known as Agent Orange. A variety of mass tort class actions followed throughout the country involving product liability, pharmaceuticals, toxic torts, medical device litigation, etc. The filing of mass tort class actions has continued and many have been successfully resolved.

APPENDIX 1: RULE 23—FEDERAL RULES OF CIVIL PROCEDURE

RULE 23. CLASS ACTIONS

(a) Prerequisites to a Class Action.

One or more members of a class may sue or be sued as representative parties on behalf of all only if (1) the class is so numerous that joinder of all members is impracticable, (2) there are questions of law or fact common to the class, (3) the claims or defenses of the representative parties are typical of the claims or defenses of the class, and (4) the representative parties will fairly and adequately protect the interests of the class.

(b) Class Actions Maintainable.

An action may be maintained as a class action if the prerequisites of subdivision (a) are satisfied, and in addition:

(1) the prosecution of separate actions by or against individual members of the class would create a risk of:

(A) inconsistent or varying adjudications with respect to individual members of the class which would establish incompatible standards of conduct for the party opposing the class, or

(B) adjudications with respect to individual members of the class which would as a practical matter be dispositive of the interests of the other members not parties to the adjudications or substantially impair or impede their ability to protect their interests; or

(2) the party opposing the class has acted or refused to act on grounds generally applicable to the class, thereby making appropriate final injunctive relief or corresponding declaratory relief with respect to the class as a whole; or

(3) the court finds that the questions of law or fact common to the members of the class predominate over any questions affecting only

individual members, and that a class action is superior to other available methods for the fair and efficient adjudication of the controversy. The matters pertinent to the findings include:

(A) the interest of members of the class in individually controlling the prosecution or defense of separate actions;

(B) the extent and nature of any litigation concerning the controversy already commenced by or against members of the class;

(C) the desirability or undesirability of concentrating the litigation of the claims in the particular forum;

(D) the difficulties likely to be encountered in the management of a class action.

(c) Determining by Order Whether to Certify a Class Action; Appointing Class Counsel; Notice and Membership in Class; Judgment; Multiple Classes and Subclasses.

(1) (A) When a person sues or is sued as a representative of a class, the court must, at an early practicable time, determine by order whether to certify the action as a class action.

(B) An order certifying a class action must define the class and the class claims, issues, or defenses, and must appoint class counsel under Rule 23(g).

(C) An order under Rule 23(c)(1) may be altered or amended before final judgment.

(2) (A) For any class certified under Rule 23(b)(1) or (2), the court may direct appropriate notice to the class.

(B) For any class certified under Rule 23(b)(3), the court must direct to class members the best notice practicable under the circumstances, including individual notice to all members who can be identified through reasonable effort. The notice must concisely and clearly state in plain, easily understood language:

the nature of the action,

the definition of the class certified,

the class claims, issues, or defenses,

that a class member may enter an appearance through counsel if the member so desires,

that the court will exclude from the class any member who requests exclusion, stating when and how members may elect to be excluded, and the binding effect of a class judgment on class members under Rule 23(c)(3).

(3) The judgment in an action maintained as a class action under subdivision (b)(1) or (b)(2), whether or not favorable to the class, shall include and describe those whom the court finds to be members of the class. The judgment in an action maintained as a class action under subdivision (b)(3), whether or not favorable to the class, shall include and specify or describe those to whom the notice provided in subdivision (c)(2) was directed, and who have not requested exclusion, and whom the court finds to be members of the class.

(4) When appropriate (A) an action may be brought or maintained as a class action with respect to particular issues, or (B) a class may be divided into subclasses and each subclass treated as a class, and the provisions of this rule shall then be construed and applied accordingly.

(d) Orders in Conduct of Actions.

In the conduct of actions to which this rule applies, the court may make appropriate orders:

(1) determining the course of proceedings or prescribing measures to prevent undue repetition or complication in the presentation of evidence or argument;

(2) requiring, for the protection of the members of the class or otherwise for the fair conduct of the action, that notice be given in such manner as the court may direct to some or all of the members of any step in the action, or of the proposed extent of the judgment, or of the opportunity of members to signify whether they consider the representation fair and adequate, to intervene and present claims or defenses, or otherwise to come into the action;

(3) imposing conditions on the representative parties or on intervenors;

(4) requiring that the pleadings be amended to eliminate therefrom allegations as to representation of absent persons, and that the action proceed accordingly;

(5) dealing with similar procedural matters. The orders may be combined with an order under Rule 16, and may be altered or amended as may be desirable from time to time.

(e) Settlement, Voluntary Dismissal, or Compromise.

(1) (A) The court must approve any settlement, voluntary dismissal, or compromise of the claims, issues, or defenses of a certified class.

(B) The court must direct notice in a reasonable manner to all class members who would be bound by a proposed settlement, voluntary dismissal, or compromise.

(C) The court may approve a settlement, voluntary dismissal, or compromise that would bind class members only after a hearing and on finding that the settlement, voluntary dismissal, or compromise is fair, reasonable, and adequate.

(2) The parties seeking approval of a settlement, voluntary dismissal, or compromise under Rule 23(e)(1) must file a statement identifying any agreement made in connection with the proposed settlement, voluntary dismissal, or compromise.

(3) In an action previously certified as a class action under Rule 23(b)(3), the court may refuse to approve a settlement unless it affords a new opportunity to request exclusion to individual class members who had an earlier opportunity to request exclusion but did not do so.

(4)(A) Any class member may object to a proposed settlement, voluntary dismissal, or compromise that requires court approval under Rule 23(e)(1)(A).

(B) An objection made under Rule 23(e)(4)(A) may be withdrawn only with the court's approval.

(f) Appeals.

A court of appeals may in its discretion permit an appeal from an order of a district court granting or denying class action certification under this rule if application is made to it within ten days after entry of the order. An appeal does not stay proceedings in the district court unless the district judge or the court of appeals so orders.

(g) Class Counsel.

(1) Appointing Class Counsel.

(A) Unless a statute provides otherwise, a court that certifies a class must appoint class counsel.

(B) An attorney appointed to serve as class counsel must fairly and adequately represent the interests of the class.

(C) In appointing class counsel, the court

(i) must consider:

the work counsel has done in identifying or investigating potential claims in the action,

counsel's experience in handling class actions, other complex litigation, and claims of the type asserted in the action, counsel's knowledge of the applicable law, and

the resources counsel will commit to representing the class;

(ii) may consider any other matter pertinent to counsel's ability to fairly and adequately represent the interests of the class;

(iii) may direct potential class counsel to provide information on any subject pertinent to the appointment and to propose terms for attorney fees and nontaxable costs; and

(iv) may make further orders in connection with the appointment.

(2) Appointment Procedure.

(A) The court may designate interim counsel to act on behalf of the putative class before determining whether to certify the action as a class action.

(B) When there is one applicant for appointment as class counsel, the court may appoint that applicant only if the applicant is adequate under Rule 23(g)(1)(B) and (C). If more than one adequate applicant seeks appointment as class counsel, the court must appoint the applicant best able to represent the interests of the class.

(C) The order appointing class counsel may include provisions about the award of attorney fees or nontaxable costs under Rule 23(h).

(h) Attorney Fees Award.

In an action certified as a class action, the court may award reasonable attorney fees and nontaxable costs authorized by law or by agreement of the parties as follows:

(1) Motion for Award of Attorney Fees.

A claim for an award of attorney fees and nontaxable costs must be made by motion under Rule 54(d)(2), subject to the provisions of this subdivision, at a time set by the court. Notice of the motion must be served on all parties and, for motions by class counsel, directed to class members in a reasonable manner.

(2) Objections to Motion.

A class member, or a party from whom payment is sought, may object to the motion.

(3) Hearing and Findings.

The court may hold a hearing and must find the facts and state its conclusions of law on the motion under Rule 52(a).

(4) Reference to Special Master or Magistrate Judge.

The court may refer issues related to the amount of the award to a special master or to a magistrate judge as provided in Rule 54(d)(2)(D).

RULE 23.1. DERIVATIVE ACTIONS BY SHAREHOLDERS

In a derivative action brought by one or more shareholders or members to enforce a right of a corporation or of an unincorporated association, the corporation or association having failed to enforce a right which may properly be asserted by it, the complaint shall be verified and shall allege:

(1) that the plaintiff was a shareholder or member at the time of the transaction of which the plaintiff complains or that the plaintiff's share or membership thereafter devolved on the plaintiff by operation of law, and

(2) that the action is not a collusive one to confer jurisdiction on a court of the United States which it would not otherwise have.

The complaint shall also allege with particularity the efforts, if any, made by the plaintiff to obtain the action the plaintiff desires from the directors or comparable authority and, if necessary, from the shareholders or members, and the reasons for the plaintiff's failure to obtain the action or for not making the effort.

The derivative action may not be maintained if it appears that the plaintiff does not fairly and adequately represent the interests of the shareholders or members similarly situated in enforcing the right of the corporation or association.

The action shall not be dismissed or compromised without the approval of the court, and notice of the proposed dismissal or compromise shall be given to shareholders or members in such manner as the court directs.

RULE 23.2. ACTIONS RELATING TO UNINCORPORATED ASSOCIATIONS

An action brought by or against the members of an unincorporated association as a class by naming certain members as representative parties may be maintained only if it appears that the representative parties will fairly and adequately protect the interests of the association and its members. In the conduct of the action the court may make appropriate orders corresponding with those described in Rule 23(d), and the procedure for dismissal or compromise of the action shall correspond with that provided in Rule 23(e).

APPENDIX 2: LIST OF PENDING/ PROPOSED CLASS ACTIONS

DEFENDANT	CLAIMS
12 Michigan Cities	illegal tax on cable users
19 Corporations	profiting from slavery
33 Banks	funding Saddam Hussein
3M Co., AL	damaging chemicals
3M Co., MN	PFC air contamination
7-Eleven Inc. and MDK, IN	leaking benzene vapors
Abbott Laboratories	increasing price of Norvir
Abercrombie & Fitch	discrimination
Abercrombie & Fitch	unpaid overtime
Aetna Health Inc. et al, price fixing	KY
AFSCME	union dues collected from non-union workers
Agilent Technologies and Hewlett-Packard	ERISA
Air Canada	employee benefits
AK Steel Corp.	discrimination in hiring practices
Alaska Communications Systems	violated calling plan terms
Alcohol Companies	marketing to minors
Allegheny General Hospital	exposure to drug-resistant bacteria
Allstate Corp.	age discrimination
Allstate Indemnity Company and Deerbrook Insurance Company	denying payment for MRIs
Al Qaeda	Bali victims
American Airlines, United Airlines and Boeing	cockpit doors did not withstand hijacking

DEFENDANT	CLAIMS
American Airlines	allegedly transmitting private information to third parties
American Airlines	keeping surcharges
American Airlines	loss of vacation time
American Business Financial Services	predatory lending
American Express Co.	charging for magazines not ordered
American Express Publishing Corp.	unfair business practices
American Express Publishing Corp. and Rodale Inc.	unfair business practices
American Express	charging late fees - Canada
American Express	unfair business practices
American Honda Finance Corporation, WFS Financial, Inc.; and Toyota Motor Credit Corporation	loan discrimination
American Honda Motor Corporation	defective CR-Vs
American Investors Life Insurance Company	selling inappropriate policies to seniors
American National Can Co.	employee benefits
AmerisourceBergen	selling recycled drugs
Anthem Inc.	medical billing
AOL Time Warner's America Online	charging for items not ordered
AOL	overbilling customers
AON Services Corp. & Cambridge Integrated Services Group, Claim Adjusters	overtime
Arcola Livestock Sales Ltd.	non-payment of calves sold at auction
AstraZeneca PLC	Seroquel diabetes onset
AT & T Wireless, TX	non-payment of overtime
AT & T Wireless	deceptive advertising
AT & T	refusing to forgive charges made by scammers
Auto Insurance Companies	not properly compensating doctors
Aventis, LA	environment
Aventis Pasteur, Canada	Thimerasol in vaccines causes autism
Baltimore City et al.	amber lights
Bank of America	breach of fiduciary duty

DEFENDANT	CLAIMS
Bank of America	mishandling trust accounts
Bank of America, Wells Fargo	$5 check cashing fee
Bank of Canada	breach of pension contract
Barclays et al.	apartheid
Baycol	liver and kidney damage
Baycol, Canada only	liver and kidney damage
Bayer Corporation et.al.	tainted blood products
Bayer Pharmaceutical	Cipro side effects
BC Hospital Employees Union	surgeries canceled
BC Hydro, Alouette River Flood	Canada
BC Rail Ltd.	improperly allocating surplus Pension funds
Bechtel Corp. et al.	exposing workers to toxic dust
Benjamin Marchese III	identity theft
Berkeley Premium Nutraceuticals	Enzyte does not work as claimed
Berkeley Unified School District	discrimination
Beverly Hills High School	toxins from oil wells on school property
Bill Heard Chevrolet	deceptive business practices
BioLab Inc.	losses due to fire at chemical plant
Bishop Guertin High School, RI	sexual abuse
Black Diamond Ranch	equity memberships
Blockbuster Inc.	misclassifying employees to avoid overtime pay
Blue Cross and Blue Shield	RICO, defrauding doctors
BMW of North America	defective air bags in BMW X5
Body Solutions	diet scam
Bon-Macy's	unauthorized credit card charges
Bouchard Transportation	oil spill damages
Brae Burn Country Club, MA	withholding tips
Briad Restaurant Group	paying less than minimum wage
Brinker Restaurant Corp.	exposing customers to salmonella
Bristol Parc	mold in houses
British Columbia College Pension Board	inappropriate distribution of funds

DEFENDANT	CLAIMS
British Ministry of Defense	rape of Kenyan women
Brown Group Retail and Redfield Rifle Scopes Inc.	chemical contamination
Business Development Bank of Canada	employee benefits
Cablevision Systems Corp.	cable piracy fraud
Cablevision Systems Corp.	unpaid labor
Caesars Entertainment Inc.	overtime pay
California Secretary of State et al.	recall process
California Banks	assisting Ponzi scheme
Cal-Shake	defective cement roof shingles
Caltrans et. al.	210 Freeway noise
Canadian Department of National Defence	soldiers exposed to chemical warefare tests
Canadian Federal Immigration Department	identity card discrimination
Canadian National Railroad, Canada	train derailment
Canadian Pacific Railway	amonia spill
Capital One	labor, age discrimination
Captain William Jackson Hospital, NF	improper sterilization of equipment
Carfax, Inc.	deceptive sales practices
Carfax	incomplete or false data on used cars
Cargill Inc.	discrimination against black employees
Car Insurance Companies, Canada	withholding deductibles
Carl Icahn, the Pension Benefit Guaranty Corporation, PBGC and the Airline Pilots Association, ALPA	ERISA
Cathedral City et al.	retaliation
CB Richard Ellis	sexual harassment of female employees
Cedar Knolls Manufactured Home Community	rent increase
Centerpoint Energy Inc. et. al.	inflated gas prices
Charlotte Russe	management overtime
Charter Communications	unfair business practices
ChevronTexaco Corp.	dumping toxic wastewater in Ecuador

DEFENDANT	CLAIMS
Chicago Housing Authority	discrimination
Chico's FAS, Inc.	requiring employees to purchase and wear company clothing
Chiron Corporation NASD: CHIR	
Choicepoint Inc., Reed Elsevier Inc.	illegal datamining
C. H. Robinson Worldwide	discrimination against women
C.H.Robinson Worldwide, Inc.	discrimination and overtime
C.H. Robinson Worldwide, Inc.	hostile work environment
Cincinnati Bell Wireless	illegal roaming charges
Cincinnati Bengals	demanding licensees buy season passes
Cintas	unpaid overtime
Citizenship and Immigration Services	discrimination
Citrus Springs County	refunding assessed funds
City of Chicago	war protesters
City of Cinncinnati	evicting poor tenants to build upscale housing
City of Detroit	detaining witnesses
City of Eugene, OR	developers fees
City of Knoxville, et.al	environmental damage
City of Oxford	forced contributions for alcohol offences
City of San Diego	overcharging sewer rates
City of San Diego	property damage
City of San Diego	sexual discrimination
City of Seattle	impounded cars
City of Seattle	temporary employee benefits
City of Toronto et al.	SARS
CKE Restaurants	not paid vacation time
Clark County, WA	overcharging builders permit fees
CNA Financial Corp.	discrimination against older workers
CNH Global	retracting health care benefits from retirees
Coca-Cola Bottling Co.	race discrimination
Colorado Lottery	selling tickets after major prizes won

DEFENDANT	CLAIMS
Combined Insurance Co. of America	sexual harassment and discrimination
Comcast	tracking customers internet websurfing habits
Comfort Inn et al.	negligence in Greenville fire
Connecticut State Medical Society Independent Practice Association	withholding physicians pay
Conseco Finance	overtime pay
Continental, American, United Airlines	discrimination
Cook County Department of Corrections	Disabilities Act violation
CortiSlim™	false advertising
Costco	gender discrimination
Countrywide Financial Corp.	workplace regulation violations
Countrywide Home Loans, Inc.	illegal $60 statement fee
County of Los Angeles, et al.	price and rent controls
Covington Pike Toyota	undisclosed interest rates
Craftmatic Organization, Inc., CA	violating consumer protection laws
Crystal Park Casino et al.	violation of minimum wage laws
Cypress Gardens	violation of WARN Act
DaimlerChrysler	Gen 3 seat belt buckle
DaimlerChrysler et al.	defective Dodge Durango
DaimlerChrysler Canada and Honda Canada	not covering all costs on recalls
Daqing Lianyi Petrochemical Co., China	financial fraud
De Beers	inflating diamond prices
Debticated Consumer Counseling	posing as a non-profit organization
Deja vu, Inc.	back pay for exotic dancers
Dell Canada	not honoring posted prices
DeMilta Iron and Metal	price fixing
Denver International Airport	exposure to mold
Department of Education, MA	MCAS exam
Department of Homeland Security	denying immigrants proof of status
Department of Homeland Security	rejecting approved immigrants

DEFENDANT	CLAIMS
Department of Mental Health	discriminatory termination
Department of Social Services, CT	discrimination
DESCO Group and DFC Group	diminishing property values
Desert Schools Federal Credit Union	discrimination against non-Mormon employees
DirecTV	demand letters
District of Columbia, et. al.	police misconduct
Dodge/Chrysler Neon	defective head gaskets
Dolphinite, Inc. and The Clean Seas Company	defective anti-fouling paint
Domain Names Australia	phony invoices
Dominion Telecom and Virginia Electric	land use
Domino's Pizza Inc.	age discrimination
DoubleClick Inc.	false advertising
Dow Chemical Co.	agent orange
Dow Chemical Co.	Tittabawassee River pollution
Dr. Sheldon Pollack, ON	using unapproved silicon injections
Drug Valet Inc.	unsolicited faxes
Dylex/Great American Group	funds owed to employees
E. Baton Rouge Sheriff's Office	DNA samples
Eastman Kodak Company	racial discrimination
Easy Heat Inc.	defective heating system
eBay	failing to protect artists
eBay	overbilling
Eckerd Drug Stores	failure to pay overtime
Educational Testing Service	mistakenly failing students
Eli Lilly, Co. and Walgreens Co.	invasion of privacy in marketing Prozac
Empire HealthChoice, Inc.	not reimbursing orthopedic surgeons
EnCana Corp. et al.	gas price fixing
Epitome Nightclub	negligence
Equifax Inc.	failed overtime payment
EquityLink, CO	predatory HomeSaver loan
Equity Residential	landlord tenant

DEFENDANT	CLAIMS
Excelsior	The Federalist, and Grill 23, Bar, retaliation
Exxon/Mobil	ERISA
Fax.com	illegal faxes in MD
Federal Government	back pay for National Guardsmen
Federal Government	immigrant data in crime database
Federal Government, Roman Catholic schools	sexual abuse
Federal Government of Canada	same-sex benefits
Federal Republic of Germany	restitution for goods seized during the Nazi regime
Federation of Medical Specialists	surgeries delayed in Quebec
FedEx	labor, race discrimination
Fidelity National Title Co. et. al.	price fixing
Finagle a Bagel	violated employment laws
First American Registry	inaccurate reports
FirstEnergy Corporation	energy blackout
Florida Department of Insurance	viaticals insurance scam
Florida Metropolitan University	unable to transfer credits
Florida Power & Light Co.	overcharging due to faulty meters
Ford Motor Co. and Magna International	faulty door latches
Ford Motor Company	police cars exploded after rear-end collisions
Formica Corp.	reduced pension checks
Fountainhead Title Group et al.	channeling kickbacks
Franklin Resources Inc.	fraudulent trading practices
Friedman's Inc.	employment discrimination
Friendly Ice Cream Corp.	exposure to hepatitis A
Fulton Homes	construction defects
Fundamentalist Church of Jesus Christ of Latter Day Saints	polygamy
Garfield Alloys Co., OH	damage from fire
GE Canola Manufacturers	damages caused to organic farmers
Geico	faulty vehicle evaluations

DEFENDANT	CLAIMS
Geico	lower-quality aftermarket vehicle parts
GEICO	unpaid overtime
General Electric Capital Assurance	not honoring long term care policies
General Motors Corporation	Piston slap
General Motors	damage caused by Dex-cool
General Motors	defective trucks
Georgia Division of Family and Children Services	deficient foster care
Ghassem, Kevin Yousefion	environmental damage
Gladney Center for Adoption	not disclosing adoption details
GlaxoSmithKline	Augmentin, antitrust
GlaxoSmithKline	supressing clinical trial info
Gold'n Plump	safety gear time
GoodTimes Entertainment	unauthorized billing
Goodyear Tire & Rubber Co.	discrimination against older workers
Google, AOL, Time Warner and Yahoo!	libel
Government of Canada	improper management of veterans funds
Greenlane Hospital, Aukland	keeping organs without consent
Guidant Corp.	Ancure Endograft System
H& R Block	charging fees for electronic filing
Hamilton County Herald et al.	lack of notification
Hamilton County, OH coroner's office	incomplete bodies
Hamilton County, Ohio	letting corpses be photographed by employee
Hamilton Health Sciences	unnecessary surgeries
Harley-Davidson	defective TC-88 engines
Health Management Associates Inc.	charging unisured more
Hewlett-Packard	defective notebooks
Hill and Associates et al.	unauthorized stock trading
Hilton Hawaiian Village's Kalia Tower	guests exposed to mold
HMO's	underpaying doctors
Hollinger International	improper use of funds

DEFENDANT	CLAIMS
Home Depot Inc.	CCA-treated wood
Home Depot	not paying employees overtime while traveling
Honeywell International, Inc., ITT Industries, Inc., and ITT-Gilfillan, Inc.	soldiers exposed to radar
Horizon Blue Cross Blue Shield	shortchanging doctors
Household Finance Corp. et.al.	overcharging on loan origination fees
IHOP	illegally deducting money from employees paychecks
ILX Resorts Inc.	selling booked timeshare rooms
Immigration and Naturalization Service, INS	discrimination
Immigration, Canada	human rights
Imperial Tobacco Canada Limited	light cigarettes
Imperial Tobacco	marketing light cigarettes as more healthful
Independence Blue Cross	reduced/denied payments
Insurance companies	Hurricane Isabel flood victims
Insurance companies	interest owed on settlements
International Brotherhood of Electrical Workers	unlawful dues
International Truck and Engine Corp.	racial discrimination
Investment Banks	false IPOs
Investor's Business Daily	sales commissions
Iowa Car Manufacturers	blocking access to less expensive cars
ISM Canada	loss of confidential information
J.P. Morgan Chase & Co.	overtime
J.S. Hovnanian & Sons	dangerous utility rooms
Jacksonville Electric Authority	hazardous material spill
Jacob K. Javits Convention Center	racial discrimination
Jefferson County Commission	sewer impact fees
Jenkens, Gilchrist et al.	illegal tax shelters
Jenkens and Gilchrist et al.	tax shelters
Jersey Central Power & Light	power outages
JetBlue Airways Corp.	dispensing private information

DEFENDANT	CLAIMS
Johnson & Johnson	discrimination against black and Hispanic employees
Kaiser Foundation	disclosing patients' private medical information
Katzman & Korr, FL	violations of Fair Debt Collections Act
KB Home and Richmond American Homes	doubling dues
Kenneth's Fine Jewelry	fraud
Kia Motors America, Inc.	Kia Sephia brakes
Kim Son Restaurants	non-payment of overtime
Kingdom of Saudi Arabia et al.	pension compensation
Kmart	devaluation of 401k plans
Kroger	violations of the Family and Medical Leave Act
Kryptonite and Ingersoll-Rand	defective locks
L & L Services	employee overtime
Lakeridge Health Corp. et al.	tuberculosis exposure
Landers Auto Sales, Inc.	sales commissions
Landry's Restaurants Inc.	deducting credit card fees from servers' tips
Landstar Inc.	truth-in-leasing
Leadenhall Bank & Trust et al.	auto-title pawn fraud
Lexmark	antitrust
LifeScan et al.	defective SureStep glucose meters
Life University	education/negligence
Limestone Correctional Facility	segregating HIV and AIDS inmates
Livescan	faulty digital fingerprint technology
Lockformer Co., IL	environment
Loews Cineplex	unfair business practices
Longs Drug Stores Corp.	overtime to managers
Los Alamos National Laboratory, NM	wage discrimination
Los Angeles County	1930s residents forcibly sent to Mexico
Louisiana school systems	overtime wage violations
Lowe's Companies, Inc.	overtime improperly calculated

DEFENDANT	CLAIMS
Lucent Technologies, Inc. and AT, T Corporation	non-compliant Y2K telecommunications equipment
Lutheran Brotherhood	life insurance vanishing premiums
Lynn University, Levitt-Weinstein Memorial Chapels	interference with dead bodies
Macomb County et al.	estate mismanagement
Macy's East, Inc.	racially profiling shoplifters
Madison taverns	fixing prices on beer and wine
Magrann Associates and Thermal Design	defective heating
Main Street Textiles	backpay
Marathon Ashland Petroleum Inc.	explosion at Detroit refinery
Marin County et al.	illegal strip searches
Match Day	exploiting medical students and violating anti-trust laws
Mayo Clinic	employees seeking back pay
MBNA Corporation	not transferring air miles
MBNA	overcharging interest
McDonald's Restaurants of Canada	withholding high level game pieces
Menorah Gardens and Funeral Chapels	unethical business practices
Mercedes-Benz	price fixing
Meriwest Credit Union and Falore Nissan, Inc.	sale of repossessed cars
Miami-Dade County	unconstitutional strip search
Microsoft and Best Buy	fraudulent billing
Microsoft	inadequate patching system
Mitel Networks Corp.	failure to give reasonable notice of termination
Mohawk Industries	hiring illegal aliens
Money Mart et al.	criminal rates of interest
Monitor Sugar Co.	odors reduce property values
National Football League et al.	heat illness
National Foundation Life Insurance	breach of contract
Neon	faulty head gasket
New England Water Heater Co.	changing terms of leases for water heaters

DEFENDANT	CLAIMS
New York City Parks Department	employment discrimination
New York State	homeless children access to education
Newmont Mining Company	Mercury spill
Newsday	overcharging for ad space based on inflated circulation
Nissan North America	Infiniti G35 brake defect
Nissan	Maxima headlights easy to steal
Nokia	defective phones
Non-Profit Hospitals	not providing charity care
Noranda Inc.	pension plan
Norfolk, Virginia school system	not paying bus drivers overtime
North American Indemnity	employee benefits
North Dakota Labor Department	delaying claims
Northshore Mining Co.	discrimination against female employees
Northwest Airlines	antitrust
Northwest Airlines	sharing personal infomation
Norvergence Lease Assignees	breach of contract
NS Govt. and Atlantic Lottery Corp	video lottery terminals
NutraSweet Corporation	hazardous Aspartame
OAO Surgutneftegaz	failing to pay dividends
Oceanview Manor Home	denying allowance
Official Reporting Services	overcharging for court recording
Ohio Bureau of Motor Vehicles	double charges to reinstate driving license
Oklahoma Transportation Authority	overbilling
Olin Corporation, CA	environment
Omni Hotels	employees alleging mold infestations made them ill
Ontario automobile insurers	insurance deductibles
Ontario Government.	civil servants health cutbacks
Ontario Trusteed Pension Plan, Canada	employee benefits
Ontario Municipal Employees Retire-ment Board	pension plan
Ontario Provincial Police	improper actions during raid

DEFENDANT	CLAIMS
Orkin Exterminating Co. Inc.	false advertising
Ortho-Clinical Diagnostics	failing to pay severance pay
Overloaded Coal Trucks, WV	health and injury risk
Pacific Coast Building Products	defective roofing shingles
Pall Life Sciences	contaminating water supply
Palm Beach Elections	discrimination against blind voters
Palm, Inc.	Palm M130 false advertising
Pan Pharmaceuticals, Australia	overdose of Travacalm
Pat and Oscar's	E. coli outbreak
Patriot Resorts Corp.	inadequate pay for salespeople
Paxil	withholding results of clinical trials
Pennsylvania Department of Transportation; et al.	damages caused by flood
Petcurean Pet Nutrition, Inc. et al.	pet food killed pets
PharmaCare Management Services Inc.	delay in paying higher prices
Philadelphia School District	breach of settlement agreement
Pilgrim's Pride	unfair business practices
Pilkington North America Inc.	alleged arsenic contamination
Pinellas County Schools	failing to educate black students
Pioneer North America, Inc.	defective TVs
Pizza Hut	unpaid overtime
P.J. Kids LLC	formaldehyde poisoning
Polo Ralph Lauren Corp.	forcing employees to pay for uniforms
Prandium, Inc.	hepatitis A contracted at Chi Chi's Restaurant
Premcor Refining Group	toxic underground plume
Prempro	alleged marked increases in invasive breast cancer, coronary heart disease, stroke and pulmonary embolism.
Prestage	pollution
PricewaterhouseCoopers LLP	discrimination
Primus Automotive Financial Service	fraud
Progressive Corp.	overtime
Province of British Columbia, et.al.	illegal strip searches
Province of Nova Scotia	Video Online Lottery addicts

DEFENDANT	CLAIMS
Province of Nova Scotia	nursing home health care
Province of Ontario	cutting health-related pension benefits
Province of Quebec	changing student loans
Prudential Life Insurance Co.	death benefits for stillborn children
Puppy Palace	selling unhealthy animals
Purdue Pharma and Abbott Laboratories	OxyContin
PyraMax	stopping interest payments
Qantas et al.	deep vein thrombosis - British only
Quest Security Services	not paying minimum wage
Qwest Communications International	non payment of overtime
R, D Enterprises Inc. et al.	debt collection misrepresentations
RadioShack	misclassifying employees
Radio Shack, PA	labor, non-payment of overtime
Ralphs Supermarket	cancelling
Register.com	illegal use of registered domain names
Reno County Jail	illegal arrests
Residential Schools in Canada	sexual and physical abuse
Resurrection Health Care Corporation	inflated insurance
Ricart	unfair business practices
Robert W. Baird, Co. Inc.	failure to pay overtime
Roche, BASF and Aventis	price fixing vitamins in Australia
Roseville Parker Hughes	inadequate notice of employee termination
Roto-Rooter, Inc.	unfair business practices
Royal Bank of Canada	computer glitch
Royal Caribbean Cruises and Celebrity Cruise Lines	fraudulent tax charges
Ryan's Family Steak Houses Inc.	overtime wages
Safeway, Albertsons and Kroger	artificially coloring farm salmon
Sally Beauty Company	deductions not spent on advertising
Salomon, Smith Barney Inc.	securities broker
Sam Goody Stores	undisclosed credit card charges
San Diego et al.	mismanaging Cedar fire

DEFENDANT	CLAIMS
Sandra Testaguzza and Dr. Alvin Pettle	spreading infection
Saturn Corp.	discrimination against older workers
SBC Communications Corp. and Cingular Wireless	denied pension benefits
SBC Communications Inc.	overcharging Yellow Page users
Salomon, Smith Barney Inc.	securities broker
Scientific Games Corporation, "Autotote"	betting fraud
Search Engines	advertising illegal gambling in CA
Sears and Whirlpool	faulty Calypso washing machines
Sears Home Improvement Products Inc., FL	overcharging vinyl siding
Second Chance Body Armor, Inc.	defective body armor
Seroxat, UK	promotes suicide
Serzone, Canada	liver damage
Sharper Image	Ionic Breeze air purifier
Sheet Metal Workers	discrimination against non-white workers
Shell Canada Limited	damaged fuel supply systems
Shell Oil	high sulfur content in gas damages fuel gauges
Shell Oil	human rights violations
Sheriff Thomas Hodgson	illegal charges to inmates
Ski Boat Companies	carbon monoxide poisoning
Slater Stainless Corp.	employee benefits
Smithfield Foods Inc.	pollution
Sodexho Marriott Services Inc.	employee discrimination against black managers
Sony Corp. of America	product liability
Sony et al.	antitrust
Sony Music et al.	copyright infringement
Sony	defective screens in widescreen TVs
South African gold companies	miners lung diseases
South Australian Government	sexual abuse to children
South Jersey Gas Co.	gas meters in dangerous locations

DEFENDANT	CLAIMS
Southern California Gas, et al.	consipring to eliminate competition
Southern Pacific Petroleum et al.	property devaluation
Sprint Corp.	discrimination against older employees
Sprint Corp	spam in Utah
Sprint	unjustified 911 fees
Stimson Lumber Company	defective Forestex Hardboard Siding
St. Joe Paper Co.	exposing people to hazardous substances
St. Jude Medical, Canada	defective Silzone mechanical heart valves
St. Paul Fire & Marine Insurance Co., IA	denying malpractice insurance
St. Thomas Development Inc. et al.,	violating constitutional rights
Starbucks	unpaid overtime
Starwood Hotels & Resorts World-wide, Inc.	improper
State Accident Insurance Fund Corp.	rebates to customers
State Farm et al.	bad faith
State Farm Fire and Casualty Co.	under-compensating policyholders
State of New Jersey, et al.	flood damage
State of Alaska	Longevity Bonus Program
State of Arizona	using Social Security number for drivers license number
State of Florida	nursing home residents insurance deductions
State of Indiana	increase in property taxes
State of Massachusetts	lack of lawyers for poor
State of Tennessee	Certificate of Driving
State of Tennessee	sex offender registry law
Stoneco Inc.	pollution decreasing property values
Stop 'N' Cash	excessive interest
Stratford Principal George McCrackin et al.	unreasonable search and seizure
Sun Life Assurance Co.	reducing disability benefits
Sun Microsystems Inc.	employment discrimination
Sunnybrook Hospital	improperly sterilization of equipment

DEFENDANT	CLAIMS
Taco Bell Corp. et al.	exposing customers to hepatitis A
Telstra, Australia	unreliable broadband service
Tenet Healthcare Corp.	breach of contract, excessive billing
Tennessee Electric Cooperative Association	conspiring to keep rates high
Tetra Tech MPS et al.	not maintaining sewers
TGF Precision Haircutters	unpaid work
Thanh Phu restaurant	food poisoning
The former Iraqi regime	beaten American citizens
The Learning Channel's reality show et al.	fraudulent film permission
Thurston County, Washington	delayed overtime
Ticketmaster and Madison Square Garden	obstructed view
Titlemax	charging excessive interest
Tobacco Companies	tobacco addiction - LA only
Top Modeling Agencies	overcharging commissions and fees
Touch America	illegal layoff of employees Jun-18-03
Transportation Security Administration, TSA	employee rights violations
Tri-State Crematory	improper cremations
Trinity Homes, IN	faulty construction
Tyson Foods, Inc. et al., OK	environmental harm from plant runoffs
Tyson Fresh Meats	price fixing
UBC	sperm lost due to negligence
Uniform Code Council, Inc.	annual fee for UPC codes
Union Central Life Insurance	lost severance benefits
United Airlines et al.	violation of labor agreements
United Equitable Insurance, and Standard Life, Accident Insurance	insurance
United Parcel Service Inc.	discrimination against employees participating in the Employee Assistance Program
United Parcel Service, Inc.	discrimination against disabled
United Parcel Service	discrimination against hearing-impared employees

DEFENDANT	CLAIMS
United Park City Mines	selling assets
University of California	illegal sale of cadavers
University of California	insufficient notice of fee increase
University of Maryland	civil rights
University System of Maryland	education
UnumProvident Corporation	ERISA
Urgent Care Pharmacy	contaminated drugs
U.S. Department of Agriculture	gender discrimination
U.S. Forest Service	discrimination against Hispanics
U.S. Government et al.	banning reimportation of drugs from Canada
U.S. Government	using Vietnam soldiers as test subjects for SHAD/Project 112
U.S. Government	veterans health care
U.S. Immigration and Naturalization Service	Solamis deportation
U.S. Postal Service	altering time slips
U.S. Treasury Department	sexual harassment and discrimination
Ustman Technologies, Inc.	unfair business practices
Utah's 3rd District Court	violating constitutional rights
VanCity Credit Union	illegal overdraft fees
Vatican	priests abuse of children
Village Voice Media	antitrust, hiking advertising rates
Volkswagen	defective Jetta spoilers
Volkswagen	defective window regulators
Wal-Mart, WA	off the clock hours
Wal-Mart	discrimination against female employees
Wal-Mart	employee insurance
Wal-Mart	immigrant labor
Wal-Mart, MN	work without pay
Wal-Mart Stores Inc.	unpaid overtime
Washington County	wrongful imprisonment
Washington D.C. Water and Sewer Authority	conceiling lead problems in water

DEFENDANT	CLAIMS
Washington Mutual, Inc.	fraudulent business practices
Washoe County, NV	raising property taxes
Wayne County Airport Authority et al.	breach of contract
Wells Fargo, MD.	charging recordation taxes on refinancing of homes
West Branch Regional Medical Center	diluted drugs
Wichita Police Department	discrimination
Women's and Children's Hospital, Australia	taking body parts
Woodland Park Hospital	insufficient notice of closure
World Airways	flight cancellation
Worldcom	settlement
W.R. Grace, CO	Zonolite asbestos insulation
Xerox	racial discrimination
Xerox	ERISA
Yahoo!	abusive postings
Yale New Haven Hospital et al.	failure to provide health care
York County Jail in Maine	strip-searching prisoners
Zapata Industries Inc.	plant closing

Source: BigClassAction.com

APPENDIX 3: NEW YORK STATE LAW GOVERNING CLASS ACTIONS

NEW YORK STATE CIVIL PRACTICE LAWS AND RULES (CPLR)

CHAPTER 8

ARTICLE 9: CLASS ACTIONS

Section 901. Prerequisites to a class action.

Section 902. Order allowing class action.

Section 903. Description of class.

Section 904. Notice of class action.

Section 905. Judgment.

Section 906. Actions conducted partially as class actions.

Section Rule 907. Orders in conduct of class actions.

Section Rule 908. Dismissal, discontinuance or compromise.

Section Rule 909. Attorneys' fees.

Section 901. Prerequisites to a class action.

a. One or more members of a class may sue or be sued as representative parties on behalf of all if:

1. the class is so numerous that joinder of all members, whether otherwise required or permitted, is impracticable;

2. there are questions of law or fact common to the class which predominate over any questions affecting only individual members;

3. the claims or defenses of the representative parties are typical of the claims or defenses of the class;

4. the representative parties will fairly and adequately protect the interests of the class; and

5. a class action is superior to other available methods for the fair and efficient adjudication of the controversy.

b. Unless a statute creating or imposing a penalty, or a minimum measure of recovery specifically authorizes the recovery thereof in a class action, an action to recover a penalty, or minimum measure of recovery created or imposed by statute may not be maintained as a class action.

Section 902. Order allowing class action.

Within sixty days after the time to serve a responsive pleading has expired for all persons named as defendants in an action brought as a class action, the plaintiff shall move for an order to determine whether it is to be so maintained. An order under this section may be conditional, and may be altered or amended before the decision on the merits on the court's own motion or on motion of the parties. The action may be maintained as a class action only if the court finds that the prerequisites under section 901 have been satisfied. Among the matters which the court shall consider in determining whether the action may proceed as a class action are:

1. the interest of members of the class in individually controlling the prosecution or defense of separate actions;

2. the impracticability or inefficiency of prosecuting or defending separate actions;

3. the extent and nature of any litigation concerning the controversy already commenced by or against members of the class;

4. the desirability or undesirability of concentrating the litigation of the claim in the particular forum;

5. the difficulties likely to be encountered in the management of a class action.

Section 903. Description of class.

The order permitting a class action shall describe the class. When appropriate the court may limit the class to those members who do not request exclusion from the class within a specified time after notice.

Section 904. Notice of class action.

(a) In class actions brought primarily for injunctive or declaratory relief, notice of the pendency of the action need not be given to the class unless the court finds that notice is necessary to protect the interests of the represented parties and that the cost of notice will not prevent the action from going forward.

(b) In all other class actions, reasonable notice of the commencement of a class action shall be given to the class in such manner as the court directs.

(c) The content of the notice shall be subject to court approval. In determining the method by which notice is to be given, the court shall consider:

I. the cost of giving notice by each method considered

II. the resources of the parties and

III. the stake of each represented member of the class, and the likelihood that significant numbers of represented members would desire to exclude themselves from the class or to appear individually, which may be determined, in the court's discretion, by sending notice to a random sample of the class.

(d) I. Preliminary determination of expenses of notification. Unless the court orders otherwise, the plaintiff shall bear the expense of notification. The court may, if justice requires, require that the defendant bear the expense of notification, or may require each of them to bear a part of the expense in proportion to the likelihood that each will prevail upon the merits. The court may hold a preliminary hearing to determine how the costs of notice should be apportioned.

II. Final determination. Upon termination of the action by order or judgment, the court may, but shall not be required to, allow to the prevailing party the expenses of notification as taxable disbursements under article eighty-three of the civil practice law and rules.

Section 905. Judgment.

The judgment in an action maintained as a class action, whether or not favorable to the class, shall include and describe those whom the court finds to be members of the class.

Section 906. Actions conducted partially as class actions.

When appropriate:

1. an action may be brought or maintained as a class action with respect to particular issues, or

2. a class may be divided into subclasses and each subclass treated as a class.

The provisions of this article shall then be construed and applied accordingly.

Rule 907. Orders in conduct of class actions.

In the conduct of class actions the court may make appropriate orders:

1. determining the course of proceedings or prescribing measures to prevent undue repetition or complication in the presentation of evidence or argument;

2. requiring, for the protection of the members of the class, or otherwise for the fair conduct of the action, that notice be given in such manner as the court may direct to some or all of the members of any step in the action, or of the proposed extent of the judgment, or of the opportunity of members to signify whether they consider the representation fair and adequate, or to appear and present claims or defenses, or otherwise to come into the action;

3. imposing conditions on the representative parties or on intervenors;

4. requiring that the pleadings be amended to eliminate therefrom allegations as to representation of absent persons, and that the action proceed accordingly;

5. directing that a money judgment favorable to the class be paid either in one sum, whether forthwith or within such period as the court may fix, or in such installments as the court may specify;

6. dealing with similar procedural matters.

The orders may be altered or amended as may be desirable from time to time.

Rule 908. Dismissal, discontinuance or compromise.

A class action shall not be dismissed, discontinued, or compromised without the approval of the court. Notice of the proposed dismissal, discontinuance, or compromise shall be given to all members of the class in such manner as the court directs.

Rule 909. Attorneys' fees.

If a judgment in an action maintained as a class action is rendered in favor of the class, the court in its discretion may award attorneys' fees to the representatives of the class based on the reasonable value of legal services rendered and if justice requires, allow recovery of the amount awarded from the opponent of the class.

APPENDIX 4: NOTICE OF PENDENCY OF CLASS ACTION, PROPOSED CLASS ACTION SETTLEMENT AND SETTLEMENT HEARING

SUPERIOR COURT OF NEW JERSEY
LAW DIVISION, CAMDEN COUNTY

CAROL KROPINSKI, JOSEPH FOULK, PATRICIA ROSINI, MARY LYNOTT and THOMAS LYNOTT, on Behalf of Themselves and All Others Similarly Situated,

CIVIL ACTION

No. L-8886-96

Plaintiffs,

vs.

JOHNSON & JOHNSON, and JOHNSON & JOHNSON VISION PRODUCTS, INC.,

Defendants.

NOTICE OF PENDENCY OF CLASS ACTION, PROPOSED CLASS ACTION SETTLEMENT AND SETTLEMENT HEARING

TO: ALL PURCHASERS OF ACUVUE® CONTACT LENSES.

You may be entitled to receive up to $3.00 in cash, $3.00 in credit towards the purchase of new contact lenses, and $1.00 towards the unreimbursed cost of an eye examination for every box of Acuvue® contact lenses you purchased from 1995 to July 31, 2001, as well as $3.00 in credit towards the purchase of new contact lenses for every box of Acuvue® contact lenses you purchased during 1994.

This notice is given pursuant to R. 4:32-2 of the New Jersey Court Rules Governing Civil Practice and the July 27, 2001, Order of the Honorable John A. Fratto, J.S.C., of the New Jersey Superior Court (hereinafter, "the Court") to all persons who are residents and domiciliaries of the United States who, between January 1, 1994 and July 31, 2001 (the "Class Period"), purchased Acuvue® contact lenses. The purpose of this notice is to inform you of this pending lawsuit, *Kropinski et al. v. Johnson & Johnson, et ano*, No. L-8886-96; to advise you of a proposed settlement and of your rights as a member of the class; and to give you notice of a hearing to be held by the Court on October 25, 2001, at 11:00 a.m., in Courtroom No. 42 of the Superior Court, Camden County, 101 South Fifth Street, Camden, New Jersey, to determine whether the proposed settlement is fair, reasonable, and adequate, and to consider such other matters as may properly come before the Court in connection with the hearing. This Settlement does not apply to those persons who purchased 1-Day Acuvue®, Surevue®, Acuvue® Bifocals or Acuvue2® lenses.

THE PURPOSE OF THIS NOTICE IS TO INFORM YOU OF YOUR RIGHTS IN CONNECTION WITH THIS CLASS ACTION LAWSUIT. PLEASE READ THIS NOTICE CAREFULLY AND IN ITS ENTIRETY.

If you have any questions with respect to the Settlement or this notice please contact the Settlement Administrator at the following address :

Acuvue® Contact Lens Settlement
Settlement Administrator
P.O. Box 9389
Garden City, NY 11530-9389
www.vistakonsettlement.com
Tel: 1-800-581-8701

PLEASE DO NOT CALL OR WRITE THE JUDGE OR CLERK OF THE COURT.

I. SUMMARY

A Proposed Settlement of a class action lawsuit relating to alleged claims for misleading statements and advertising regarding the use of Acuvue® and 1-Day Acuvue® lenses, has been reached in *Kropinski et al. v. Johnson & Johnson et ano*, Docket No. L-8886-96. The Court has preliminarily approved the Settlement by an Order dated July 27, 2001. As is more fully described below, under the terms of the Settlement, Defendants will pay to each Class Member, upon presentation of an appropriate proof of claim, a cash payment as well as certain credits towards purchases of contact lenses and eye exams after July 31, 2001. The details of the compensation to the Class are discussed in full in paragraph VI.A below. Additionally, Defendants have agreed to certain disclosures and injunctive relief in the form of guidelines for future promotional activity, labeling and packaging of the Acuvue® and 1-Day Acuvue® contact lenses. The details of the disclosure and injunctive relief part of the Settlement are discussed in full in paragraph VI.B below. Furthermore, Defendants have agreed to pay attorneys' fees and expenses to those law firms representing the Class in this litigation (herein referred to as "Class Counsel"). These fees, costs and expenses are to be paid entirely by Defendants and in no way reduce the amount received by each Class Member under the terms of the Settlement. Finally, Defendants agreed to pay each Representative Plaintiff $15,000 over and above the consideration paid to Class Members and to pay all costs of administration of the Settlement, including the costs of Notice to the Class Members.

II. THE CLASS

By Order dated February 11, 1998, the Court determined that this lawsuit may be maintained as a class action pursuant to R. 4:32-1. The class was defined as "[a]ll persons who are residents and domiciliaries of the United States who, between 1993 and the present, purchased disposable contact lenses marketed under the name Acuvue®." That Order was affirmed on appeal by the Appellate Division of the Superior Court for the State of New Jersey by Order dated January 7, 1999. Defendants sought leave from the New Jersey Supreme Court to take an interlocutory appeal from that Order. On March 26, 1999, the New Jersey Supreme Court denied Defendants' Motion for Leave to Take an Interlocutory Appeal. During the course of discovery, plaintiffs discovered that although 1-Day Acuvue® lenses were test-marketed in two cities in late 1993, the lenses were distributed for sale only on a limited basis in 1994. Nationwide distribution of 1-Day Acuvue® lenses began in early 1995. Accordingly, by Order dated March 20, 2001, the Court modified the class definition to the following: "All persons who are residents and domiciliaries of the United States who, between January 1, 1994, and the present, purchased disposable contact lenses marketed under the name Acuvue®." If you have purchased Acuvue® contact lenses between January 1, 1994 and July 31, 2001, you are a member of the Class. Excluded from the Class are Defendants and their officers, directors, affiliates, legal representatives, heirs, successors, subsidiaries and/or assigns, any entity in which Defendants have a controlling interest and the officers, directors, affiliates, legal representatives, heirs, successors, subsidiaries and/or assigns of any such entity or entities.

III. SUMMARY OF THE CLAIMS

The above lawsuit was filed on October 30, 1996. Carol Kropinski, Joseph Foulk, Patricia Rosini, Mary Lynott and Thomas Lynott (the "Representative Plaintiffs") each wears Acuvue® contact lenses manufactured, distributed and placed into the stream of commerce by Vistakon®, Division of Johnson & Johnson Vision Care, Inc., a wholly-owned subsidiary of Johnson and Johnson ("J&J"). Vistakon and J&J are herein referred to collectively as "Defendants." The lawsuit was brought by the Representative Plaintiffs on behalf of all persons similarly situated. The lawsuit asserts claims for fraud and deceit, negligent misrepresentation, violation of consumer protection statutes and negligence *per se*, and seeks compensatory and punitive damages. In summary, the lawsuit alleges that during the Class Period (from January 1, 1994 to July 31, 2001), Defendants have produced contact lenses under the names Acuvue® and 1-Day Acuvue® and advertised and marketed Acuvue® and 1-Day Acuvue® lenses as unique and suited only for different purposes. According to Defendants' marketing and advertising, the Acuvue® lens should be worn for between seven and fourteen days either as a disposable lens or as a frequent replacement lens. The Defendants' marketing and advertising stated that the 1-Day Acuvue® contact lens is suited for daily disposable wear only. In fact, Acuvue® and 1-Day Acuvue® contact lenses are made of the same material, marketed pursuant to the same approval from the Food and Drug Administration, and there is no known clinical reason why 1-Day Acuvue® contact lenses cannot be worn for more than one day. In marketing Acuvue® and 1-Day Acuvue®, Defendants adopted disparate advertising schemes and retail price structures. Although prices varied during the course of the Class Period, the Acuvue® lenses sell at retail for approximately $4.16 each, while the 1-Day Acuvue® lenses sell at retail for approximately $0.82 each. As a result, consumers who purchase contact lenses marketed under the name Acuvue® are paying more than five times the price they could be paying for a 1-Day Acuvue® lens suitable for the same purpose. Defendants deny these allegations, however, and have asserted various affirmative defenses. Among other things, Defendants have observed that Acuvue® and 1-Day Acuvue® lenses are different in a number of respects. They have different base curves, different diameters, and are available in somewhat different power ranges. Because of these parameter differences, an Acuvue® lens user cannot switch to 1-Day Acuvue® lenses without obtaining a new prescription from a qualified eye care professional, and not every patient who is successfully fit with Acuvue? lenses can appropriately wear 1-Day Acuvue® lenses. Acuvue® lenses also have two features - a light blue visibility tint and an inversion mark—that facilitate cleaning and reuse; these features were not present on 1-Day

Acuvue® lenses. Defendants deny that they have misrepresented either the similarities or the differences between the two lenses. The Court has not ruled on the merits of the lawsuit's allegations or on the Defendants' defenses.

IV. PLAINTIFFS' POSITION REGARDING THE SETTLEMENT

The attorneys for the Class believe the Settlement to be fair and adequate and in the Class' best interest. They have entered into the agreement after weighing its substantial benefits against the probabilities of success or failure, and the long delays in obtaining any recovery if the case went to trial.

V. DEFENDANTS' POSITION REGARDING THE SETTLEMENT

Defendants maintain that they have valid defenses to all the claims in the litigation, deny all wrongdoing or liability with respect to the claims asserted and maintain that the certification of the Class was improper. Nonetheless, Defendants have decided to settle the Class' claims pursuant to the terms set out below in order to avoid the costs, risks and expenses of further litigation.

VI. THE TERMS OF THE SETTLEMENT

A. COMPENSATION TO CLASS MEMBERS

1. Upon presentation of an appropriate proof of claim, for every box of Acuvue® contact lenses purchased between January 1, 1995 and July 31, 2001, each Class Member will receive:

(a) Three dollars ($3.00) in cash;

(b) Three dollars ($3.00) credit towards purchases after July 31, 2001, of contact lenses manufactured or distributed by Defendants, subject to the following terms:

(i) The credits are valid for use on the purchase of any contact lens now or in the future manufactured or distributed by Defendants, including, by way of example: Acuvue®, Surevue®, 1-Day Acuvue®, Acuvue2® and Acuvue® Bifocal lenses.

(ii) The credits will be redeemable for cash when submitted to the Settlement Administrator with appropriate proof of purchase of Vistakon contact lenses.

(iii) Up to three credits (a total of $9.00) may be redeemed for each box of Vistakon contact lenses purchased after July 31, 2001, except that up to nine credits (a total of $27.00) may be redeemed toward the purchase of any 90-pack box of 1-Day Acuvue® lenses.

(iv) The credits are valid until two years after the date of their issuance.

(v) The credits are not transferable, and can only be used by the Class Member to whom they are issued.

(c) One dollar ($1.00) cash for the otherwise unreimburseable (i.e. through insurance or other third-party payment) portion of the cost of an examination by a qualified eye care professional from July 31, 2001 until two years after the date of issuance of a credit form by the Settlement Administrator.

2. In addition, for every box of Acuvue® lenses purchased between January 1, 1994 and December 31, 1994, each Class Member will receive three dollars ($3.00) credit towards purchases after July 31, 2001, of contact lenses manufactured or distributed by defendants, on the terms set forth above in Paragraph 1(b).

3. If the Class Member and the eye care professional agree that the Class Member need not pay the eye care professional in full or part for the lenses and/or the eye examination subject to the Settlement, defendants will compensate the eye care professional directly for amounts otherwise payable to the Class Member under the Settlement.

B. DISCLOSURES AND INJUNCTIVE RELIEF

1. Defendants have agreed that they will not make or cause to be made any future statement

(i) that 1-Day Acuvue® lenses cannot be slept in or used for more than one day, or

(ii) that there is any lack of scientific data showing that 1-Day Acuvue® lenses can be slept in or used for more than one day.

2. Defendants have agreed to remove the words "Disposable" and "For Single Use Only" from the 1-Day Acuvue® box.

3. Defendants have agreed to make changes in their packaging and other marketing materials to eliminate anything that could be construed to suggest that 1-Day Acuvue® lenses cannot safely be slept in or used for more than a single day, or that there is any lack of scientific data showing that 1-Day Acuvue® lenses can be slept in or used for more than one day.

4. Defendants will inform eye care professionals who have purchased Defendants' products in the past of the information described above by way of a detailed letter to the eye care professionals, sent by first class

mail and posted on the Professional Information Section of the Vistakon website, and through changes to the Patient Instruction Guides and the Fitting and Patient Management Guides.

5. Defendants have further agreed to change their sales training materials, change the information contained on the Defendants' website, and to follow an agreed-upon script on their toll-free consumer information line to reflect the information described above.

6. Defendants' agreements regarding disclosures and injunctive relief are subject to the continuing approval of applicable regulatory authorities, including the FDA and nothing in the Settlement will prevent Defendants from complying with the expressed requirements of such authorities. In addition, it is recognized that Defendants may from time to time alter their labeling and marketing materials for business reasons, and nothing in the Settlement shall prevent them from doing so provided that no such alteration could be construed to suggest that 1-Day Acuvue® cannot safely be used for more than a single day, or that there is any lack of scientific data showing that 1-Day Acuvue® lenses can be slept in or used for more than one day.

C. VALUE OF THE SETTLEMENT TO THE AVERAGE PARTICIPATING CLASS MEMBER

The value of the Settlement (described in VI(A) above) to each member of the Class is dependent upon the number of boxes of Acuvue® contact lenses such Class Member purchased during the Class Period. It is estimated that the average Class Member purchased approximately 20 boxes during the Class Period. By way of example, this average Class Member would, upon submitting an appropriate Claim Form, receive $60 in cash; $60 in credit towards purchases of Defendants' contact lenses after July 31, 2001; and the right to a $20 refund on the otherwise unreimbursed cost of an examination by a qualified eye care professional after July 31, 2001.

D. CLAIMS PROCESS

If you want to participate in the Settlement, you must submit to the Settlement Administrator, postmarked no later than April 30, 2002, a Claim Form together with appropriate supporting documentation. If you received this Notice by mail, a copy of the Claim Form will be enclosed. To obtain a Claim Form, please call 1 (800)-581-8701; write to P.O. Box 9389, Garden City, New York 11530-9389, or request it through the Settlement Website at www.vistakonsettlement.com. Complete directions for making a claim are provided on the Claim Form and in an accompanying Instruction Sheet.

IF YOU DO NOT TIMELY AND PROPERLY SUBMIT ONE OF THESE CLAIM FORMS YOU WILL NOT BE ALLOWED TO PARTICIPATE IN THE BENEFITS OF THE SETTLEMENT BUT YOU WILL BE BOUND BY THE TERMS OF THE SETTLEMENT AND THE FINAL RELEASE OF CLAIMS AGAINST DEFENDANTS JUST AS IF YOU HAD FILED A PROOF OF CLAIM.

E. RELEASE

If and when the Settlement becomes final, the parties will exchange mutual releases. Such releases extend to Defendants, their shareholders, officers, successors, subsidiaries, assigns and affiliates, to their employees, distributors, agents and representatives and to all optical stores, opticians, optometrists and ophthalmologists with respect to the issues raised in this litigation regarding the sale of Defendants' Acuvue® contact lenses to Class Members from January 1, 1994 to the date of the release, excluding Defendants' obligations under the terms of the Settlement. The releases will exclude any claims relating to physical injuries arising from use of Acuvue® lenses, as well as any claims presently being asserted in *In re Disposable Contact Lens Antitrust Litigation*, 94-MDL-1030-J-20A (M.D. Fla.).

F. ATTORNEYS' FEES, COSTS AND EXPENSES

Class Counsel have been aggressively prosecuting this case on behalf of the Class since its inception on a contingency basis, without charge to the Class. In addition to the settlement amounts described above, Defendants have also agreed to pay to Class Counsel attorneys' fees and expenses up to $20 million (which includes approximately $3 million in expenses), subject to Court approval of the fees and the Settlement. Such attorneys' fees and expenses as may be awarded by the Court will not reduce the class benefits in any way.

G. COMPENSATION TO REPRESENTATIVE PLAINTIFFS

Defendants will make a cash payment in the amount of $15,000 to each Representative Plaintiff. This amount is over and above the settlement amount to be paid to Class Members and will not reduce the class benefits in any way.

H. COSTS OF NOTICE AND ADMINISTERING THE SETTLEMENT

All costs of administering the Settlement, including the cost of Notice to the Class Members, are to be paid directly by Defendants. The cost of the settlement administration and the cost of the Notice to be paid by Defendant is over and above the settlement amount to be paid to Class Members and will not reduce the class benefits in any way.

VII. SETTLEMENT ADMINISTRATION

The Garden City Group, Inc. has been selected as the Settlement Administrator for the purposes of the administration of this Settlement. The Settlement Administrator has total authority to determine the extent, if any, to which each claim will be allowed, subject to review by the Court. Defendants will not have any authority with regard to the acceptance or denial of any claim. The Settlement Administrator will notify all Claimants whose claims have been rejected, in whole or in part, and will set forth the reasons for the rejection, subject to a reasonable opportunity to cure the deficiency. If any Claimant whose claim has been rejected, in whole or in part, desires to contest that rejection, the Claimant must, within thirty (30) days after the mailing of the Notice of Rejection, in writing notify the Settlement Administrator of the Claimant's reasons for contesting the rejection along with any supporting documentation, and requesting a review of the rejection. In the event that such a dispute is not resolved, Class Counsel will present all such requests to the Court for review. Subject to and following final approval of the Settlement, claims will be paid on a periodic basis throughout and after the claims period.

VIII. NOTICE TO THE CLASS

The Class shall be given notice of the Settlement as follows:

A. Between July 31, 2001, and September 15, 2001, a summary notice shall appear in 10 publications with nationwide circulation, as well as 62 regional newspapers throughout the country and 3 national medical publications.

B. This Notice, together with the Claim Form, will be mailed by first class mail to approximately 700,000 Class Members whose addresses are known.

C. This Notice, together with the Claim Form, will be sent by first class mail to all Class Members who request it from the Settlement Administrator either in writing, by calling the settlement toll free number, or by completing a form at www.vistakonsettlement.com. The complete notice will also be posted at www.vistakonsettlement.com, and Vistakon's own website (www.jnjvision.com) (including links both on the home page and webpages giving information about Acuvue® Contact Lenses).

D. A letter will be sent by first class mail to approximately 24,000 Eye Care Professionals, outlining the terms of the settlement and the claims process. The letter will enclose a copy of this Notice, an example of the Claim Form, and the summary notice, and will request that the Eye Care Professionals post the summary notice in their offices.

This letter will also be posted on the Professional Information Section of the Vistakon website.

E. Publication will also include website advertising in the form of 21 million screen appearances on at least six leading websites of a banner advertisement linked to the Settlement Website.

IX. EXCLUSION FROM THE SETTLEMENT

You may request that the Court exclude you from the Class. Persons who request exclusion will not be entitled to share in the settlement proceeds, nor will they be bound by the final judgment in this action. If you wish to be excluded from the Class on whose behalf this action is being maintained, please mail a letter postmarked by October 15, 2001 requesting exclusion to the Claims Administrator at the following address:

Acuvue® Contact Lens Settlement
Settlement Administrator
P.O. Box 9389
Garden City, NY 11530-9389

X. OBJECTIONS TO THE SETTLEMENT

You may appear, in person or through your counsel, at your own expense, and be heard in opposition to: (i) the fairness, adequacy or reasonableness of the Settlement; (ii) the payment of attorneys' fees and reimbursement of expenses; or (iii) awards to the Representative Plaintiffs. Any Objection must be in the form of a written statement from a Class Member and must set forth: (i) the heading referring to this case, Civil Action Docket Number L-8886-96, to the Superior Court of New Jersey, Law Division, Camden County; (ii) the objector's name; (iii) a statement as to whether the Class Member intends to appear at the Settlement Hearing either in person or through counsel; (iv) a detailed statement of the specific basis for the objection, including identification of all papers the objector intends to rely on at the hearing; (v) the names of all witnesses the objector intends to call at the fairness hearing; (vi) the objector's current address; (vii) the objector's current telephone number; (viii) the objector's signature or that of his or her authorized representative; (ix) verification, in the form of receipts for the purchase of Acuvue® contact lenses, that the objector is a Class Member.

The written objection must be filed with the Clerk of New Jersey Superior Court, Law Division, Camden County, 101 South Fifth Street, Camden, New Jersey 08103, and copies served on Counsel for the parties postmarked no later than October 15, 2001 at the following address:

Counsel for Plaintiffs:

Peter L. Masnik
KALIKMAN & MASNIK
P.O. Box 1067
Haddonfield, NJ 08033

Counsel for Defendants:

KRAMER LEVIN NAFTALIS & FRANKEL LLP
FDR Station
P.O. Box 8047
New York, NY 10150-8047
Attn: Vistakon Settlement

DUANE MORRIS & HECKSCHER LLP,
A PENNSYLVANIA LIMITED LIABILITY PARTNERSHIP
P.O. Box 59000
Philadelphia, PA 19102

XI. SETTLEMENT HEARING

The Court has scheduled a fairness hearing on October 25, 2001 at 11:00 a.m. in Courtroom 42 of the New Jersey Superior Court, Law Division, Camden County, 101 South Fifth Street, Camden, New Jersey 08103, before the Honorable John A. Fratto, J.S.C.

At the fairness hearing, the Court will consider, among other issues, whether the Settlement should be granted final approval as fair, adequate and reasonable, and is in the best interests of the Class. Although you may attend this hearing, you are not required to do so in order to participate in the Settlement. The fairness hearing may from time to time and without further notice to Class Members be continued or adjourned by Order of the Court.

XI. SCOPE OF THIS NOTICE AND ADDITIONAL INFORMATION

The foregoing description of the litigation, the terms of the Settlement, and other matters described herein provides a summary of the litigation and the Settlement and is qualified by the full terms of the Stipulation of Settlement. For further details of the litigation and the full terms of the Settlement, you are referred to the Stipulation of Settlement, the pleadings, records and other papers on file in this litigation, which may be inspected during regular business hours at the New Jersey Superior Court, Camden County Hall of Justice, 101 South Fifth Street, Suite 430, Camden, New Jersey 08103. Additional information will be available by calling 1 (800) 581-8701, or writing to Settlement Administrator, P.O. Box 9389, Garden City, NY 11530-9389, or on the internet at www.vistakonsettlement.com.

PLEASE DO NOT CONTACT THE COURT.

Dated: July 27, 2001
Camden, New Jersey
By Order of the Superior Court of New Jersey, Law Division, Camden County

APPENDIX 5: CERTIFICATION ORDER

IN THE CIRCUIT COURT FOR THE FIRST JUDICIAL CIRCUIT
WILLIAMSON COUNTY, ILLINOIS

TAMMY SNIDER and MICHAEL AVERY,
On Behalf of Themselves and All Others
Similarly Situated,

Plaintiffs,

CLASS ACTION

No. 97-L-114

vs.

STATE FARM MUTUAL AUTOMOBILE
INSURANCE COMPANY,

Defendant.

ORDER AND FINDINGS THAT ACTION MAY BE MAINTAINED AS A CLASS ACTION FOR BREACH OF CONTRACT, CONSUMER FRAUD AND EQUITABLE RELIEF CLAIMS

I. SUMMARY OF THE CASE

The representative plaintiffs ("Plaintiffs") in this class action allege that defendant State Farm Mutual Automobile Insurance Company ("State Farm") has breached its contract with its auto insurance policyholders, and violated the provisions of Illinois' Consumer Fraud and Deceptive Business Practices Act (the "CFA"), 815 ILCS 505/1 *et seq.* Plaintiffs seek certification of a class (the "Class") composed of: All persons in the United States, except those residing in Arkansas and Tennessee, who:

(1) were insured by a vehicle casualty insurance policy issued by Defendant State Farm and

(2) made a claim for vehicle repairs pursuant to their policy and had imitation that is, non-factory-authorized and/or non-OEM parts installed on their vehicles or else received monetary compensation determined in relation to the cost of imitation parts.

Excluded from the class are employees of Defendant State Farm, its officers, its directors, its subsidiaries, or its affiliates.

In addition, the following persons are excluded from the class:

(1) persons who resided in Illinois and whose policies were issued/executed prior to April 16, 1994, and

(2) persons who resided in California and whose policies were issued/executed prior to September 26, 1996.

Plaintiffs' claims concern contractual language in standard form State Farm automobile insurance policies issued nationwide. This language either obligates State Farm to restore a policyholder's vehicle to "its pre-loss condition" after an accident, or for State Farm to "pay to repair or replace the property or part with like kind and quality." While State Farm has designed form policies specific to each state, the contractual obligations at issue in this case are stated in substantially identical form in State Farm policies issued nationwide.

Notwithstanding this language, State Farm's uniform policy specifies the use of certain non-original equipment manufacture (non-OEM) replacement parts (referred to as "quality replacement parts" by State Farm and "imitation parts" by Plaintiffs) when these parts are priced lower than original equipment manufacturer's (OEM) parts. Whether this policy violates the above-referenced provisions of State Farm's insurance contracts with its policyholders is the central issue of this litigation.

In their Second Amended Class Action Complaint (the "Complaint"), their submissions, and their arguments before the Court, Plaintiffs contend that non-OEM parts are neither of "like kind and quality," nor are they sufficient to restore a policyholder's vehicle to its "pre-loss condition." For this reason, Plaintiffs contend that State Farm has breached its contract with its policyholders. Plaintiffs seek damages for breach of contract and for State Farm's alleged violation of CFA. Plaintiffs also seek equitable relief against State Farm as set forth in Plaintiffs' Complaint.

State Farm contends that non-OEM parts (particularly those certified by the Certified Auto Parts Association ("CAPA")) are of "like kind and quality" to OEM parts, and that they fully restore a policyholder's vehicle to its "pre-loss condition." State Farm also contends that its policyholders are informed whenever non-OEM parts are used, and that its use of the term "quality replacement parts" is not misleading.

II. GOVERNING LEGAL STANDARD

Certification of a class action in the State of Illinois is governed by 735 ILCS 5/2-801, which provides as follows:

An action may be maintained as a class action in any court of this State and a party may sue or be sued as a representative party of the class only if the court finds:

(1) The class is so numerous that joinder of all members is impractical.

(2) There are questions of fact or law common to the class, which common questions predominate over any questions affecting only individual members.

(3) The representative parties will fairly and adequately protect the interests of the class.

(4) The class action is an appropriate method for the fair and efficient adjudication of the controversy.

Plaintiffs request class certification under 5/2-801. The Court hascarefully considered the testimony adduced over the course of the evidentiary hearing on class certification conducted in November, 1997, the affidavits filed by Plaintiffs and State Farm, the pleadings and briefs submitted to the Court, the voluminous exhibits introduced at the certification hearing, and the argumentsby counsel. *See Gordon v. Boden*, 224 Ill. App. 195, 199, 586 N.E.2d 461, 464 (1991).

In considering class certification the Court has assigned to Plaintiffs the burden of satisfying the four requirements of 5/2-801. *Wheatley v. Board of Ed. of District 205*, 99 Ill. 2d 481, 486, 459 N.E.2d 1364, 1367 (1984).

The Court has not considered the possibility of success on the underlying merits, but only whether the statutory requisites for class certification are satisfied at this time. *See Purcell & Wardrope Chartered v. Hertz Corp.*, 175 Ill. App. 3d 1069, 1075, 530 N.E. 2d 994, 998 (1988)("hypothetical problems that may arise in the future***[are] not a sufficient basis to refuse to certify an otherwise properly pleaded class action.") Applying this standard, the Court makes the following findings of fact, and the following conclusions, with respect to each of the four statutory requirements for certification of a class action in Illinois.

III. CERTIFICATION ISSUES

A. Numerosity and Impracticality of Joinder

735 ILCS 5/2-801(1) requires not only that the number of plaintiffs be numerous, but also that joinder of plaintiffs in one individual action be impractical. "In general the question of numerosity depends on the particular facts of each case and no arbitrary rules regarding the size of class have been established by the courts." *In re Application of Edward J. Rosewell*, 236 Ill. App.3d 165, 174, 603 N.E. 2d 681, 686 (1992).

Where there are a number of potential claimants, and the individual amount of each claim is small, making redress on an individual level difficult, if not impossible, Illinois courts have been particularly receptive to proceeding on a class action basis. *Miner v. Gillette Co.*, 87 Ill. 2d 7, 428 N.E. 2d 478 (1981), *cert. dismissed*, 459 U.S. 86 (1982).

Testimony at the certification hearing indicates that State Farm's practice of using non-OEM parts affects a large number of policyholders. State Farm is the largest auto insurer in the United States, with over 34 million auto policies in effect nationwide. Affidavit of Kathleen M. Pechan, Defendant's Exhibit 8, p. 3. State Farm paid approximately 5.1 million separate collision and comprehensive claims in 1996. Affidavit of David W. Gibson, Jr., Defendant's Exhibit 5, p. 3. In 1993, 49.4% of State Farm's repair estimates nationwide included CAPA certified non-OEM parts. Plaintiffs' Exhibit 177.

It is clear from the exhibits introduced by both Plaintiffs and State Farm that millions of people are affected by State Farm's current claims settlement practices. The Court therefore finds the potential class members are sufficiently numerous.

In reaching its determination that joinder is impracticable the Court is guided by the number of potential class members. The Court finds that, first, the potential class members are widely distributed.

Second, the class is large and its members cannot be easily identified, located and informed of the pendency of this action for purposes of formal joinder.

Third, the potential class members are average consumers, not "sophisticated" entities.

Fourth, the individual damages alleged in this action are, for the most part, small. They involve accelerated vehicle deterioration after repair, inferior fit and finish of repaired areas, and loss of value at resale. The dollar value of individual claims, although not nominal, is not large. *See, e.g.*, Plaintiffs' Exhibit 94 ($1,670 diminution in value upon resale when non-OEM parts used).

Finally, it should be noted that this is the type of consumer class action on behalf of smaller claimants to which Illinois courts have been particularly receptive. *Gordon*, 224 Ill. App. 3d at 204, 586 N.E.2d at 467.

The Court finds that more localized litigation, either on an individual or localized class basis, would be a waste of scarce judicial resources both in this and other states. Addressing the common issues in one litigation would aid judicial administration. Therefore, the Court finds that requirements for certification of a class action under 5/2-801(1) are satisfied.

B. Common Questions of Fact or Law

735 ILCS 5/2-801(2) requires that there be "questions of fact or law common to the class." However, "[c]ertification require[s] only that there be either a predominating common issue of law or fact, not both." *Martin v. Heinold Commodities, Inc.*, 117 Ill. 2d 67, 81 510 N.E. 2d. 840, 846 (1987).

While Plaintiffs must demonstrate that the common questions predominate over individual issues, "the hypothetical existence of individual issues is not a sufficient reason to deny the right to bring a class action. Where it appears that the common issue is dominant and pervasive, something more than the assertion of hypothetical variations of a minor character should be required to bar the action." *Harrison Sheet Steel Co. v. Lyons*, 15 Ill. 2d 532, 538, 155 N.E. 2d 595, 598 (1959).

Common questions arising from the interpretation of standard contract provisions or other uniform documents may be found to predominate; accordingly, the inability of some members of the class to obtain relief due to particular factors unique to them, is to be resolved at trial and does not impair certification of the class. *Steinberg*, 69 Ill. 2d at 338, 371 N.E. 2d at 643; *Rosen v. Village of Dowwer's Grove*, 19 Ill. 2d 448, 456, 167 N.E. 2d. 230, 235 (1960).

Testimony at the class certification hearing highlighted the common factual pattern in this case. James Ford, employed by State Farm as a divisional claims superintendent, testified that State Farm's claims policies are communicated through a series of "general claims memos" issued from State Farm's headquarters in Bloomington, Illinois, which governs claims policy nationwide.

Certification Hearing at 0120-0124. General Claims Memo #430, introduced at the hearing as Defendant's Exhibit 23, governs the use of non-OEM parts.

In resolving customer claims, an estimate is prepared at a local State Farm claims office. When a particular part is needed to complete a repair, the part number is input into a computer program. This program contains a database maintained by, respectively, Mitchell, C.C.C. or A.D.P, *Id.* at 0142, which contains information on the availability of, and price for, various parts from suppliers State Farm has approved. *Id.* at 0144. The computer's software then automatically searches what was referred to as "the matrix," and locates the cheapest available part. *Id.* at 0143-44. This part, whether it is an OEM or non-OEM part, is then automatically specified on the repair estimate. *Id.* at 0143-44. The State Farm adjuster has no authority to override the computer's choice of the cheapest part. *Id.* at 0153-54. It appears that this practice is uniform throughout the United States wherever non-OEM parts are used. *Id.* at 0155. Defendant's Exhibit 23. The policyholder is neither informed, nor consulted when a non-OEM part is specified. Certification Hearing at 0132. If the policy holder does not want non-OEM parts placed on their car, they must convince a body shop to absorb the price difference, or pay for the difference in price themselves. *Id.* at 0151.

As to the consumer fraud allegations, the facts presented at the certification hearing on State Farm's methods of disclosing to policyholders its use of non-OEM parts also demonstrates a course of conduct common to all class members. When such parts are used on an estimate, the policyholder is given a State Farm brochure discussing the use of non-OEM parts. Defendant's Exhibit 24; Certification Hearing at 0124-25. The estimate is then stamped indicating the use of non-OEM parts. Defendant's Exhibit 27. State Farm has also promoted the use of the term"quality replacement parts" nationwide in an effort to promote its substitution of non-OEM for OEM parts. Plaintiffs' Exhibits 115, 116.

The Court finds that the evidence introduced at the certification hearing demonstrate "a series of essentially identical transactions," *Miner*, 87 Ill. 2d at 19, 428 N.E. 2d at 484, between State Farm and its insureds, which transactions routinely result in the use of non-OEM parts.

In reaching its conclusion that the class claims are essentially factually identical, the Court acknowledges the significant evidence presented at the hearing regarding the varying availability and use of non-OEM parts in each of State Farm's regional offices. Affidavit of David A. Gibson, Jr., Defendant's Exhibit 5; Certification Hearing at 0121, 0124. The Court notes that varying availability of non-OEM parts affects how many policyholders did or did not receive non-OEM parts, but it does not affect the common pattern with respect to class members, who always received such parts if they were available. Any person whose car was repaired only with OEM parts is not part of the class for which certification is sought. Therefore, any variations in OEM part use is irrelevant to certification.

Given State Farm's common and ongoing course of conduct in repairing its insureds' vehicles with cheaper non-OEM parts whenever these parts were available, potential class members have a common interest in determining State Farm's obligations under its contractual provisions. "A class action can properly be prosecuted where a defendant is alleged to have acted wrongly in the same basic manner as to an entire class. In such circumstances, the common class questions still dominate the case." *Brooks v. Midas-International Corp.*, 47 Ill. App. 3d 266, 273, 361 N.E. 2d 815, 820 (1977).

Here the class members have a common interest in determining if State Farm's policy violates its contractual obligations, and this issue of contractual interpretation predominates over other issues. *See, e.g.*, *Carrao v. Healthcare Service Corp.*, 118 Ill. App. 3d 417, 428, 454 N.E. 2d 781, 790 (1983). Similarly, the question of whether State Farm's practice of using non-OEM parts constitutes a violation of the CFA is a common issue appropriate for resolution. *See, e.g.*, *Brooks*, 47 Ill. App. 3d at 272, 361 N.E. 2d at 820.

In determining if this common question predominates, the Court has carefully considered State Farm's contention that it has no standard form auto insurance policy, as each individual state's policy is tailored to comply with the requirements of that state. *See* Affidavit of Everett J. Truttmann, Defendant's Exhibit 9. Therefore, State Farm contends there is no common question to be interpreted.

The Court finds, however, that the policies' specific form is immaterial, provided that the operative contractual language contained in each policy is susceptible to uniform interpretation. Whether particular language in its policies authorizes State Farm's use of non-OEM parts or is in conflict with the "like kind and quality" or "pre-loss condition" language of the policies is not a question to be resolved during class certification. It is a question for resolution on the merits.

State Farm has placed particular emphasis on its practice of using CAPA-certified non-OEM parts. Under this practice, State Farm will specify only a CAPA-certified part in place of an OEM part when that type of part was subject to CAPA certification. Affidavit of David A. Gibson, Jr., Defendant's Exhibit 5, p. 8. Although considerable testimony was received as to the difference between CAPA-certified non-OEM parts, non-CAPA-certified non-OEM parts, and OEM parts, this testimony all addresses the merits of whether non-OEM parts satisfy State Farm's contractual obligations.

This ultimate issue is irrelevant to class certification, where the common treatment of the class members in having received non-OEM parts is the central question.

The Court heard substantial testimony as to the number of different non-OEM parts. Since the Court finds that a common question concerning the use of non-OEM parts has been established, the number of different parts and their relative quality is a question that goes to the merits of whether non-OEM parts are equal to OEM parts. Plaintiffs' submissions that non-OEM parts are categorically inferior in performance and safety, because of inferior design, manufacture and quality control, and evidence that they are commonly perceived by the marketplace as inferior, with a resulting negative effect on policyholders' cars' ultimate resale value are factors in the Court's determination that the requirements of 2-801(2) have been established.

In *Phillips Petroleum Co. v. Shutts*, the United States Supreme Court discussed the constitutional limitations on the application of a particular state's substantive law to the claims of out-of-state plaintiffs, finding that a state may apply its substantive law beyond its borders where it has "'significant contact or aggregation of contacts' to the claims asserted by each member of the plaintiff class, contacts 'creating, state interests'* * * insur[ing] that the choice of [law] is not arbitrary or unfair." 472 U.S. 797, 821-22, 105 S. Ct. 2965, 2979 (1985) (quoting *Allstate Ins. Co. v. Hague*, 449 U.S. 302, 312-12, 101 S. Ct. 633, 640 (1981)). Illinois courts have approved the application of the CFA, § 815 ILCA 505/1 *et seq.*, to the claims of out-of-state plaintiffs. *See, e.g., Gordon*, 224 Ill. App. 3d at 202-03, 586 N.E. 2d at 466; *Martin* 117 Ill. 2d 67, 510 N.E.2d 840. In *Martin*, a class composed of in state and out-of-state plaintiffs sued an Illinois corporation for fraud and for violations of the Illinois CFA. Relying upon *Phillips*, the Illinois Supreme Court noted that defendant's principal place of business was Illinois and stated:

> "Applying the Phillips Petroleum standard to the instant case, it is apparent that Illinois substantive law can be applied to resolve the underlying common factual dispute. Here each member of the plaintiff class asserts the same breach of defendant's fiduciary duty with regard to the same nondisclosure of the same fact. This common allegation implicates the legitimate interests of the State of Illinois in insuring that persons and entities within its jurisdiction, insofar as they undertake to act as agents, do so in accordance with its law." 117 Ill. 2d at 82, 510 N.E.2d at 847.

> The Illinois Supreme Court concluded that "there can be no doubt that the claim of each member of the plaintiff class implicates the legitimate interests of Illinois in applying its law to adjudicate a dispute involving a business principally situated in its jurisdiction and which, by its own efforts, insistently has sought to avail itself of both the courts and the laws of the forum State." 117 Ill. 2d at 83, 510 N.E. 2d at 847.
>
> Under *Phillips* and *Martin*, given the fact that State Farm is situated and headquartered in Illinois and affirmatively uses Illinois courts and law, this Court could apply Illinois substantive laws, including the CFA to the entire class.
>
> While it is not necessary for the Court at this time to decide upon choice of law as to the breach of contract claim, it does note that the eventual decision as to choice of law will not prevent the certification of the Class in this case. *Gordon*, 224 Ill. App. 3d at 202, 586 N.E. 2d at 466.
>
> The Court retains the right to divide the litigation into a manageable number of sub-classes under 2-802(b) should differences in law present themselves. The Court finds that the requirements of Section 2-801(2) are met as "common issues of fact or law predominate."
>
> **C. The Representative Plaintiffs Fairly and Adequately Protect the Interest of the Class**

735 ILCS 5/2-801(3) conditions class certification upon a finding that "[t]he representative parties will fairly and adequately protect the interest of the class." "The purpose . . . of the adequate representation requirement is merely to ensure that all class members will receive proper, efficient, and appropriate protection of their interests in the presentation of the claim." *Gordon*, 224 Ill. App. at 203, 586 N.E. 2d at 466. Judicial evaluation of the quality of the representation, as well as class certification in general, rests within the sound discretion of the trial court. *McCabe v. Burgess*, 75 Ill. 2d 457, 389 N.E. 2d 565, 568 (1979).

Adequate representation assures compliance with due process requirements. "The test applied to determine the adequacy of representation is whether the interests of those who are parties are the same as those who are not joined and whether the litigating parties fairly represent those not joined." *Miner*, 87 Ill. 2d at 14, 428 N.E.2d at 482. Essentially, the determination focuses on whether the absentee members are so represented by the persons before the court "that their interests will receive actual and efficient protection." *Brooks*, 47 Ill. App. 3d at 274, 361 N.E. 2d at 820, quoting *State Life Insurance Co. v. Board of Education*, 394 Ill. 301, 308, 68 N.E.2d 525, 529 (1946).

Finally, unlike in Federal Rule of Civil Procedure 23, there is no "typicality" requirement in 5/2-801(3). The Illinois rule is more liberal than the federal rule in this regard and ". . . a class representative may not be disqualified merely because his claim is not exactly the same as the claims of other potential class members." *Carrao*, 118 Ill. App. 3d at 428, 454 N.E.2d at 790. The Court finds that the requirement of adequate representation under 735 ILCS 5/2-801(3) has been satisfied.

After a rigorous analysis of Plaintiffs' Complaint, Plaintiffs' affidavits and Plaintiffs' counsels' affidavits or résumés, the Court concludes that Plaintiffs have zealously pursued their claims since learning of State Farm's alleged wrongful conduct and that Plaintiffs have sufficient financial resources to absorb the expenses involved in being the named representatives.

The Court further finds that no conflicting interests exist between Plaintiffs and the Plaintiff Class as it is clear from the Court's review of the material submitted in support of class certification that the representatives herein and Class members share common objectives and legal and factual positions. Other than the dates and specific amounts concerning Plaintiffs' repairs and Class members' repairs, the proof, objectives, legal and factual positions will be essentially identical from plaintiff to plaintiff and class member to class member.

In determining the adequacy of representation, the Court may also consider the quality and experience of the attorneys for the Class. The Court finds, after a rigorous analysis and review of the pleadings and résumés submitted by Plaintiffs' counsel and having observed their conduct in open Court, that they are able advocates for the Class. Counsel for Plaintiffs have regularly engaged in major complex consumer litigation of size, scope and complexity similar to this case. Counsel have successfully prosecuted many and varied class actions or other complex litigation. They have the experience and sophistication that the Plaintiffs and Class members lack. The Court finds that counsel for Plaintiffs are well suited for this case and that Plaintiffs will fairly and adequately protect the interest of the Class in compliance with the mandate of 735 ILCS 5/2-801(3).

D. The Class Action Is an Appropriate Method to Resolve the Class Issues

735 ILCS 5/2-801(4) conditions class certification on a finding that "[t]he class action is an appropriate method for the fair and efficient adjudication of the controversy." In applying the fourth prerequisite, the Court has considered whether a class action can best secure economies of time, effort, and expense and promote uniformity of decision or accomplish other ends of equity and justice. *Gordon*, 224 Ill. App. 3d at 203, 586 N.E.2d at 467.

While Federal Rule of Civil Procedure 23(b)(3) requires that a class action be *superior* to other available methods of adjudication, the Illinois statute requires that the trial court find that the class action is an *appropriate* method of litigating the controversy. Section 5/2-801(4). This standard allows the trial court a more flexible measure of discretion in determining whether to permit the class action to proceed. A significant factor in the case at bar is that a class action is the only practical means for State Farm policyholders to present their claims and for State Farm to achieve finality as to their claims.

Illinois courts have historically recognized that class actions are an appropriate method of fairly and efficiently adjudicating controversies involving numerous small claims. In *Wood River Area Development Corporation v. Germania Federal Savings and Loan*, 198 Ill. App. 3d 445, 452; 555 N.E.2d 1150, 1154 (1990), the Court stated "[t]he class action is particularly appropriate where those who have allegedly been injured 'are in poor position to seek legal redress, either because they do not know enough or because such redress is disproportionately expensive. . . . Its 'historic mission' has been to take care of the smaller guy." The *Wood River* court concluded,:

> "No matter how refined, how revised, or how evolved" [the class action becomes], ". . . the goal of the class action remains the same—justice for the lowly, the tenants, the parishioners, the multitudes." 198 Ill. App. 3d at 448, 555 N.E.2d at 1152.

The United States Supreme Court recently acknowledged not only the appropriateness, but the necessity, of class treatment of small consumer claims in *AmChem Prods. Inc. v. Windsor*, ___ U.S. ___, 117 S. Ct. 2231, 2250 (1997), . . . stating. . .

> "Predominance is a test readily met in certain cases alleging consumer or securities fraud or violations of the antitrust laws."

With respect to "small claims" class actions in general, the Court stated:

> "The policy at the very core of the class action mechanism is to overcome the problem that small recoveries do not provide the incentive for any individual to bring a solo action prosecuting his or her rights. A class action solves this problem by aggregating the relatively paltry potential recoveries into something worth someone's (usually an attorney's) labor." 117 S. Ct. at 2246, quoting *Mace v. Van Ru Credit Corp.*, 109 F.3d 338, 344 (7th Cir. 1997).

The evidence presented to the Court supports the conclusion that, not only is a class action an appropriate method for the fair adjudication of the disputes between Defendant State Farm and its millions of automobile insurance policyholders, but also that it may be the only means by which these disputes may be efficiently resolved.

Defendant State Farm provides automobile insurance coverage to one out of every five insured drivers in the United States, making it the nation's number one auto insurer. Plaintiffs' Exhibit 102. The evidence submitted by Plaintiffs indicates that State Farm achieved a savings of

$32 million in 1994 from the use of non-OEM parts. Plaintiffs' Exhibit 92. Accordingly, this action qualifies for class resolution both in terms of the dollar amount in controversy and the number of claims involved.

State Farm has previously settled two lawsuits challenging its non-OEM parts practices—the Illinois case entitled *Krusinski v. State Farm*, No. 87 CH 10253, in the Circuit Court of Cook County ("*Krusinski*"), and the California case entitled *Krinsk v. State Farm Mutual Automobile Insurance Company*, No. 626412, in San Diego County Superior Court ("*Krinsk*"). Defendant's Exhibit 1. State Farm has settled both the *Krusinski* and *Krinsk* actions but has continued its practice of utilizing non-OEM parts in its repairs of policyholders' vehicles. In addition to other relief, Plaintiffs at bar seek an injunction prohibiting State Farm from continuing its practice of settling policyholders' repair claims based upon the use and cost of non-OEM parts.

Proof of Plaintiffs' claims against Defendant State Farm may be made on a class-wide basis. After a rigorous review of the pleadings, exhibits and affidavits submitted by Plaintiffs, the only proof that might differ from Plaintiff to Plaintiff and class member to class member would appear to be the amount of damages suffered by each class member. It is well settled, in Illinois and elsewhere, that differences in the amount of damages suffered by individual class members will not defeat class certification. *Gordon*, 224 Ill. App. 3d at 202, 586 N.E.2d at 465-66.

Individual lawsuits for small amounts would be too expensive, and absent a class action, individual lawsuits run a substantial likelihood of adjudications. Upon consideration of the pleadings, exhibits and affidavits submitted by Plaintiffs, the Court concludes that the proposed Class is manageable. The Court concludes, pursuant to 735 ILCS 5/2-801(4), that a class action is an appropriate method for the for the fair and efficient adjudication of this controversy.

IV. CONCLUSION

Pursuant to 735 ILCS 5/2-801, this Court concludes that Plaintiffs have adequately satisfied the four requirements for class certification of this action under Illinois law. Plaintiffs will now have the opportunity to try and prove the merits of their claims, which is an entirely different matter from establishing the requirements for class certification.

The Court notes that class certification will allow all State Farm policyholders to seek redress for their claims and will also provide State Farm with finality as to the claims. State Farm has, for years, had class actions filed against it concerning the matters involved in this litigation and has been forced to defend itself in numerous jurisdictions.

Since this case has been filed, the parties have made the Court aware of several cases which have recently been filed, including the *Dorries* action in Champaign County, Illinois (No. 97-L- 88), which has now been terminated by Judge Green's November 10, 1997 order in *"Krusinski"*. The Court has learned that the attorneys prosecuting the *Dorries* case in Illinois had also filed an identical class action case in Alabama. Such a multiplicity of suits is an inefficient use of judicial resources and places State Farm in the unenviable position of trying to defend itself on multiple fronts.

The Court believes that Illinois is the one State where a national class can be maintained and where all issues between State Farm and State Farm's policyholders concerning the use of non-OEM parts can finally be resolved. The Court is unaware of any other class action cases pending in Illinois concerning the issues involved in this litigation and is unaware of any other class action case in any other State which has certified a national class after a full evidentiary hearing on class certification.

The following described Plaintiff Class is hereby ordered certified for purposes of litigation and trial:

> All persons in the United States, except those residing in Arkansas and Tennessee, who
>
> > (1) were insured by a vehicle casualty insurance policy issued by Defendant State Farm and
> >
> > (2) made a claim for vehicle repairs pursuant to their policy and had non-factory-authorized and/or non-OEM (Original Equipment Manufacturer) "crash parts" installed on their vehicles or else received monetary compensation determined in relation to the cost of such parts.

Excluded from the class are employees of Defendant State Farm, its officers, its directors, its subsidiaries, or its affiliates.

In addition, the following persons are excluded from the class:

> (1) persons who resided or garaged their vehicles in Illinois and whose Illinois insurance policies were issued/executed prior to April 16, 1994, and
>
> (2) persons who resided in California and whose policies were issued/executed prior to September 25, 1996.

ENTERED: December 5, 1997
JOHN SPERONI, ASSOCIATE CIRCUIT JUDGE
[February 11, 1998]

APPENDIX 6: NOTICE OF CLASS ACTION

IN THE CIRCUIT COURT FOR THE FIRST JUDICIAL CIRCUIT
WILLIAMSON COUNTY, ILLINOIS

TAMMY SNIDER and MICHAEL AVERY, On Behalf of Themselves and All Others Similarly Situated,	CLASS ACTION
Plaintiffs,	No. 97-L-114
vs.	
STATE FARM MUTUAL AUTOMOBILE INSURANCE COMPANY,	
Defendant.	

NOTICE OF CLASS ACTION

If you have had vehicle repairs under your State Farm auto insurance policy, this notice may affect your rights.

Please read this Court Ordered Class Action Notice carefully.

In the Circuit Court for the First Judicial Circuit, Williamson County, Illinois, a lawsuit is now pending titled: *Tammy Snider and Michael Avery, on behalf of themselves and all other similarly situated, Plaintiffs, vs. State Farm Mutual Automobile Insurance Company, Defendant, No. 97-L-114.*

This Notice is directed to all members of the Plaintiff Class, defined as:

> All persons in the United States, except those residing in Arkansas and Tennessee, who:
>
> > (1) were insured by a vehicle casualty insurance policy issued by Defendant State Farm and
> >
> > (2) made a claim for vehicle repairs pursuant to their policy and had non-factory-authorized and/or non-OEM (Original Equipment Manufacturer) "crash parts"* installed on their vehicles or else received monetary compensation determined in relation to the cost of such parts.

Excluded from the Class are employees of Defendant State Farm, its officers, its directors, its subsidiaries, or its affiliates.

In addition, the following persons are excluded from the Class:

> (1) persons who resided or garaged their vehicles in Illinois and whose Illinois insurance policies were issued/executed prior to April 16, 1994, and
>
> (2) persons who resided in California and whose policies were issued/executed prior to September 26, 1996.

Notice of this lawsuit is given pursuant to Illinois statutes, and by order of the Court, to inform you of the Court's decision to certify a Plaintiff Class, the nature of Plaintiffs' claims, and your right to participate in or exclude yourself from the Class.

Individual and representative Plaintiffs Tammy Snider and Michael Avery have been appointed by the Court to function as representatives of the Plaintiff Class.

Plaintiffs' claims concern the contractual language contained in standard form State Farm automobile insurance policies issued nationwide, which, either obligate State Farm to restore a policyholder's vehicle to "its pre-loss condition" after an accident, or to "pay to repair or replace the property or part with like kind and quality."

While State Farm has designed form policies specific to each state, the contractual obligations at issue in this case are stated in substantially identical form in State Farm policies issued nationwide.

Under this contractual language, State Farm uniformly specifies the use of certain non-original equipment manufacturer ("non-OEM") replacement parts (referred to as "quality replacement parts" by State Farm and "imitation parts" by Plaintiffs) when these parts are available and priced lower than original equipment manufacturer's (OEM) parts.

Plaintiffs contend that non-OEM crash parts are neither of "like kind and quality," nor are they sufficient to restore a policyholder's vehicle to its "pre-loss condition." For this reason, Plaintiffs contend that State Farm has breached its contract with its policyholders.

Plaintiffs also contend that State Farm's use of non-OEM crash parts and the term "quality replacement parts" are violations of the Illinois Consumer Fraud and Deceptive Business Practices Act (815 ILCS 505/1 *et seq.*)

Plaintiffs request compensatory damages and an injunction against State Farm.

State Farm denies any wrongdoing and contends that non-OEM parts are of "like kind and quality" to OEM crash parts, and that they fully restore a policyholder's vehicle to its "pre-loss condition."

State Farm also contends that its policyholders are informed whenever non-OEM crash parts are used, and that its use of the term "quality replacement parts" is not misleading.

The Court has certified for litigation and trial the Plaintiff Class of State Farm policy holders described above. The Court's class certification order does not decide the merits of Plaintiffs' claims or State Farm's defenses. Plaintiffs will be required to prove the Class claims at trial set to commence on February 2, 1999.

Class Counsel have been appointed by the Court to represent the interests of the Class. Class Counsel include G. Patrick Murphy, Barrett Law Offices, the Rose Law Firm, Much Shelist Freed Denenberg Ament Bell & Rubenstein, P.C., and Lieff, Cabraser, Heimann & Bernstein, LLP. You will not be charged for Class Counsel's services. Instead, if they obtain a recovery for the Class, Class Counsel may apply to the Court for payment of their reasonable attorneys' fees and costs by State Farm or out of any funds recovered before distribution of the net proceeds to the Class. You have the right to hire your own attorney. If you hire your own attorney, you will be responsible for paying that attorney's fee. You also have the right to seek to intervene or appear in the action with the Court's permission.

If you wish to remain a member of the Class, YOU NEED NOT DO ANYTHING AT THIS TIME. As Class members, you will be bound by all orders and judgments of the Court, and your claims will be terminated by the judgment in this case.

You may exclude yourself from the Class by writing to the address below, and expressly stating in a letter postmarked by June 5, 1998, that you wish to be excluded from the Class.

If you exclude yourself from the Class, you cannot participate in any recovery for the Class, and you will not be bound by any Court orders or judgments. If you wish to remain a Class member, DO NOT send an exclusion letter.

If you have questions regarding this litigation, you may write to: Snider, et al. v. State Farm, Plaintiffs' Class Counsel, P.O. Box 1500, Marion, Illinois 62959. You may also call 1-888-299-9777, or see the website at http://www.sfparts.com.

PLEASE DO NOT CONTACT THE COURT.

Dated: February 25, 1998.
Honorable John Speroni, Associate Circuit Judge.

APPENDIX 7: LONG FORM LANGUAGE NOTICE—SECURITIES CLASS ACTION

UNITED STATES DISTRICT COURT FOR THE DISTRICT OF STATE

If you bought XYZ Corporation stock in 1999, you could get a payment from a class action settlement

A federal court authorized this notice. This is not a solicitation from a lawyer.

- The settlement will provide $6.99 million to pay claims from investors who bought shares of XYZ Corporation stock during 1999.
- The settlement resolves a lawsuit over whether XYZ misled investors about its future earnings.
- Your legal rights are affected whether you act, or don't act. Read this notice carefully.

YOUR LEGAL RIGHTS AND OPTIONS IN THIS SETTLEMENT:	
SUBMIT A CLAIM FORM	The only way to get a payment.
EXCLUDE YOURSELF	Get no payment. This is the only option that allows you to ever be part of any other lawsuit against XYZ, about the legal claims in this case.
OBJECT	Write to the Court about why you don't like the settlement.
GO TO A HEARING	Ask to speak in Court about the fairness of the settlement.
DO NOTHING	Get no payment. Give up rights.

- These rights and options—**and the deadlines to exercise them**—are explained in this notice.

- The Court in charge of this case still has to decide whether to approve the settlement. Payments will be made if the Court approves the settlement and after appeals are resolved. Please be patient.

1. WHY DID I GET THIS NOTICE PACKAGE?

You or someone in your family may have purchased shares of XYZ Corporation stock during 1999.

The Court sent you this notice because you have a right to know about a proposed settlement of a class action lawsuit, and about all of your options, before the Court decides whether to approve the settlement. If the Court approves it and after objections and appeals are resolved, an administrator appointed by the Court will make the payments that the settlement allows. You will be informed of the progress of the settlement.

This package explains the lawsuit, the settlement, your legal rights, what benefits are available, who is eligible for them, and how to get them.

The Court in charge of the case is the United States District Court for the District of State, and the case is known as *North et al v. XYZ Corporation and Anne Adams,* Case No. CV-00-5678. The people who sued are called Plaintiffs, and the company and the person they sued, XYZ and Anne Adams, are called the Defendants.

2. WHAT IS THIS LAWSUIT ABOUT?

The lawsuit claimed that XYZ and its Chief Executive Officer, Anne Adams, misled investors by intentionally overstating the profits that the company expected to earn in the future. The lawsuit also claimed that XYZ issued press releases and financial statements that had false and misleading information about XYZ's income and earnings per share for 1999, and that XYZ executives sold their personally held shares of XYZ stock at inflated prices during that time. XYZ and Ms. Adams deny they did anything wrong.

3. WHY IS THIS A CLASS ACTION?

In a class action, one or more people called Class Representatives (in this case Mary North), sue on behalf of people who have similar claims. All these people are a Class or Class Members. One court resolves the issues for all Class Members, except for those who exclude themselves from the Class. U.S. District Judge Jane Jones is in charge of this class action.

4. WHY IS THERE A SETTLEMENT?

The Court did not decide in favor of Plaintiffs or Defendants. Instead, both sides agreed to a settlement. That way, they avoid the cost of a trial, and the people affected will get compensation. The Class Representative and the attorneys think the settlement is best for all Class Members.

WHO IS IN THE SETTLEMENT

To see if you will get money from this settlement, you first have to decide if you are a Class Member.

5. HOW DO I KNOW IF I AM PART OF THE SETTLEMENT?

Judge Jones decided that everyone who fits this description is a Class Member: *All people who purchased shares of XYZ Corporation stock during 1999.*

6. ARE THERE EXCEPTIONS TO BEING INCLUDED?

You are not a Class Member if you are an officer or director of XYZ, or were one during 1999. Also, immediate family members of XYZ officers and directors are not in the Class.

If one of your mutual funds owns shares of XYZ stock, that alone does not make you a Class Member. You are a Class Member only if you purchased shares of XYZ stock individually. Contact your broker to see if you have or held XYZ stock.

If you sold XYZ stock during 1999, that alone does not make you a Class Member. You are a Class Member only if you bought shares in 1999.

7. I'M STILL NOT SURE IF I AM INCLUDED.

If you are still not sure whether you are included, you can ask for free help. You can call 1-800-000- 0000 or visit www.XYZsettlement.com for more information. Or you can fill out and return the claim form described on page 5, in question 10, to see if you qualify.

THE SETTLEMENT BENEFITS—WHAT YOU GET

8. WHAT DOES THE SETTLEMENT PROVIDE?

XYZ has agreed to create a $6.99 million fund to be divided among all Class Members who send in a valid claim form.

9. HOW MUCH WILL MY PAYMENT BE?

Your share of the fund will depend on the number of valid claim forms that Class Members send in, how many shares of XYZ stock you bought, and when you bought and sold them. Here's how it works:

There were about 40,000,000 shares of XYZ stock bought during 1999. For each day of that year, the settlement specifies that the stock price was "Artificially Inflated" by a certain amount. These amounts per share are listed on pages 11 and 12 of the "Understanding Your Payment" section of this Notice.

By following the instructions on page 10 of this Notice, you can calculate what is called your Net Recognized Loss. It's unlikely that you will get a payment for all of your Net Recognized Loss. After all Class Members have sent in their claim forms, the payment you get will reflect your Net Recognized Loss in relation to everyone's Net Recognized Loss. See the instructions on page 10 for more information on your Net Recognized Loss.

So those who bought more shares and have a larger Net Recognized Loss will get more money, and those who bought fewer shares and have a smaller Net Recognized Loss will get less. All of the $6.99 million available will be distributed.

If every eligible Class Member sends in a valid claim form, the average payment will be 17 ½ cents ($6,990,000 ÷ 40,000,000 shares) for each share bought in 1999. The number of claimants who send in claims varies widely from case to case. If less than 100% of the Class sends in a claim form, you could get more money.

HOW YOU GET A PAYMENT—SUBMITTING A CLAIM FORM

10. HOW CAN I GET A PAYMENT?

To qualify for payment, you must send in a claim form. A claim form is attached to this Notice. You may also get a claim form on the Internet at www.XYZsettlement.com. Read the instructions carefully, fill out the form, include all the documents the form asks for, sign it, and mail it postmarked no later than **Month 00, 0000**.

11. WHEN WOULD I GET MY PAYMENT?

The Court will hold a hearing on Month 00, 0000, to decide whether to approve the settlement. If Judge Jones approves the settlement after that, there may be appeals. It's always uncertain whether these appeals can be resolved, and resolving them can take time, perhaps more than a year. Everyone who sends in a claim form will be informed of the progress of the settlement. Please be patient.

12. WHAT AM I GIVING UP TO GET A PAYMENT OR STAY IN THE CLASS?

Unless you exclude yourself, you are staying in the class, and that means that you can't sue, continue to sue, or be part of any other lawsuit against XYZ about the legal issues in *this* case. It also means that all of the Court's orders will apply to you and legally bind you. If you sign the claim form, you will agree to a "Release of Claims," attached to the claim form, which describes exactly the legal claims that you give up if you get settlement benefits.

EXCLUDING YOURSELF FROM THE SETTLEMENT

If you don't want a payment from this settlement, but you want to keep the right to sue or continue to sue XYZ, on your own, about the legal issues in this case, then you must take steps to get out. This is called excluding yourself—or is sometimes referred to as opting out of the settlement Class.

13. HOW DO I GET OUT OF THE SETTLEMENT?

To exclude yourself from the settlement, you must send a letter by mail saying that you want to be excluded from *North v. XYZ*. Be sure to include your name, address, telephone number, and your signature. You must mail your exclusion request postmarked no later than **Month 00, 0000** to:

XYZ Exclusions
P.O. Box 0000
City, ST 00000-0000

You can't exclude yourself on the phone or by e-mail. If you ask to be excluded, you will not get any settlement payment, and you cannot object to the settlement. You will not be legally bound by anything that happens in this lawsuit. You may be able to sue (or continue to sue) XYZ in the future.

14. IF I DON'T EXCLUDE MYSELF, CAN I SUE XYZ FOR THE SAME THING LATER?

No. Unless you exclude yourself, you give up any right to sue XYZ for the claims that this settlement resolves. If you have a pending lawsuit speak to your lawyer in that case immediately. You must exclude yourself from *this* Class to continue your own lawsuit. Remember, the exclusion deadline is **Month 00, 0000**.

15. IF I EXCLUDE MYSELF, CAN I GET MONEY FROM THIS SETTLEMENT?

No. If you exclude yourself, do not send in a claim form to ask for any money. But, you may sue, continue to sue, or be part of a different lawsuit against XYZ.

THE LAWYERS REPRESENTING YOU

16. DO I HAVE A LAWYER IN THIS CASE?

The Court asked the law firm of Lawfirm LLP in City, ST, to represent you and other Class Members. These lawyers are called Class Counsel. You will not be charged for these lawyers. If you want to be represented by your own lawyer, you may hire one at your own expense.

17. HOW WILL THE LAWYERS BE PAID?

Class Counsel will ask the Court for attorneys' fees and expenses up to $3,010,000, and a payment of $10,000 to the Class Representative, Mary North. The Court may award less than these amounts. XYZ will separately pay the fees and expenses that the Court awards. These amounts will not come out of the funds for payments to Class Members. XYZ has agreed not to oppose these fees and expenses. XYZ will also separately pay the costs to administer the settlement.

OBJECTING TO THE SETTLEMENT

You can tell the Court that you don't agree with the settlement or some part of it.

18. HOW DO I TELL THE COURT THAT I DON'T LIKE THE SETTLEMENT?

If you're a Class Member, you can object to the settlement if you don't like any part of it. You can give reasons why you think the Court should not approve it. The Court will consider your views. To object, you must send a letter saying that you object to *North v. XYZ*. Be sure to include your name, address, telephone number, your signature, and the reasons you object to the settlement. Mail the objection to these three different places postmarked no later than **Month 00, 0000**:

COURT	CLASS COUNSEL	DEFENSE COUNSEL
Clerk of the Court United States District Court for the District of State 100 Court Street City, ST 00000-0000	Herman Green Lawfirm LLP 100 Main Street Suite 100 City, ST 00000-0000	John Simmons Defensefirm LLP 200 Broad Street Suite 200 City ST, 00000-0000

19. WHAT'S THE DIFFERENCE BETWEEN OBJECTING AND EXCLUDING?

Objecting is simply telling the Court that you don't like something about the settlement. You can object only if you stay in the Class. Excluding yourself is telling the Court that you don't want to be part of the Class. If you exclude yourself, you have no basis to object because the case no longer affects you.

THE COURT'S FAIRNESS HEARING

The Court will hold a hearing to decide whether to approve the settlement. You may attend and you may ask to speak, but you don't have to.

20. WHEN AND WHERE WILL THE COURT DECIDE WHETHER TO APPROVE THE SETTLEMENT?

The Court will hold a Fairness Hearing at 9:00 AM on Tuesday, Month 00, 0000, at the United States District Court for the District of State, 100 Court Street, City, State, in Courtroom One. At this hearing the Court will consider whether the settlement is fair, reasonable, and adequate. If there are objections, the Court will consider them. Judge Jones will listen to people who have asked to speak at the hearing. The Court may also decide how much to pay to Class Counsel. After the hearing, the Court will decide whether to approve the settlement. We do not know how long these decisions will take.

21. DO I HAVE TO COME TO THE HEARING?

No. Class Counsel will answer questions Judge Jones may have. But, you are welcome to come at your own expense. If you send an objection, you don't have to come to Court to talk about it. As long as you mailed your written objection on time, the Court will consider it. You may also pay your own lawyer to attend, but it's not necessary.

22. MAY I SPEAK AT THE HEARING?

You may ask the Court for permission to speak at the Fairness Hearing. To do so, you must send a letter saying that it is your "Notice of Intention to Appear in *North v. XYZ.*" Be sure to include your name, address, telephone number, and your signature. Your Notice of Intention to Appear must be postmarked no later than **Month 00, 0000**, and be sent to the Clerk of the Court, Class Counsel, and Defense Counsel, at the three addresses on page 7, in question 18. You cannot speak at the hearing if you excluded yourself.

IF YOU DO NOTHING

23. WHAT HAPPENS IF I DO NOTHING AT ALL?

If you do nothing, you'll get no money from this settlement. But, unless you exclude yourself, you won't be able to start a lawsuit, continue with a lawsuit, or be part of any other lawsuit against XYZ about the legal issues in this case, ever again.

GETTING MORE INFORMATION

24. ARE THERE MORE DETAILS ABOUT THE SETTLEMENT?

This notice summarizes the proposed settlement. More details are in a Settlement Agreement. You can get a copy of the Settlement Agreement by writing to Herman Green, Lawfirm LLP, 100 Main Street, Suite 100, City, ST 00000-0000, or by visiting www.XYZsettlement.com.

25. HOW DO I GET MORE INFORMATION?

You can call 1-800-000-0000 toll free; write to XYZ Settlement, P.O. Box 0000, City ST 00000-0000; or visit the website at www.XYZsettlement.com, where you will find answers to common questions about the settlement, a claim form, plus other information to help you determine whether you are a Class Member and whether you are eligible for a payment.

DATE: MONTH 00, 0000.

UNDERSTANDING YOUR PAYMENT

STEP 1: Go to the table on the next page, find the date you bought your XYZ shares, and see what the artificial inflation rate per share ("Artificial Inflation") was on that date.

STEP 2: Multiply the number of shares you bought by the Artificial Inflation for that date. This result is your Recognized Loss. Skip to STEP 6 if you did not sell this stock during the class period. If you sold any of your XYZ stock during 1999, continue with STEP 3.

STEP 3: Go to the table on the next page, find the date you sold your shares of XYZ stock that you had purchased in 1999, and see the Artificial Inflation for that date.

STEP 4: Multiply the number of shares you sold by the Artificial Inflation for that date.

STEP 5: Subtract the amount calculated in STEP 4 from the amount calculated in STEP 2. This is your Net Recognized Loss. If your Net Recognized Loss is less than zero, you do not have a claim in this settlement.

STEP 6: Your Net Recognized Loss is a percentage of the total Net Recognized Losses from all Class Members claims. This percentage is the same percentage of the settlement fund that you will get. This amount can be estimated only after the claims administrator receives all the claim forms. If less than 100% of the Class sends in a claim form, you could get more money.

STEP 7: The claims administrator will calculate your payment from the settlement fund.

EXAMPLE—PAYMENT CALCULATION	
Suppose John Smith bought 500 shares of XYZ stock on March 31, 1999, and sold 400 shares of XYZ stock on August 27, 1999:	
STEP 1:	On 3/31/99 the Artificial Inflation = $8.03
STEP 2:	500 shares bought x $8.03 = $4,015 Recognized Loss
STEP 3:	On 8/27/99 the Artificial Inflation = $5.89
STEP 4:	400 shares sold x $5.89 = $2,356 to deduct from John Smith's Recognized Loss
STEP 5:	$4,015 - $2,356 = $1,659, John Smith's Net Recognized Loss
STEP 6:	Suppose in this example that there is a total Net Recognized Loss of $20 million claimed by all Class Members who send in claim forms: $1,659 ÷ $20,000,000 = John Smith's Net Recognized Loss per share is .0000829 of the total.
STEP 7:	.0000829 x $6,990,000 = John Smith's payment would be $579.47

Date	Artificial Inflation Rate Per Share
01/02/1999	$3.01
01/05/1999	$2.67
01/06/1999	$2.67
01/07/1999	$2.62
01/08/1999	$2.50
01/09/1999	$2.41
01/12/1999	$2.44
01/13/1999	$2.52
01/14/1999	$2.52
01/15/1999	$2.48
01/16/1999	$2.45
01/20/1999	$4.11
01/21/1999	$4.07
01/22/1999	$4.15
01/23/1999	$4.07
01/26/1999	$3.94
01/27/1999	$3.88
01/28/1999	$4.18
01/29/1999	$4.15
01/30/1999	$4.09
02/02/1999	$3.99
02/03/1999	$3.96
02/04/1999	$4.09
02/05/1999	$4.35
02/06/1999	$4.88
02/09/1999	$4.94
02/10/1999	$5.00
02/11/1999	$5.02
02/12/1999	$4.96
02/13/1999	$5.19
02/17/1999	$5.60
02/18/1999	$5.53
02/19/1999	$5.47
02/20/1999	$5.30
02/23/1999	$5.45
02/24/1999	$5.43
02/25/1999	$5.49
02/26/1999	$5.87
02/27/1999	$5.87
03/02/1999	$5.53
03/03/1999	$5.60
03/04/1999	$5.53
03/05/1999	$5.43

Date	Artificial Inflation Rate Per Share
03/06/1999	$5.41
03/09/1999	$5.76
03/10/1999	$5.64
03/11/1999	$5.49
03/12/1999	$5.74
03/13/1999	$5.74
03/16/1999	$5.72
03/17/1999	$5.72
03/18/1999	$5.93
03/19/1999	$5.94
03/20/1999	$5.83
03/23/1999	$5.93
03/24/1999	$6.13
03/25/1999	$6.47
03/26/1999	$6.95
03/27/1999	$7.12
03/30/1999	$7.57
03/31/1999	$8.03
04/01/1999	$7.95
04/02/1999	$8.37
04/03/1999	$7.95
04/06/1999	$8.10
04/07/1999	$8.08
04/08/1999	$8.08
04/09/1999	$8.18
04/13/1999	$8.14
04/14/1999	$8.16
04/15/1999	$8.25
04/16/1999	$8.25
04/17/1999	$8.31
04/20/1999	$8.14
04/21/1999	$8.22
04/22/1999	$8.07
04/23/1999	$8.07
04/24/1999	$7.97
04/27/1999	$7.46
04/28/1999	$7.35
04/29/1999	$7.12
04/30/1999	$7.50
05/01/1999	$7.80
05/04/1999	$7.95
05/05/1999	$7.88
05/06/1999	$7.72

Date	Artificial Inflation Rate Per Share
05/07/1999	$7.57
05/08/1999	$7.46
05/11/1999	$7.50
05/12/1999	$7.46
05/13/1999	$7.46
05/14/1999	$7.36
05/15/1999	$7.40
05/18/1999	$7.42
05/19/1999	$7.19
05/20/1999	$7.08
05/21/1999	$7.36
05/22/1999	$7.35
05/26/1999	$7.36
05/27/1999	$7.36
05/28/1999	$7.33
05/29/1999	$7.38
06/01/1999	$7.40
06/02/1999	$7.42
06/03/1999	$7.54
06/04/1999	$7.69
06/05/1999	$7.84
06/08/1999	$8.29
06/09/1999	$8.42
06/10/1999	$8.67
06/11/1999	$8.90
06/12/1999	$9.03
06/15/1999	$8.73
06/16/1999	$8.67
06/17/1999	$8.50
06/18/1999	$8.41
06/19/1999	$8.75
06/22/1999	$8.90
06/23/1999	$9.11
06/24/1999	$9.64
06/25/1999	$9.60
06/26/1999	$9.77
06/29/1999	$9.56
06/30/1999	$8.86
07/01/1999	$9.14
07/02/1999	$9.20
07/06/1999	$9.05
07/07/1999	$9.01
07/08/1999	$8.97

Date	Artificial Inflation Rate Per Share
07/09/1999	$8.92
07/13/1999	$8.84
07/14/1999	$8.90
07/15/1999	$8.88
07/16/1999	$8.86
07/17/1999	$8.86
07/20/1999	$9.69
07/21/1999	$8.48
07/22/1999	$8.25
07/23/1999	$7.65
07/24/1999	$7.76
07/27/1999	$7.76
07/29/1999	$7.42
07/30/1999	$7.50
07/31/1999	$7.27
08/03/1999	$7.06
08/04/1999	$7.16
08/05/1999	$7.46
08/06/1999	$7.78
08/07/1999	$7.93
08/10/1999	$7.86
08/11/1999	$7.55
08/12/1999	$7.57
08/13/1999	$7.55
08/14/1999	$7.50
08/17/1999	$7.50
08/18/1999	$8.03
08/19/1999	$8.08
08/20/1999	$7.99
08/21/1999	$7.82
08/24/1999	$7.57
08/25/1999	$7.08
08/26/1999	$6.27
08/27/1999	$5.89
08/28/1999	$5.66
08/31/1999	$5.13
09/01/1999	$5.36
09/02/1999	$6.19
09/03/1999	$5.83
09/04/1999	$5.77
09/08/1999	$6.21
09/09/1999	$6.02
09/10/1999	$5.59

Date	Artificial Inflation Rate Per Share
09/11/1999	$5.47
09/14/1999	$5.74
09/15/1999	$6.04
09/16/1999	$5.91
09/17/1999	$5.93
09/18/1999	$6.44
09/21/1999	$6.36
09/22/1999	$6.78
09/23/1999	$6.76
09/24/1999	$6.53
09/25/1999	$5.89
09/28/1999	$5.72
09/29/1999	$5.43
09/30/1999	$5.15
10/01/1999	$3.99
10/05/1999	$4.20
10/06/1999	$4.18
10/07/1999	$3.90
10/08/1999	$3.75
10/09/1999	$3.64
10/12/1999	$4.05
10/13/1999	$3.98
10/14/1999	$3.86
10/15/1999	$3.86
10/16/1999	$3.79
10/19/1999	$3.84
10/20/1999	$4.39
10/21/1999	$3.90
10/22/1999	$3.94
10/23/1999	$3.64
10/26/1999	$3.64
10/27/1999	$3.84
10/28/1999	$4.24
10/29/1999	$4.37
10/30/1999	$4.54
11/02/1999	$4.81
11/03/1999	$5.30
11/04/1999	$5.60
11/05/1999	$5.96
11/06/1999	$5.98
11/09/1999	$6.06
11/10/1999	$5.89
11/11/1999	$5.72

Date	Artificial Inflation Rate Per Share
11/12/1999	$5.45
11/13/1999	$5.51
11/16/1999	$5.70
11/17/1999	$5.76
11/18/1999	$5.93
11/19/1999	$6.10
11/20/1999	$6.04
11/23/1999	$6.06
11/24/1999	$5.85
11/25/1999	$5.76
11/27/1999	$5.76
11/30/1999	$5.83
12/01/1999	$5.72
12/02/1999	$5.68
12/03/1999	$5.66
12/04/1999	$3.49
12/07/1999	$1.54
12/08/1999	$1.58
12/10/1999	$1.58
12/11/1999	$1.65
12/14/1999	$1.54
12/15/1999	$1.61
12/16/1999	$1.56
12/17/1999	$1.54
12/18/1999	$1.64
12/21/1999	$1.70
12/22/1999	$1.60
12/23/1999	$1.63
12/24/1999	$1.63
12/28/1999	$1.72
12/29/1999	$1.74
12/30/1999	$1.76
12/31/1999	$1.86

APPENDIX 8: SUMMARY LEGAL PUBLICATION NOTICE—SECURITIES CLASS ACTION

COURT-ORDERED LEGAL NOTICE

If you bought XYZ Corp. stock in 1999, you could get a payment from a class action settlement

Para una notificación en Español, llamar o visitar nuestro website.

A settlement has been proposed in a class action lawsuit about the price of XYZ Corporation stock. The settlement will provide $6.99 million to pay claims from XYZ investors who bought the company's stock during 1999. If you qualify, you may send in a claim form to get benefits, or you can exclude yourself from the settlement, or object to it.

The United States District Court for the District of State authorized this notice. The Court will have a hearing to decide whether to approve the settlement, so that the benefits may be paid.

WHO'S INCLUDED?

You are a Class Member and could get benefits if you bought shares of XYZ stock during 1999. You are a Class Member only if you bought shares of XYZ stock individually, not simply through a mutual fund. If you sold XYZ stock during 1999, you are a Class Member only if those shares you sold were purchased in 1999. XYZ officers and directors, as well as immediate family members of directors of XYZ during1999, are not Class Members.

Contact your broker to see if you hold or held shares of XYZ stock. If you're not sure whether you are included, you can get more information, including a detailed notice, at www.XYZsettlement.com or by calling toll free 1-800-000-0000.

WHAT'S THIS ABOUT?

The lawsuit claimed that XYZ and its Chief Executive Officer, Anne Adams, misled investors by intentionally overstating the profits that the company expected to earn in the future. The lawsuit also claimed that XYZ issued false and misleading information about XYZ's income and earnings per share for 1999, and that XYZ executives sold their personal shares at inflated prices during that time. XYZ and Ms. Adams deny they did anything wrong. The Court did not decide which side was right. But both sides agreed to the settlement to ensure a resolution and to provide benefits to Class Members.

WHAT DOES THE SETTLEMENT PROVIDE?

XYZ agreed to create a fund of $6.99 million to be divided among all Class Members who send in valid claim forms. A Settlement Agreement, available at the website below, describes all of the details about the proposed settlement.

Your share of the fund will depend on the number of valid claim forms that Class Members send in, how many shares of XYZ stock you bought, and when you bought and sold them. Generally, if you bought more shares and have more Net Recognized Losses (as explained in the detailed notice), you will get more money. If you bought fewer shares and have fewer Net Recognized Losses, you will get less. All of the $6.99 million will be paid out.

If every eligible Class Member sends in a valid claim form, the average payment will be 17 ½ cents for each share of stock bought in 1999. The number of claimants who send in claims varies widely from case to case. If less than 100% of the Class sends in a claim form, you could get more money.

HOW DO YOU ASK FOR A PAYMENT?

A detailed notice and claim form package contains everything you need. Just call or visit the website below to get one. To qualify for a payment, you must send in a claim form. **Claim forms are due by Month 00, 0000.**

WHAT ARE YOUR OTHER OPTIONS?

If you don't want settlement benefits or don't want to be legally bound by the settlement, you must exclude yourself by **Month 00, 0000**, or you won't be able to sue, or continue to sue, XYZ about the legal claims in this case. If you exclude yourself, you can't get any benefits from this settlement. If you stay in the settlement, you may object to it by

Month 00, 0000. The detailed notice explains how to exclude yourself or object.

The Court will hold a hearing in this case (*North v. XYZ Corp.*, Case No. CV-00-5678) on **Month 00, 0000**, to consider whether to approve the settlement and a request by the lawyers representing all Class Members (Lawfirm LLP, of City, ST) for attorneys' fees and costs. The fees and costs won't reduce the settlement fund. You may ask to appear at the hearing, but you don't have to. For more information, call toll free 1-800-000-0000, visit the website www.XYZsettlement.com, or write to XYZ Settlement, P.O. Box 000, City, ST 0000-0000.

APPENDIX 9: LONG FORM LANGUAGE NOTICE—PRODUCT LIABILITY CLASS ACTION

UNITED STATES DISTRICT COURT FOR THE DISTRICT OF STATE

If you were ever exposed to asbestos in ABC Corporation products, you could get a payment from a class action settlement

A federal court authorized this notice. This is not a solicitation from a lawyer.

- The settlement will provide $270 million to pay claims from those who are currently suffering from an asbestos-related disease, as well as those exposed but not sick, who need medical monitoring.
- To qualify, you must have been exposed to asbestos in ABC Corporation products. Your exposure may have happened in different ways:
  - **Homeowners may have had ABC's Xinsulation in their attics or walls.**
  - **Workers may have installed ABC building products like Xbestos.**
- Your legal rights are affected whether you act or don't act. Read this notice carefully.

YOUR LEGAL RIGHTS AND OPTIONS IN THIS SETTLEMENT:	
SUBMIT A CLAIM FORM	The only way to get a payment.
EXCLUDE YOURSELF	Get no payment. This is the only option that allows you to ever be part of any other lawsuit against ABC, about the legal claims in this case.
OBJECT	Write to the Court about why you don't like the settlement.

GO TO A HEARING	Ask to speak in Court about the fairness of the settlement.
DO NOTHING	Get no payment. Give up rights.

- These rights and options—**and the deadlines to exercise them**—are explained in this notice.
- The Court in charge of this case still has to decide whether to approve the settlement. Payments will be made if the Court approves the settlement and after appeals are resolved. Please be patient.

BASIC INFORMATION

1. WHY DID I GET THIS NOTICE PACKAGE?

You or someone in your family may have owned or lived in a home or other property with Xinsulation. Or you or a family member may have worked around Xbestos, Xinsulation, or other asbestos-containing products made or sold by ABC Corporation.

The Court sent you this notice because you have a right to know about a proposed settlement of a class action lawsuit, and about your options, before the Court decides whether to approve the settlement. If the Court approves it and after objections and appeals are resolved, an administrator appointed by the Court will make the payments that the settlement allows. You will be informed of the progress of the settlement.

This package explains the lawsuit, the settlement, your legal rights, what benefits are available, who is eligible for them, and how to get them.

The Court in charge of the case is the United States District Court for the District of State, and the case is known as *Smith et al v. ABC Corporation*, Case No. CV-00-1234. The people who sued are called Plaintiffs, and the company they sued, ABC, is called the Defendant.

2. WHAT IS THIS LAWSUIT ABOUT?

The lawsuit claimed that ABC made and sold products knowing that the asbestos fibers contained in them posed a danger to the health and safety of anyone exposed to them. The lawsuit claimed that exposure increased the risk of developing asbestosis, mesothelioma, lung cancer, or other diseases that scientists have associated with exposure to asbestos. ABC denies they did anything wrong.

3. WHY IS THIS A CLASS ACTION?

In a class action, one or more people, called Class Representatives (in this case Frederick Smith), sue on behalf of people who have similar claims. All these people are a Class or Class Members. One court resolves the issues for all Class Members, except for those who exclude themselves from the Class. U.S. District Judge Jane Jones is in charge of this class action.

4. WHY IS THERE A SETTLEMENT?

The Court did not decide in favor of Plaintiffs or Defendants. Instead, both sides agreed to a settlement. That way, they avoid the cost of a trial, and the people affected will get compensation. The Class Representative and the attorneys think the settlement is best for everyone who was injured or exposed.

WHO IS IN THE SETTLEMENT

To see if you will get money from this settlement, you first have to decide if you are a Class Member.

5. HOW DO I KNOW IF I AM PART OF THE SETTLEMENT?

Judge Jones decided that everyone who fits this description is a Class Member: *All people exposed to asbestos fibers in any ABC Corporation product any time before Month 00, 0000.*

6. WHICH ABC PRODUCTS ARE INCLUDED?

If you're not sure whether you were exposed to ABC products, look at these pictures and captions:

DID YOU WORK AROUND OR INSTALL ABC BUILDING PRODUCTS?

ABC made Xbestos, Xinsulation, and other building products called Ybestos and Zbestos. These products were sprayed on during the construction of high-rise office buildings and many other structures and homes. You may have been exposed to asbestos by either installing the products directly, or simply by working at the site. You may have brought asbestos fibers home on your clothing, exposing your family.

DID YOUR HOME EVER HAVE XINSULATION?

Xinsulation is in the attics and walls of older homes. It's loose, white, and fluffy. It's shaped like a small cotton ball, varying from silver-blue to gray-black. It is layered with a glittery, puffy appearance that may have a translucent or brownish hue. After years in the attic, the granules may darken to black or gray. **Be careful not to disturb it.** It may be underneath other types of insulation. The settlement provides for someone to come and test it for you, if you call and ask.

DID A FAMILY MEMBER EVER WORK AROUND ABC'S ASBESTOS PRODUCTS? HE OR SHE MAY BE INCLUDED.

Did your home or property ever have Xinsulation?

You're included even if you don't live there anymore.

7. IF I WAS EXPOSED BUT DO NOT HAVE ANY DISEASE, AM I INCLUDED?

Yes. You don't have to have a disease to be part of this settlement. The Class includes all those who have certain asbestos-related diseases. The Class also includes those who were exposed but are not currently suffering from an asbestos-related disease and who may need medical monitoring—even those who haven't visited a doctor. The settlement payments are different for sick and for healthy people.

8. I'M STILL NOT SURE IF I AM INCLUDED.

If you are still not sure whether you are included, you can ask for free help. You can call 1-800-000-0000 and ask for an independent inspector to come see if your insulation is Xinsulation. **Some government agencies warn that the asbestos in Xinsulation is dangerous to your health, so do not disturb it.** For more information, you can also visit the website, www.ABCsettlement.com. Or you can fill out and return the claim form described on page 7, in question 12, to see if you qualify.

THE SETTLEMENT BENEFITS—WHAT YOU GET

9. WHAT DOES THE SETTLEMENT PROVIDE?

ABC has agreed to create an Injury Compensation Fund of $200 million for Class Members who have been diagnosed with an asbestos-related disease, and another $70 million Medical Monitoring Fund for assessing the health of those who were exposed but not currently suffering from an asbestos-related disease. ABC will also pay claims for future injuries among Class Members already exposed who request medical monitoring.

10. WHAT CAN I GET FROM THE SETTLEMENT?

ARE YOU INJURED?

If you have been diagnosed with an asbestos-related disease, you may be eligible for payment from the Injury Compensation Fund. These are the payment amounts for specific asbestos-related diseases:

INJURY COMPENSATION FUND PAYMENTS			
Disease	**Minimum**	**Maximum**	**Average**
Mesothelioma	$10,000	$100,000	$20,000-$30,000
Lung Cancer	$5,000	$43,000	$9,000-$15,000
Other Cancer	$2,500	$16,000	$4,000-$6,000
Non-Malignant	$1,250	$15,000	$3,000-$4,000

If, after everyone sends in claim forms, the injury compensation claims total more than $200 million, the payments will be reduced. If the injury compensation claims are less than $200 million, the payments will be increased.

Your payment will be based on how severe your disease is, your medical expenses, and your lost earnings. To get the minimum payment in the table above, you do not have to detail your expenses or lost earnings. To get larger amounts up to the maximum amount, you'll have to prove your medical expenses and document your lost earnings.

WERE YOU EXPOSED TO ASBESTOS? HAVE YOU BEEN TESTED?

If you were exposed to one or more of ABC's asbestos-containing products, but you are *not* currently suffering from an asbestos-related disease, you may be eligible for payment from the Medical Monitoring Fund according to this table:

MEDICAL MONITORING FUND PAYMENTS		
Exposure to Asbestos	Medical Expenses	Payment
You have evidence of exposure to asbestos in an ABC product.	You *do* have evidence of your medical expenses to test for an asbestos-related disease.	$1,000 or your actual expenses, whichever is greater.
	You *don't* have evidence of your medical expenses to test for an asbestos-related disease.	$1,000

If, after everyone sends in claim forms, the medical monitoring claims total more than $70 million, the payments will be reduced. If the total medical monitoring claims are less than $70 million, the payments will be increased.

11. WHAT IF I GET SICK, OR I AM EXPOSED TO ASBESTOS IN ABC PRODUCTS, IN THE FUTURE?

If you were exposed to asbestos in ABC products before Month 00, 0000, you must send in a claim form now, or you will not be able to get a payment under this settlement for injuries that develop in the future. If you do send a claim form now, and in the future you develop symptoms of the diseases listed in the table on page 5, in question 10, you will be eligible for a payment as shown in that table.

If, in the future, you determine that you need medical monitoring from exposure that took place *after* Month 00, 0000, then you are not bound by this settlement for those claims. This means you can pursue your claims separately from this settlement with your own lawyer.

HOW YOU GET A PAYMENT—SUBMITTING A CLAIM FORM

12. HOW CAN I GET A PAYMENT?

To qualify for payment, you must send in a claim form. A claim form is attached to this Notice. You can also get a claim form on the Internet at www.ABCsettlement.com. Read the instructions carefully, fill out the form, include all the documents the form asks for, sign it, and mail it postmarked no later than **Month 00, 0000**.

For an injury compensation claim, you'll have to send in a statement from a doctor with a description of your current medical condition, including a diagnosis of one of the types of diseases in the table on page 5, in question 10. For a medical monitoring claim, you have to show that you were exposed to ABC products. You may be asked for additional documentation. Follow all the instructions on the claim form.

13. WHEN WOULD I GET MY PAYMENT?

The Court will hold a hearing on Month 00, 0000, to decide whether to approve the settlement. If Judge Jones approves the settlement after that, there may be appeals. It's always uncertain whether these appeals can be resolved, and resolving them can take time, perhaps more than a year. Everyone who sends in a claim form will be informed of the progress of the settlement. Please be patient.

14. WHAT AM I GIVING UP TO GET A PAYMENT OR STAY IN THE CLASS?

Unless you exclude yourself, you are staying in the Class, and that means that you can't sue, continue to sue, or be part of any other lawsuit against ABC about the legal issues in *this* case. It also means that all of the Court's orders will apply to you and legally bind you. If you sign the claim form, you will agree to a "Release of Claims," attached to the claim form, which describes exactly the legal claims that you give up if you get settlement benefits.

EXCLUDING YOURSELF FROM THE SETTLEMENT

If you don't want a payment from this settlement, but you want keep the right to sue or continue to sue ABC, on your own, about the legal issues in this case, then you must take steps to get out. This is called excluding yourself—or is sometimes referred to as opting out of the settlement Class.

15. HOW DO I GET OUT OF THE SETTLEMENT?

To exclude yourself from the settlement, you must send a letter by mail saying that you want to be excluded from *Smith v. ABC*. Be sure to include your name, address, telephone number, and your signature. You must mail your exclusion request postmarked no later than **Month 00, 0000**, to:

ABC Exclusions
P.O. Box 0000
City, ST 00000-0000

You can't exclude yourself on the phone or by e-mail. If you ask to be excluded, you will not get any settlement payment, and you cannot object to the settlement. You will not be legally bound by anything that happens in this lawsuit. You may be able to sue (or continue to sue) ABC in the future.

16. IF I DON'T EXCLUDE MYSELF, CAN I SUE ABC FOR THE SAME THING LATER?

No. Unless you exclude yourself, you give up the right to sue ABC for the claims that this settlement resolves. If you have a pending lawsuit, speak to your lawyer in that lawsuit immediately. You must exclude yourself from *this* Class to continue your own lawsuit. Remember, the exclusion deadline is **Month 00, 0000**.

17. IF I EXCLUDE MYSELF, CAN I GET MONEY FROM THIS SETTLEMENT?

No. If you exclude yourself, do not send in a claim form to ask for any money. But, you may sue, continue to sue, or be part of a different lawsuit against ABC.

THE LAWYERS REPRESENTING YOU

18. DO I HAVE A LAWYER IN THIS CASE?

The Court asked the law firms of Lawfirm One LLP, of City, ST, and Lawfirm Two P.C., of City, ST, to represent you and other Class Members. Together, the lawyers are called Class Counsel. You will not be charged for these lawyers. If you want to be represented by your own lawyer, you may hire one at your own expense.

19. HOW WILL THE LAWYERS BE PAID?

Class Counsel will ask the Court for attorneys' fees and expenses up to $23,990,000, and a payment of $10,000 to the Class Representative, Frederick Smith. The Court may award less than these amounts. ABC will separately pay the fees and expenses that the Court awards. These amounts will not come out of the funds for payments to Class Members. ABC has agreed not to oppose these fees and expenses. ABC will also separately pay the costs to administer the settlement.

OBJECTING TO THE SETTLEMENT

You can tell the Court that you don't agree with the settlement or some part of it.

20. HOW DO I TELL THE COURT THAT I DON'T LIKE THE SETTLEMENT?

If you're a Class Member, you can object to the settlement if you don't like any part of it. You can give reasons why you think the Court should not approve it. The Court will consider your views. To object, you must send a letter saying that you object to *Smith v. ABC*. Be sure to include your name, address, telephone number, your signature, and the reasons you object to the settlement. Mail the objection to these three different places postmarked no later than **Month 00, 0000**:

COURT	CLASS COUNSEL	DEFENSE COUNSEL
Clerk of the Court United States District Court for the District of State 100 Court Street City, ST 00000-0000	Herman Green Lawfirm One LLP 100 Main Street Suite 100 City, ST 00000-0000	Mary Jones Defensefirm LLP 200 Broad Street Suite 200 City ST, 00000-0000

21. WHAT'S THE DIFFERENCE BETWEEN OBJECTING AND EXCLUDING?

Objecting is simply telling the Court that you don't like something about the settlement. You can object only if you stay in the Class. Excluding yourself is telling the Court that you don't want to be part of the Class. If you exclude yourself, you have no basis to object because the case no longer affects you.

THE COURT'S FAIRNESS HEARING

The Court will hold a hearing to decide whether to approve the settlement. You may attend and you may ask to speak, but you don't have to.

22. WHEN AND WHERE WILL THE COURT DECIDE WHETHER TO APPROVE THE SETTLEMENT?

The Court will hold a Fairness Hearing at 10:00 a.m. on Tuesday, Month 00, 0000, at the United States District Court for the District of State, 100 Court Street, City, State, in Courtroom One. At this hearing the Court will consider whether the settlement is fair, reasonable, and adequate. If there are objections, the Court will consider them. Judge Jones will listen to people who have asked to speak at the hearing. The Court may also decide how much to pay Class Counsel. After the hearing, the Court will decide whether to approve the settlement. We do not know how long these decisions will take.

23. DO I HAVE TO COME TO THE HEARING?

No. Class Counsel will answer questions Judge Jones may have. But, you are welcome to come at your own expense. If you send an objection, you don't have to come to Court to talk about it. As long as you mailed your written objection on time, the Court will consider it. You may also pay your own lawyer to attend, but it's not necessary.

24. MAY I SPEAK AT THE HEARING?

You may ask the Court for permission to speak at the Fairness Hearing. To do so, you must send a letter saying that it is your "Notice of Intention to Appear in *Smith v. ABC*." Be sure to include your name, address, telephone number, and your signature. Your Notice of Intention to Appear must be postmarked no later than **Month 00, 0000**, and be sent to the Clerk of the Court, Class Counsel, and Defense Counsel, at the three addresses on page 9, in question 20. You cannot speak at the hearing if you excluded yourself.

IF YOU DO NOTHING

25. WHAT HAPPENS IF I DO NOTHING AT ALL?

If you do nothing, you'll get no money from this settlement. But, unless you exclude yourself, you won't be able to start a lawsuit, continue with a lawsuit, or be part of any other lawsuit against ABC about the legal issues in this case, ever again.

GETTING MORE INFORMATION

26. ARE THERE MORE DETAILS ABOUT THE SETTLEMENT?

This notice summarizes the proposed settlement. More details are in a Settlement Agreement. You can get a copy of the Settlement Agreement by writing to Herman Green, Lawfirm One LLP, 100 Main Street, Suite 100, City, ST 00000-0000, or by visiting www.ABCsettlement.com.

27. HOW DO I GET MORE INFORMATION?

You can call 1-800-000-0000 toll free; write to ABC Settlement, P.O. Box 000, City, ST 00000-0000; or visit the website at www.ABCsettlement.com, where you will find answers to common questions about the settlement, a claim form, plus other information to help you determine whether you are a Class Member and whether you are eligible for a payment.

DATE: MONTH 00, 0000.

APPENDIX 10: SUMMARY LEGAL PUBLICATION NOTICE—PRODUCT LIABILITY CLASS ACTION

LEGAL NOTICE

If you were exposed to Xbestos or other ABC products, you may have a claim in a proposed class action settlement

A settlement of a class action lawsuit affects you if you were ever exposed to asbestos in Xinsulation, Xbestos, or other ABC Corporation products. The settlement will pay people who are suffering from an asbestos-related disease, as well as those who were exposed, but not sick, who need medical monitoring. If you qualify, you may send in a claim form to ask for payment, or you can exclude yourself from the settlement, or object.

The United States District Court for the District of State authorized this notice. The Court will have a hearing to consider whether to approve the settlement, so that the benefits may be paid.

WHO'S AFFECTED?

Construction workers who installed, or worked around, Xbestos, Xinsulation, and other ABC products (pictured and described to the right) are included in the settlement. Homeowners whose homes have or had Xinsulation are also included, as described in separate notices. *You're a 'Class Member' if you were exposed to asbestos fibers in any ABC Corporation products any time before Month 00,0000.*

WHAT'S THIS ABOUT?

The lawsuit claimed that ABC made and sold products knowing that the asbestos fibers contained in them posed a danger to the health and safety of anyone exposed to them. The suit claimed that exposure increased the risk of developing Asbestosis, Mesothelioma, Lung Cancer, or other diseases that scientists have associated with exposure to asbestos. ABC denies all allegations and has asserted many defenses. The settlement is not an admission of wrongdoing or an indication that any law was violated.

WHAT CAN YOU GET FROM THE SETTLEMENT?

There will be an Injury Compensation Fund of $200 million for Class Members who have been diagnosed with an asbestos-related disease, and a $70 million Medical Monitoring Fund for checking the health of those who were exposed but are not currently suffering from an asbestos-related disease. Compensation for injuries will be in varying amounts for specific diseases:

DISEASE	MINIMUM	MAXIMUM	AVERAGE
MESOTHELIOMA	$10,000	$100,000	$20,000-$30,000
LUNG CANCER	$5,000	$43,000	$9,000-$15,000
OTHER CANCER	$2,500	$16,000	$4,000-$6,000
NON-MALIGNANT	$1,250	$15,000	$3,000-$4,000

Medical monitoring payments will be $1,000 or the amount of your actual medical expenses, whichever is greater.

HOW DO YOU GET A PAYMENT?

A detailed notice and claim form package contains everything you need. Just call or visit the website below to get one. **Claim forms are due by Month 00, 0000**. For an injury compensation claim, you'll have to submit a statement from a doctor that describes your current medical condition and confirms that you have one of the diseases in the box above. For a medical monitoring claim, you'll have to show proof of your exposure to an ABC asbestos-containing product.

WHAT ARE YOUR OPTIONS?

If you don't want a payment and you don't want to be legally bound by the settlement, you must exclude yourself by **Month 00, 0000**, or you won't be able to sue, or continue to sue, ABC about the legal claims in this case. If you exclude yourself, you can't get a payment from this settlement. If you stay in the Class, you may object to the settlement by **Month 00, 0000**. The detailed notice describes how to exclude yourself or object. The Court will hold a hearing in this case (*Smith v. ABC Corp.*, Case No. CV-00-1234) on **Month 00, 0000**, to consider whether to approve the settlement and attorneys' fees and expenses totalling no more than $30 million. You may appear at the hearing, but you don't have to. For more details, call toll free 1-800-000-0000, go to www.ABCsettlement.com, or write to ABC Settlement, P.O. Box 000, City, ST 00000.

APPENDIX 11: LONG FORM LANGUAGE NOTICE— EMPLOYMENT DISCRIMINATION

UNITED STATES DISTRICT COURT FOR THE DISTRICT OF STATE

If you are a woman and are or were employed by MNO, a class action lawsuit may affect your rights.

A court authorized this notice. This is not a solicitation from a lawyer.

- Female employees have sued MNO, Inc., alleging discrimination against women.
- The Court has allowed the lawsuit to be a class action on behalf of all women employed by MNO as account executives at any time from June 6, 1996, through July 15, 2003.
- The Court has not decided whether MNO did anything wrong. There is no money available now, and no guarantee there will be. However, your legal rights are affected, and you have a choice to make now:

YOUR LEGAL RIGHTS AND OPTIONS IN THIS LAWSUIT	
DO NOTHING	**Stay in this lawsuit. Await the outcome. Give up certain rights.** By doing nothing, you keep the possibility of getting money or benefits that may come from a trial or a settlement. But, you give up any rights to sue MNO separately about the same legal claims in this lawsuit.
ASK TO BE EXCLUDED	**Get out of this lawsuit. Get no benefits from it. Keep rights.** If you ask to be excluded and money or benefits are later awarded, you won't share in those. But, you keep any rights to sue MNO separately about the same legal claims in this lawsuit.

- Your options are explained in this notice. To ask to be excluded, you must act before **Month 00,0000.**
- Lawyers must prove the claims against MNO at a trial set to start Month 00, 0000. If money or benefits are obtained from MNO, you will be notified about how to ask for a share.
- **Any questions? Read on and visit www.mnoclassaction.com.**

BASIC INFORMATION

1. WHY DID I GET THIS NOTICE?

MNO's records show that you currently work, or previously worked, for MNO, Inc. This notice explains that the Court has allowed, or "certified," a class action lawsuit that may affect you. You have legal rights and options that you may exercise before the Court holds a trial. The trial is to decide whether the claims being made against MNO, on your behalf, are correct. Judge Jane Jones of the United States District Court for the District of State is overseeing this class action. The lawsuit is known as *Johnson, et al., v. MNO, Inc.*, Civil Action No. CV-00-1234.

2. WHAT IS THIS LAWSUIT ABOUT?

This lawsuit is about whether MNO discriminated against female account executives based on their gender, by making it harder for them to advance in their careers. More information about federal laws prohibiting job discrimination can be found at the website of the *U.S. Equal Employment Opportunity Commission, www.eeoc.gov.*

3. WHAT IS A CLASS ACTION AND WHO IS INVOLVED?

In a class action lawsuit, one or more people called "Class Representatives" (in this case Mary Johnson and Louise Smith) sue on behalf of other people who have similar claims. The people together are a "Class" or "Class Members." The women who sued—and all the Class Members like them—are called the Plaintiffs. The company they sued (in this case MNO, Inc.) is called the Defendant. One court resolves the issues for everyone in the Class—except for those people who choose to exclude themselves from the Class.

4. WHY IS THIS LAWSUIT A CLASS ACTION?

The Court decided that this lawsuit can be a class action and move towards a trial because it meets the requirements of Federal Rule of Civil

Procedure 23, which governs class actions in federal courts. Specifically, the Court found that:

- There are more than 90,000 women who are or were employed by MNO as account executives;
- There are legal questions and facts that are common to each of them;
- Mary Johnson's and Louise Smith's claims are typical of the claims of the rest of the Class; "Ms. Johnson, Ms. Smith, and the lawyers representing the Class will fairly and adequately represent the Class' interests;
- The common legal questions and facts are more important than questions that affect only individuals; and
- This class action will be more efficient than having many individual lawsuits.

More information about why the Court is allowing this lawsuit to be a class action is in the *Court's Order Certifying the Class*, which is available at *www.mnoclassaction.com.*

THE CLAIMS IN THE LAWSUIT

5. WHAT DOES THE LAWSUIT COMPLAIN ABOUT?

In the lawsuit, the Plaintiffs say that MNO discriminated against women account executives. They claim that these women received less pay than men in similar jobs. They also say that MNO made promotions to account supervisor positions more difficult for women because they had to demonstrate greater achievements than men. You can read the Plaintiffs' *Class Action Complaint at www.mnoclassaction.com.*

6. HOW DOES MNO ANSWER?

MNO denies that it did anything wrong and says that opportunities for hiring and promotion are equally available to women and men. MNO says that its policies are clear and that they neither allow, nor condone, discrimination against women. MNO says that women advanced as often as men, and that greater achievements are not necessary for women to qualify for a promotion. MNO's *Answer to the Complaint* is also at the website.

7. HAS THE COURT DECIDED WHO IS RIGHT?

The Court hasn't decided whether MNO or the Plaintiffs are correct. By establishing the Class and issuing this Notice, the Court is not suggesting that the Plaintiffs will win or lose this case. The Plaintiffs must prove their claims at a trial starting Month 00, 0000. (See "The Trial" below on page 7.)

8. WHAT ARE THE PLAINTIFFS ASKING FOR?

The Plaintiffs are asking for changes in MNO's policies to ensure that women are treated fairly and equally in the workplace. They want MNO's policies to say that discrimination based on gender is banned. The Plaintiffs also want lost wages and money for emotional distress for Class Members.

9. IS THERE ANY MONEY AVAILABLE NOW?

No money or benefits are available now because the Court has not yet decided whether MNO did anything wrong, and the two sides have not settled the case. There is no guarantee that money or benefits ever will be obtained. If they are, you will be notified about how to ask for a share.

WHO IS IN THE CLASS

You need to decide whether you are affected by this lawsuit.

10. AM I PART OF THIS CLASS?

Judge Jones decided that all women who were employed by MNO, Inc. as account executives (full time or part time) at any time from June 6, 1996, through July 15, 2003, are Class Members. She also specified that "temp" employees and independent contractors are *not* part of the class. See question 12 below.

11. WHICH CURRENT AND FORMER EMPLOYEES ARE INCLUDED?

Former employees are in the Class as long as they were employed by MNO any time from June 6, 1996, through July 15, 2003. If you were hired after July 15, 2003—even if you are a current employee—you are not included. In other words, these women are included:

- **Women account executives currently employed by MNO who were hired on or before July 15, 2003.**
- **Women account executives no longer employed by MNO but who were employed by MNO any time from June 6, 1996, through July 15, 2003.**

12. ARE ANY WOMEN WHO WORKED AT MNO NOT INCLUDED IN THE CLASS?

If you *worked at* MNO during the time period in question 10, but you were not directly *employed by* MNO, you are NOT a Class Member. Think about whether you were paid for your work at MNO by a temporary staffing service or an independent contractor for MNO. If so, you were not employed by MNO. If you were later hired by MNO after a temporary period, you may be part of the Class as long as MNO hired you on or before July 15, 2003.

13. I'M STILL NOT SURE IF I AM INCLUDED.

If you are still not sure whether you are included, you can get free help at www.mnoclassaction.com, or by calling or writing to the lawyers in this case, at the phone number or address listed in question 23.

YOUR RIGHTS AND OPTIONS

You have to decide whether to stay in the Class or ask to be excluded before the trial, and you have to decide this now.

14. WHAT HAPPENS IF I DO NOTHING AT ALL?

You don't have to do anything now if you want to keep the possibility of getting money or benefits from this lawsuit. By doing nothing you are staying in the Class. If you stay in and the Plaintiffs obtain money or benefits, either as a result of the trial or a settlement, you will be notified about how to apply for a share (or how to ask to be excluded from any settlement). Keep in mind that if you do nothing now, regardless of whether the Plaintiffs win or lose the trial, you will not be able to sue, or continue to sue, MNO—as part of any other lawsuit—about the same legal claims that are the subject of this lawsuit. This means that if you do nothing, you may only be able to sue for gender discrimination that occurred *before* June 6, 1996 or occurs *after* July 15, 2003 only. You will also be legally bound by all of the Orders the Court issues and judgments the Court makes in this class action.

15. WHY WOULD I ASK TO BE EXCLUDED?

If you already have your own gender discrimination lawsuit against MNO and want to continue with it, you need to ask to be excluded from the Class. If you exclude yourself from the Class—which also means to remove yourself from the Class, and is sometimes called "opting-out" of the Class— you won't get any money or benefits from this lawsuit even if the Plaintiffs obtain them as a result of the trial or from any settlement (that may or may not be reached) between MNO and the Plaintiffs. However, you may then be able to sue or continue to sue MNO for employment discrimination that occurred or occurs at any time. If you exclude yourself, you will not be legally bound by the Court's judgments in this class action.

If you start your own lawsuit against MNO after you exclude yourself, you'll have to hire and pay your own lawyer for that lawsuit, and you'll have to prove your claims. If you do exclude yourself so you can start or continue your own lawsuit against MNO, you should talk to your own lawyer soon, because your claims may be subject to a statute of limitations.

Note that if you exclude yourself from this lawsuit and you are currently employed by MNO, any changes made to MNO's policies about the treatment of women would still apply to you.

16. HOW DO I ASK THE COURT TO EXCLUDE ME FROM THE CLASS?

To ask to be excluded, you must send an "Exclusion Request" in the form of a letter sent by mail, stating that you want to be excluded from *Johnson v. MNO*. Be sure to include your name and address, and sign the letter. You must mail your Exclusion Request postmarked by **Month 00, 0000,** to: Johnson v. MNO Exclusions, P.O. Box 0000, City, ST 00000-0000. You may also get an *Exclusion Request* form at the website, *www.mnoclassaction.com.*

THE LAWYERS REPRESENTING YOU

17. DO I HAVE A LAWYER IN THIS CASE?

The Court decided that the law firms of Lawfirm One, LLP, of City, ST, and Lawfirm Two, P.C., of City, ST, are qualified to represent you and all Class Members. Together the law firms are called "Class Counsel." They are experienced in handling similar cases against other employers. More information about these law firms, their practices, and their lawyers' experience is available at *www.lawfirmone.com* and *www.lawfirmtwo.com*.

18. SHOULD I GET MY OWN LAWYER?

You do not need to hire your own lawyer because Class Counsel is working on your behalf. But, if you want your own lawyer, you will have to pay that lawyer. For example, you can ask him or her to appear in Court for you if you want someone other than Class Counsel to speak for you.

19. HOW WILL THE LAWYERS BE PAID?

If Class Counsel get money or benefits for the Class, they may ask the Court for fees and expenses. You won't have to pay these fees and expenses. If the Court grants Class Counsels' request, the fees and expenses would be either deducted from any money obtained for the Class or paid separately by MNO.

THE TRIAL

The Court has scheduled a trial to decide who is right in this case.

20. HOW AND WHEN WILL THE COURT DECIDE WHO IS RIGHT?

As long as the case isn't resolved by a settlement or otherwise, Class Counsel will have to prove the Plaintiffs' claims at a trial. The trial is set to start on Tuesday, Month 00, 0000, in the United States District Court for the District of State, 100 Court Street, City, State, in Courtroom 1. During the trial, a Jury or the Judge will hear all of the evidence to help them reach a decision about whether the Plaintiffs or Defendant are right about the claims in the lawsuit. There is no guarantee that the Plaintiffs will win, or that they will get any money for the Class.

21. DO I HAVE TO COME TO THE TRIAL?

You do not need to attend the trial. Class Counsel will present the case for the Plaintiffs, and MNO will present the defenses. You or your own lawyer are welcome to come at your own expense.

22. WILL I GET MONEY AFTER THE TRIAL?

If the Plaintiffs obtain money or benefits as a result of the trial or a settlement, you will be notified about how to participate. We do not know how long this will take.

GETTING MORE INFORMATION

23. ARE MORE DETAILS AVAILABLE?

Visit the website, *www.mnoclassaction.com*, where you will find the Court's *Order Certifying the Class*, the Complaint that the Plaintiffs submitted, the Defendant's *Answer to the Complaint*, as well as an *Exclusion Request form*. You may also speak to one of the lawyers by calling 1-000-000-0000, or by writing to: MNO Class Action, P.O. Box 000, City, ST 00000-0000.

DATE: MONTH 00, 0000.

APPENDIX 12: SUMMARY LEGAL PUBLICATION NOTICE—EMPLOYMENT DISCRIMINATION

LEGAL NOTICE

If you are a woman and are or were employed by MNO, a class action lawsuit may affect your rights.

You may be affected by a class action lawsuit about whether MNO, Inc. discriminated against women.

The lawsuit is called *Johnson v. MNO, Inc.*, No. CV-00-1234, and is in the United States District Court for the District of State. The Court decided this lawsuit should be a class action on behalf of a "Class," or group of people, that could include you. This notice summarizes your rights and options before an upcoming trial. More information is in a detailed notice available at the website below. If you're included, you have to decide whether to stay in the Class and be bound by whatever results, or ask to be excluded and keep your right to sue MNO. **There is no money available now and no guarantee that there will be.**

Who's affected?

Women account executives employed by MNO, Inc. any time from June 6, 1996, through July 15, 2003, including current and former employees, and full and part-time employees.

ARE YOU AFFECTED?

Women employed as account executives by MNO, Inc. at any time from June 6, 1996, through July 15, 2003, are Class members. This includes women currently employed, as long as they were hired on or before July 15, 2003, as well as those no longer employed, but who were employed any time from June 6, 1996, through July 15, 2003. Those who worked at MNO as independent contractors are NOT included.

WHAT IS THIS CASE ABOUT?

The lawsuit claims that MNO discriminated against female account executives. The suit claims women received less pay than men in similar jobs. It also says that MNO required women to achieve more than men to get promoted. The lawsuit seeks to ensure an equal workplace for women, as well as money or benefits for the Class.

MNO denies it did anything wrong and says it has a fair workplace that gives women the same opportunities as men. **The Court has not decided whether the Class or MNO is right.** The lawyers for the Class will have to prove their claims at a trial set to begin on Month 00, 0000.

WHO REPRESENTS YOU?

The Court asked Lawfirm One, LLP of City, ST and Lawfirm Two, P.C. of City, ST, to represent you as "Class Counsel." You don't have to pay Class Counsel, or anyone else, to participate. Instead, if they get money or benefits for the Class, they may ask the Court for attorneys' fees and costs, which would be paid by MNO or out of any money recovered, before giving the rest to the Class. You may hire your own lawyer to appear in Court for you; if you do, you have to pay that lawyer. Mary Johnson and Louise Smith are Class members like you, and the Court accepted them as the "Class Representatives."

WHAT ARE YOUR OPTIONS?

You have a choice of whether to stay in the Class or not, and **you must decide this now.** If you stay in the Class, you will be legally bound by all orders and judgments of the Court, and you won't be able to sue, or continue to sue, MNO—as part of any other lawsuit—for gender discrimination that occurred from June 6, 1996, through July 15, 2003. If money or benefits are obtained, you will be notified about how to get a share. To stay in the Class, you do not have to do anything now.

If you ask to be excluded from the Class, you cannot get any money or benefits from this lawsuit if any are awarded, but you will keep any rights to sue MNO for these claims, now or in the future, and will not be bound by any orders or judgments of the Court. To ask to be excluded, send a letter to the address below, postmarked by **Month 00, 0000,** that says you want to be excluded from *Johnson v. MNO, Inc.* Include your name, address, and telephone number.

HOW CAN YOU GET MORE INFORMATION?

If you have questions or want a detailed notice or other documents about this lawsuit and your rights, visit www.mnoclassaction.com, or write to: MNO Class Action, P.O. Box 000, City, ST 00000-0000.

www.mnoclassaction.com

APPENDIX 13:
LIST OF CLASS ACTION SETTLEMENTS AND VERDICTS

DEFENDANT	PLAINTIFFS	CLAIMS	VALUE OF SETTLEMENT/VERDICT
Aetna Inc.	American Dental Association o/b/o dentists	interference with dental procedures in order to cut costs	$4,000,000 to dentists and $1,000,000 to ADA Foundation
AT&T	Digital One Rate Calling Plan customers	overcharges for airtime usage	$1,987,000
Austrian government and industry	surviving victims of Nazi regime	slave and forced labor	$380,000,000
Bausch & Lomb	purchasers of company's common stock	misleading financial expectations	$12.5 million
Boston Chicken Inc.	investors	concealment of true financial condition	$2.18 million
Bridgestone-Firestone	tire owners	tire safety concerns	$149 million settlement
Bristol-Myers Squibb	patients who used cancer drug Taxol	price fixing conspiracy	$62.5 million

DEFENDANT	PLAINTIFFS	CLAIMS	VALUE OF SETTLEMENT/VERDICT
Chrysler	owners of Chrysler minivans	defect rear hatch door locks	$120,000,000
Cigna	physicians	the company systematically cheated on payments	$540,000,000
City of New York	Latino and black officers	discrimination in hiring and employment practices	$20,000,000
Computer Associates	investors	accounting fraud	$144,000,000
Cosmetics Manufacturers and Retailers	consumers	price-fixing	$175,000,000
Dow Corning	women who suffered damages due to silicon breast implants	defective breast implants	$2.35 billion
DuPont	residents in area near West Virginia plant	contamination of drinking water	$343 million
EarthLink	Oregon customers	internet service outages	$42 to each qualifying customer
Enron	former and current workers	pension fund stock losses	$66.5 million
Experian	TransUnion and Equifax, consumers	bankruptcy notation appeared on credit report of persons who had joint accounts with someone who had filed for bankruptcy	amendment of to remove bankruptcy notation from existing credit reports of approximately 2 to 3 million persons who had not actually filed for bankruptcy
Ferdinand Marcos	9,539 Filipino victims	human rights abuses under Marcos rule	$40,000,000
German industry	surviving victims of Nazi regime	slave and forced labor	$5 billion

DEFENDANT	PLAINTIFFS	CLAIMS	VALUE OF SETTLEMENT/VERDICT
Home Depot	employees	hostile work environment based on gender, race and national origin	$5.5 million
Honeywell International	employees	violation of the Age Discrimination in Employment Act	$2.15 million
Hyundai Motor Co.	consumers	allegations that the company overstated the horsepower of 1.3 million vehicles and inflated the value of models	between $76 and $127 million dollars
Infant formula manufacturers	consumers	price fixing conspiracy	$125,760,000
Jack-in-the-Box	consumers	injury resulting from consumption of food products contaminated with E coli	$13,000,000
KB Toys	consumers	deceptive pricing	30% discount on qualifying products
KPMG International	shareholders	accounting malpractice	$115,000,000
Lucent Technologies	shareholders	federal and state securities violations	$600,000,000
Lutheran Medical Center, New York	51 female victims of sexual abuse	sexual abuse by doctor performing medical examinations on new employees	$5.4 million
Macy's	disabled customers	narrow aisles violated Americans with Disabilities Act	store agreed to widen store aisles

DEFENDANT	PLAINTIFFS	CLAIMS	VALUE OF SETTLEMENT/VERDICT
McDonald's	members of the vegetarian community	deception in the marketing of french fries and hash browns which were cooked using beef by-products	$8.6 million dollars awarded to 23 organizations
MCI Worldcom	California customers	underhanded business practices	$8,500,000
Miss Cleo's Psychic Hotline	consumers	deceptive practices	cancellation of $500 million in customer bills
Music distributors and retailers	CD purchasers	conspiracy to increase prices	refunds ranging from $5 to $20
Nissan	owners of Nissan minivans	engine failures and fires	$200,000,000
Pfizer Inc.	Illinois purchasers of Rezulin	sale of diabetes drug Rezulin	$60,000,000
Philip Morris	consumers	fraud about dangers of smoking light cigarettes	$10.1 billion
Poland Spring Water	consumers	company's bottled water does not come from a spring and is not completely safe	$12,000,000
Premier Cruise Lines	qualifying customers	excessive port charges	$30 to $40 discount vouchers from Ocean Club Cruise Line
Roman Catholic Archdiocese of Louisville, KY	sexual abuse victims	sexual abuse and cover up over past 50 years	$27.5 million
Salton Inc.	consumers	violation of federal anti-trust laws by fixing price of George Foreman grills	$8.2 million

DEFENDANT	PLAINTIFFS	CLAIMS	VALUE OF SETTLEMENT/VERDICT
Sony Pictures Entertainment	filmgoers	reviews from fictitious film critic invented by Sony subsidiary tricked filgoers into seeing mediocre films	settlement value unknown at this time
Sotheby's and Christie's Auction Houses	certain buyers and ssellers	antitrust	$20,000,000
Taco Bell Corp.	fromer employees	overtime and meal break violations	$1.5 million
Target Corp.	consumers	failure to stamp prices on merchandise in violation of Massachusetts law	$1,000,000
Tyson Fresh Meats Inc.	cattlemen	unfair manipulation of cattle prices	$1.28 billion
US Federal Government	descendants of the Sisseton-Wahpeton Sioux tribe	recovery of treaty-related payments	$1,000,000
Various food companies	consumers	the sale of products containing corn made from Starlink a genetically-engineered seed known as StarLink that had been approved by the EPA for use only in animal feed	$6,000,000 in coupons
Verizon Wireless	customers	improper billing and failure to disclose fees and terms	$30-$45 credit

* Source: BigClassAction.com

APPENDIX 14: SECURITIES CLASS ACTION CLASS ACTION COMPLAINT

UNITED STATES DISTRICT COURT
NORTHERN DISTRICT OF CALIFORNIA

GREGORY D. CALLENDER, on behalf of himself and All others similarly situated, Civil Action No.

Plaintiff,

vs.

CRITICAL PATH, INC., DOUGLAS HICKEY, DAVID HAYDEN, DAVID THATCHER, LARRY REINHOLD and MARCK J. RUBASH,

Defendants.

CLASS ACTION COMPLAINT

JURY TRIAL DEMANDED

Plaintiff, individually and on behalf of all other persons similarly situated, by his undersigned counsel, for his complaint alleges upon personal knowledge as to himself and his own acts and upon information and belief as to all other matters, based upon, *inter alia,* the investigation made by and through his attorneys, as follows:

NATURE OF ACTION

1. Plaintiff brings this action as a class action on behalf of himself and all other persons who purchased the common stock of Critical Path, Inc. ("Critical Path" or the "Company") on the open market during the period April 20, 2000 through and including February 2, 2001 (the

"Class Period") to recover damages caused by defendants' violations of the federal securities laws. During the Class Period, defendants issued false and misleading financial statements and press releases concerning Critical Path's publicly reported revenue and net income to the investing public.

2. The materially false and misleading statements, which are described in detail below, concerned the Company's financial condition, and were contained in public statements, filings with the Securities and Exchange Commission ("SEC") and press releases. As a result of these false and misleading statements, the market price of the Company's common stock was artificially inflated during the Class Period and plaintiff and the Class purchased their stock at artificially inflated prices to their financial detriment.

3. These materially false and misleading statements allowed the Company to engage in a number of acquisitions in which it acquired the target companies in exchange for Critical Path stock. Such acquisitions would have been impossible without Company's artificial inflation of its stock price.

4. On January 18, 2001, Critical Path announced its results for its fourth quarter and year ended December 31, 2000. Revenue for the quarter reached $52.0 million, a 16 percent sequential increase over revenue of $45.0 million in the third quarter of 2000, and a 534 percent increase over revenue of $8.2 million in the fourth quarter of 1999. The Company announced that its net loss for the quarter, excluding special charges, was $11.5 million, or $0.16 per share, compared with a net loss, excluding special charges, of $8.7 million, or $0.14 per share, in the third quarter of 2000, and a net loss of $11.0 million, or $0.26 per share, in the fourth quarter of 1999. The Company also reported gross profit, excluding special charges, of $29.1 million, a 15 percent increase over gross profit of $25.3 million in the third quarter of 2000.

5. These results, along with lower estimates going forward, surprised the investment community, and the Company's stock price dropped from $19.5625 per share on January 18, 2001 to $9.00 per share on January 19, 2001, on volume of 37,950,800—over 7 times the prior day's volume.

6. Then, on February 2, 2001, Critical Path shocked the investment community when it announced that it had discovered that a number of transactions had put into question its financial results, and that, as a result, its Board of Directors (the "Board") had formed a special committee to investigate the Company's revenue recognition practices.

7. The Company also announced that its revenue of $52 million and net loss of $11.5 million for its fourth quarter ended December 31, 2000, may have been materially misstated.

8. The Company further stated that the Board, effective immediately, had placed on "administrative leave" David Thatcher, Critical Path's President, and William Rinehart, its Vice President of Worldwide Sales, and was working with its independent auditors, PriceWaterhouseCoopers and its outside counsel, Wilson Sonsini Goodrich & Rosati, to investigate these financial reporting matters.

9. Upon the announcement of the "bad news," the NASDAQ securities exchange halted trading in shares of Critical Path on February 2, 2001, for "additional information requested." The price of Critical Path stock closed at $10.0625 per share.

10. As a result, throughout the Class Period, Critical Path's financial statements were materially false and misleading in that they overstated revenue and net income. Based upon Critical Path's materially false and misleading financial results, the Company's common stock price rose to a high of $58.125 per share during the Class Period.

JURISDICTION AND VENUE

11. The claims asserted below arise under Sections 10(b) of the Securities Exchange Act of 1934 (the "Exchange Act"), 15 U.S.C. § 78j(b), Rule 10b-5 promulgated thereunder by the SEC, 17 C.F.R. § 240.10b-5, and Section 20(a) of the Exchange Act, 15 U.S.C. § 78t(a).

12. Jurisdiction is conferred upon this Court by Section 27 of the Exchange Act, 15 U.S.C. §78aa, 28 U.S.C. §§ 1331 and 1337.

13. Venue is proper in this District pursuant to Section 27 of the Exchange Act and 28 U.S.C. § 1391(b) since Critical Path has its principal place of business in this District in San Francisco, California, and many of the acts alleged herein, including the dissemination of the misleading statements at issue to the investing public, occurred in substantial part in this District.

14. In connection with the acts, transactions and conduct alleged herein, defendants used the means and instrumentalities of interstate commerce, including the United States mails, interstate telephone communications and the facilities of national securities exchanges and markets.

THE PARTIES

15. Plaintiff purchased shares of Critical Path in the NASDAQ market, an open and efficient market, during the Class Period, as set forth in the annexed certification.

16. Defendant Critical Path maintains its principal executive offices at 320 1st Street, San Francisco, CA 94105. Critical Path is a leading provider of complete end-to-end Internet messaging and collaboration solutions for Internet service providers ("ISPs"), telecommunications providers, web hosting companies, web portals and corporations. The Company provides services and products, both on a hosted and licensed basis, that enable its customers to provide feature-rich e-mail, messaging, collaboration and directory services to their customers and employees. Its solutions enable customers to improve messaging performance, reduce the cost of providing messaging services and focus on other aspects of their businesses. Critical Path stock trades on the NASDAQ stock exchange, an open and efficient market. As of April October 31, 2000, Critical Path had approximately 73,651,212 shares outstanding.

17. Defendant Douglas Hickey ("Hickey") is and was at all relevant times Critical Path's Chief Executive Officer and a member of its Board of Directors.

18. Defendant David Hayden ("Hayden") is and was at all relevant times Chairman of Critical Path's Board of Directors. Hayden took advantage of his insider knowledge and sold approximately 350,000 shares during the Class Period at artificially inflated prices, reaping proceeds of approximately $10 million.

19. Defendant David Thatcher ("Thatcher") was at all relevant times President of Critical Path. As set forth below, on February 2, 2001, the Company placed Thatcher on administrative leave.

20. Defendant Mark J. Rubash ("Rubash") was Critical Path's Chief Financial Officer ("CFO") from the start of the Class Period until December 6, 2000. Rubash signed Critical Path's Form 10-Q for the quarterly periods ended March 31, 2000 (the "March 31, 2000 10-Q"), June 30, 2000 (the "June 30, 2000 10-Q") and September 30, 2000 (the "September 30, 2000 10-Q"). On or about December 6, 2000, Rubash resigned as CFO of the Company for personal reasons.

21. Defendant Larry Reinhold ("Reinhold") was appointed CFO of the Company upon Rubash's resignation on December 6, 2000.

22. Defendants Hickey, Hayden, Thatcher, Rubash and Reinhold (collectively the "Individual Defendants"), as officers and/or directors of the Company, are controlling persons of the Company within the mean-

ing of Section 20 of the Exchange Act. By reason of their positions with the Company, they were able to and did, directly or indirectly, in whole or in material part, control the content of public statements issued by or on behalf of the Company. They participated in and approved the issuance of such statements made throughout the Class Period, including the materially false and misleading statements identified herein.

23. By reason of their positions with the Company, the Individual Defendants had access to internal Company documents, reports and other information, including the adverse non-public information concerning the Company's services, financial condition, and future prospects, and attended management and/or board of directors meetings. As a result of the foregoing, they were responsible for the truthfulness and accuracy of the Company's public reports and releases described herein.

24. The Individual Defendants, as officers of a publicly held company, had a duty to promptly disseminate truthful and accurate information with respect to Critical Path and to promptly correct any public statements issued by or on behalf of the Company which had become false or misleading.

25. Critical Path and the Individual Defendants knewor with deliberate recklessness disregarded that the misleading statements and omissions complained of herein would adversely affect the integrity of the market for the Company's stock and would cause the price of the Company's common stock to become artificially inflated. Each of the defendants acted knowingly or in such a deliberately reckless manner as to constitute a fraud and deceit upon plaintiff and the other members of the Class.

26. Defendants are liable, jointly and severally, as direct participants in and co-conspirators of, the wrongs complained of herein.

CLASS ACTION ALLEGATIONS

27. Plaintiff brings this action as a class action pursuant to Federal Rules of Civil Procedure 23(a) and (b)(3) on behalf of a class consisting of all persons who purchased Critical Path common stock on the open market during the period from April 20, 2000, through and including February 2, 2001, (the "Class Period") and who suffered damages thereby. Excluded are the defendants, members of the Individual Defendants' families, any entity in which any defendant has a controlling interest or is a parent or subsidiary of or is controlled by the Company, and the officers, directors, employees, affiliates, legal representatives, heirs, predecessors, successor and assigns of any of the defendants (the "Class").

28. The members of the Class are so numerous that joinder of all members is impracticable. While the exact number of Class members is unknown to Plaintiff at this time and can only be ascertained through appropriate discovery, plaintiff believes there are, at a minimum, thousands of members of the Class who traded during the Class Period. The Company had more than 73 million shares of its common stock outstanding as of October 31, 2000.

29. Common questions of law and fact exist as to all members of the Class and predominate over any questions solely affecting individual members of the Class. Among the questions of law and fact common to the Class are:

a) whether the federal securities laws were violated by defendants' acts as alleged herein;

b) whether Critical Path issued materially false and misleading financial statements in the Registration Statement and/or during the Class Period;

c) whether the Individual Defendants caused Critical Path to issue materially false and misleading financial statements during the Class Period;

d) whether defendants acted knowingly or with deliberate recklessness in issuing false and misleading financial statements;

e) whether the market prices of Critical Path securities during the Class Period were artificially inflated because of the defendants' conduct complained of herein; and

f) whether the members of the Class have sustained damages and, if so, what is the proper measure of damages.

30. Plaintiff's claims are typical of the claims of the members of the Class as plaintiff and members of the Class sustained damages arising out of defendants' wrongful conduct in violation of federal law as complained of herein.

31. Plaintiff will fairly and adequately protect the interests of the members of the Class and has retained counsel competent and experienced in class actions and securities litigation. Plaintiff has no interests antagonistic to or in conflict with those of the Class.

32. A class action is superior to other available methods for the fair and efficient adjudication of the controversy since joinder of all members of the Class is impracticable. Furthermore, because the damages suffered by the individual Class members may be relatively small, the expense and burden of individual litigation make it impossible for the

Class members individually to redress the wrongs done to them. There will be no difficulty in the management of this action as a class action.

33. Plaintiff will rely, in part, upon the presumption of reliance established by the fraud-on-the-market doctrine in that:

a) defendants made public misrepresentations or failed to disclose material facts during the Class Period;

b) the omissions and misrepresentations were material;

c) the securities of the Company traded in an efficient market;

d) the misrepresentations and omissions alleged would tend to induce a reasonable investor to misjudge the value of the Company's securities; and

e) plaintiff and members of the Class purchased their stock between the time the defendants failed to disclose or misrepresented material facts and the time the true facts were disclosed, without knowledge of the omitted or misrepresented facts.

34. Based upon the following, plaintiff and members of the Class are entitled to the presumption of reliance upon the integrity of the market.

DEFENDANTS' MATERIAL MISSTATEMENTS AND OMISSIONS

35. As reported in the *PR Newsire* on or about April 20, 2000, Critical Path announced its financial results for its first quarter ended March 31, 2000. For the quarter, the Company reported that revenues for the first quarter marked the largest quarter in Critical Path's history at $24.6 million, a 200 percent increase over revenue of $8.2 million in the previous quarter ended December 31, 1999, and more than a 2,200 percent increase over revenue of $1.05 million for the same quarter of the prior year. The Company announced that its net loss for the quarter, excluding special charges, was $16.8 million, or $0.33 per share, beating the First Call consensus estimate of a loss of $0.41 per share. During the corresponding quarter in 1999, the net loss, excluding special charges, was $5.4 million, or $0.77 per share. Including special charges, net loss for the first quarter ended March 31, 2000, was $76.9 million or a loss of $1.52 per share.

36. In the April 20, 2000 press release, defendant Hickey stated: We continued to increase gross margin in the quarter, reflecting the success of our business model and maintaining our path to profitability.

37. These results were substantially repeated in the Company's March 31, 2000, 10-Q that was signed by defendant Rubash and filed with the SEC on or about May 15, 2000.

38. As reported in the *PR Newswire* on or about July 19, 2000, Critical Path announced its financial results for the quarterly period ended June 30, 3000. The Company reported revenues for the quarter of $33.5 million, a 36 percent sequential increase over revenue of $24.6 million in the first quarter, and more than a 1,500 percent increase over revenue of $2.0 million in the same quarter of the prior year. The net loss for the quarter, excluding special charges, was $20.2 million, or $0.34 per share, compared with a net loss, excluding special charges, of $16.8 million, or $0.33 per share, in the first quarter this year, and a net loss of $6.9 million, or $0.21 per share, in the same quarter a year prior. The Company also reported gross margin of $16.0 million, a 74 percent increase over gross margin of $9.2 million in the quarter ended March 31, 2000.

39. In the July 19, 2000 press release, defendant Hickey touted the Company's "firm[ ] path to profitability:

> "We are extremely pleased with our operating performance and the strength of our business across geographic regions, customers and product lines," said Doug Hickey, Critical Path's CEO. "Through increased penetration of the enterprise market and the market acceptance of key value-added products and services, we remain firmly on a path to profitability."

40. Hickey further touted the fact that approximately 40 percent of the company's revenue in the second quarter came from international customers. Hickey also noted that approximately 40 percent of the revenue in the second quarter came from international customers:

> "We saw significant growth in both Europe and Latin America, and our Critical Path Pacific joint venture with Mitsui, NTT, and NEC will accelerate our penetration of the rapidly growing Asian market."

41. The results announced on July 19, 2000, were substantially repeated in the Company's June 30, 2000, 10-Q that was signed by defendant Rubash and filed with the SEC on or about August 14, 2000.

42. As reported in the *PR Newswire* on or about October 19, 2000, Critical Path announced its financial results for the quarterly period ended September 30, 2000. The Company reported revenue for the quarter of nearly $45.0 million, a 34 percent sequential increase over revenue of $33.5 million in the second quarter, and an 815 percent increase over revenue of $4.9 million in the same quarter of the prior year. The net loss for the quarter, excluding special charges, was $8.7 million, or $0.14 per share, compared with a net loss, excluding special charges, of $20.2 million, or $0.34 per share, in the second quarter of this year, and a net loss of $6.2 million, or $0.17 per share, in the same quarter a year prior. The Company also reported gross margin, excluding special charges, of $25.3 million, a 58 percent increase over gross margin of $16.0 million in the quarter ended June 30, 2000.

43. In the October 19, 2000, news article, defendant Hickey touted the Company's "rapidly growing revenue and stronger margins":

> "All of our business areas contributed to the outstanding performance in the third quarter," said Doug Hickey, Critical Path's CEO. "Rapidly growing revenue and stronger margins demonstrate the strength of our product and service offerings across several broad horizontal markets. At the same time, cutting the operating loss by more than half from the prior quarter reflects the leverage achieved in each operating expense category."

44. Hickey further announced increased expectations for the Company:

> "As a result of our acquisition of PeerLogic and the strength we see in our business going forward, we are increasing our estimates for revenue for the fourth quarter of this year, and revenue and earnings per share for the full year 2001," said Hickey. The Company expects revenue for the fourth quarter ending December 31, 2000 of between $54 million and $56 million, and fully diluted earnings per share, excluding special charges, for the period estimated at $0.01. For the year 2001, revenue is expected between $300 million and $310 million, with fully diluted earnings per share, excluding special charges, of $0.39 to $0.41.

45. These results were substantially repeated in the Company's September 30, 2000 10-Q that was signed by defendant Rubash and filed with the SEC on or about November 14, 2000.

46. As reported in the *Business Wire* on or about November 2, 2000, in a meeting in New York City with over 100 investors and analysts, Critical Path provided to the investing public "financial guidance for the fourth quarter 2000 and the full year 2001." The Company stated that "This guidance, which was provided is intended to provide all investors with information the Company believes is important in evaluating Critical Path's business."

47. The Company stated that it expected revenue for the fourth quarter ending December 31, 2000, to be between $54 million and $56 million, representing growth of approximately 22 percent over the third quarter of 2000. The Company also stated that it expected pro forma earnings per share for the period to improve from a loss of $0.14 to a gain of approximately $0.01 per share. For the year 2001, the Company stated that revenue is expected to grow approximately 95 percent over 2000, to between $300 million and $310 million, with pro forma earnings per share growing to a level ranging between $0.39 and $0.41.

48. Defendant Hickey touted Critical Path's financial future:

> "The fourth quarter of 2000 is a pivotal one for Critical Path, one in which we join an elite group of profitable 'new economy' companies. Critical Path is executing across all product segments and target markets," said Doug Hickey, Critical Path's CEO. "We anticipate continued high demand for our product and service offerings, and leverage in our operations to deliver initial profitability in Q4 2000 and increases in our profitability in 2001."

49. As reported in the Business Wire on or about January 18, 2001, Critical Path announced "record" financial results for the quarter and year ended December 31, 2000. The Company reported revenue for the quarter of $52.0 million, a 16 percent sequential increase over revenue of $45.0 million in the third quarter of 2000, and a 534 percent increase over revenue of $8.2 million in the fourth quarter of 1999. The Company reported that the net loss for the quarter, excluding special charges, was $11.5 million, or $0.16 per share, compared with a net loss, excluding special charges, of $8.7 million, or $0.14 per share, in the third quarter of 2000, and a net loss of $11.0 million, or $0.26 per share, in the fourth quarter of 1999. The Company also reported gross profit, excluding special charges, of $29.1 million, a 15 percent increase over gross profit of $25.3 million in the third quarter of 2000.

50. In the same January 18, 2001, press release, defendant Hickey stated:

> "Despite a difficult economic environment, Critical Path achieved solid revenue growth and improved gross margins, while adding over 200 new customers and further solidifying our category leadership position," said Doug Hickey, Critical Path's CEO.

51. Defendants failed to disclose that the true reason behind the Company's results was accounting violations, but rather stated that the reasons for the results were: deferred revenue, a non-operating foreign exchange loss, higher than expected operating expenses in the recently acquired PeerLogic business and the provision of a significant allowance for doubtful accounts: According to Chief Financial Officer Larry Reinhold, other factors in addition to . . . deferred revenue . . . had an impact on results in the fourth quarter of 2000. These factors included a non-operating foreign exchange loss due primarily to currency fluctuations in U.S. dollar-denominated European revenues, higher than expected operating expenses in the recently acquired PeerLogic business as full synergies have not yet been achieved, and the provision of a significant allowance for doubtful accounts. "While we are disappointed with the bottom-line impact of these charges, we are evaluating and will be taking concrete steps to control the underlying factors impacting these areas," said Reinhold.

52. Defendant Hickey lowered expectations for the Company going forward, yet failed to disclose the true nature of Critical Path's problems. Hickey stated,

> "Taking into account economic indicators that seem to be affecting the technology sector across the board, we are also reevaluating our guidance for 2001 and taking a very conservative stance toward the Company's financial expectations. The Company expects revenue for the first quarter 2001 of between $54 million and $56 million, and a loss per share, excluding special charges, estimated between $0.15 and $0.16. For the full year

2001, revenue is expected between $255 million and $260 million, with the Company becoming profitable in the third quarter."

"It's disappointing to lower the expectations for Critical Path, but macroeconomic forecasts and reports from leaders in the technology space lead us to believe it is prudent to be conservative at this time," said Hickey. "It is our strategy to make this move now and position the Company to execute effectively throughout the year." Hickey went on to discuss the positive indications for the quarter and the year. "Regardless of near term uncertainty, I continue to be excited at the size and potential of the Internet messaging solutions market, and my confidence is bolstered by our success in addressing that market. We have the best and broadest suite of messaging solutions, the most flexible delivery capability and the unique ability to scale to meet the demands of the largest customers," he said.

53. As a result of these announcements, the Company's stock price dropped from $19.5625 per share on January 18, 2001, to $9.00 per share on January 19, 2001, on volume of 37,950,800 - over 7 times the prior day's volume.

THE TRUTH BEGINS TO EMERGE

54. On February 2, 2001, Critical Path shocked the investment community by announcing that its Board of Directors had formed a special committee to investigate the Company's revenue recognition practices.

55. The Company also announced that its revenue of $52 million and net loss of $11.5 million for its fourth quarter ended December 31, 2000, may have been materially misstated.

56. Critical Path also stated that it had "discovered a number of transactions that put into question the company's financial results."

57. The Company further stated that the Board, effective immediately, had placed on "administrative leave" David Thatcher, Critical Path's President, and William Rinehart, its Vice President of Worldwide Sales, and was working with its independent auditors, PriceWaterhouseCoopers and its outside counsel Wilson Sonsini Goodrich & Rosati to investigate these financial reporting matters.

58. Upon the announcement of the "bad news," the NASDAQ stock exchange halted trading in Critical Path for "additional information requested." The price of Critical Path stock closed at $10.0625 per share.

ANALYSTS' REACTION UNDERSCORES THE MAGNITUDE OF THE FRAUD

59. The magnitude of the fraud was made clear by the analysts covering the Company. On February 2, 2001, as reported in the Dow Jones Business News, such analysts were utterly misled by the Company:

> When Critical Path reported fourth-quarter results that missed analysts' estimates, Robertson Stephens analyst Rick Juarez [("Juarez")] said the visibility regarding future revenue had been clouded. "We had no idea that visibility was in fact zero," Mr. Juarez said[.]

60. Juarez further stated, as set forth in Reuters English News Service on or about February 2, 2001, that "You can't trust anything the management has said so far[.]"

61. As reported in the New York Times on or about February 3, 2001, Bert Hochfeld, a managing director at Josephtal & Company, stated "Companies miss all the time[.] . . . I'm familiar with that. I'm not familiar with being the victim of a con game."

62. As a result, throughout the Class Period Critical Path's financial statements were materially false and misleading in that they overstated revenue and net income.

63. Each of the statements identified above in paragraphs 35-53 were materially false and misleading when made. Throughout the Class Period, Critical Path reported artificially inflated revenue and net income in violation of Generally Accepted Accounting Principles ("GAAP").

64. Critical Path's practices violated GAAP. The realization principle of GAAP requires that revenue be earned before it is recognized. Under GAAP, revenue is recognized when the earnings process is complete and an exchange has taken place (Statement of Financial Accounting Concepts No. 5, Recognition and Measurement in Financial Statements of Business Enterprises, pp. 83, 84). The earnings process is not complete until collection of the sales price is reasonably assured. (Id.)

STATUTORY SAFE HARBOR

65. The statutory safe harbor that provides for forward-looking statements under certain circumstances does not apply to any of the allegedly false forward-looking statements pleaded in this Complaint to the extent that said forward-looking statements were not identified as a "forward-looking statement" when made or to the extent that meaningful cautionary statements identifying important factors that could cause actual results to differ materially from those in the forward-looking statements did not accompany those forward-looking statements. Alternatively, to the extent that the statutory safe harbor

does apply to any forward-looking statements, because at the time each of those forward-looking statements was made, the speaker knew the forward-looking statement was false and the forward-looking statement was authorized and/or approved by an executive officer of the Company who knew that those statements were false when made, the safe harbor does not apply.

COUNT I
(Against All Defendants For Violation of Section 10(b) of the Exchange Act and Rule 10b-5 of the Securities and Exchange Commission)

66. Plaintiff repeats and realleges each and every allegation contained in the foregoing paragraphs as if fully set forth herein.

67. This Count is asserted against all defendants and is based upon Section 10(b) of the Exchange Act, 15 U.S.C. § 78j(b), and Rule 10b-5 promulgated thereunder.

68. During the Class Period, defendants, singularlyand in concert, directly engaged in a common plan, scheme, and unlawful course of conduct, pursuant to which they knowingly or with deliberate recklessness engaged in acts, transactions, practices, and courses of business which operated as a fraud and deceit upon plaintiff and the other members of the Class, and made various deceptive and untrue statements of material facts and omitted to state material facts necessary in order to make the statements made, in light of the circumstances under which they were made, not misleading to plaintiff and the other members of the Class. The purpose and effect of said scheme, plan, and unlawful course of conduct was, among other things, to induce plaintiff and the other members of the Class to purchase Critical Path common stock during the Class Period at artificially inflated prices.

69. During the Class Period, defendants, pursuant to said scheme, plan, and unlawful course of conduct, knowingly and with deliberate recklessness issued, caused to be issued, participated in the issuance of, and in the preparation and issuance of, deceptive and materially false and misleading statements to the investing public as particularized above.

70. Throughout the Class Period, Critical Path acted through the Individual Defendants, whom it portrayed and represented to the financial press and public as its valid representative. The willfulness, motive, knowledge, and deliberate recklessness of the Individual Defendants are therefore imputed to Critical Path, which is primarily liable for the securities law violations made by them while acting in their official capacities as Company representatives, or, in the alternative, which is li-

able for the acts of the Individual Defendants under the doctrine of respondeat superior.

71. As a result of the dissemination of the false and misleading statements set forth above, the market price of Critical Path common stock was artificially inflated during the Class Period. In ignorance of the false and misleading nature of the statements described above and the deceptive and manipulative devices and contrivances employed by said defendants, plaintiff and the other members of the Class relied, to their detriment, on the integrity of the market price of the stock in purchasing Critical Path common stock. Had plaintiff and the other members of the Class known the truth, they would not have purchased said shares or would not have purchased them at the inflated prices that were paid.

72. Plaintiff and the other members of the Class have suffered substantial damages as a result of the wrongs herein alleged in an amount to be proved at trial.

73. By reason of the foregoing, defendants directly violated Section 10(b) of the Exchange Act and Rule 10b-5 promulgated thereunder in that they: (a) employed devices, schemes, and artifices to defraud; (b) made untrue statements of material facts or omitted to state material facts necessary in order to make the statements made, in light of the circumstances under which they were made, not misleading; or (c) engaged in acts, practices, and a course of business which operated as a fraud and deceit upon plaintiff, and the other members of the Class, in connection with their purchases of Critical Path common stock during the Class Period.

COUNT II
(Against The Individual Defendants For Violation of Section 20(a) of the Exchange Act)

74. Plaintiff repeats and realleges each and every allegation contained in each of the foregoing paragraphs as if set forth fully herein.

75. The Individual Defendants, by virtue of their positions, stock ownership and/or specific acts described above, were, at the time of the wrongs alleged herein, controlling persons within the meaning of Section 20(a) of the 1934 Act.

76. The Individual Defendants had the power and influence and exercised the same to cause Critical Path to engage in the illegal conduct and practices complained of herein.

77. By reason of the conduct alleged in Count I of the Complaint, the Individual Defendants are liable for the aforesaid wrongful conduct, and are liable to plaintiff and to the other members of the Class for the sub-

stantial damages which they suffered in connection with their purchases of Critical Path common stock during the Class Period.

PRAYER FOR RELIEF AND JURY DEMAND

WHEREFORE, plaintiff, on his own behalf and on behalf of the Class, prays for judgment as follows:

A. Declaring this action to be a proper class action and certifying plaintiff as class representative under Rule 23 of the Federal Rules of Civil Procedure;

B. Awarding compensatory damages in favor of plaintiff and the other members of the Class against all defendants, jointly and severally, for the damages sustained as a result of the wrongdoings of defendants, together with interest thereon;

C. Awarding plaintiff the fees and expenses incurred in this action, including reasonable allowance of fees for plaintiff's attorneys and experts; and

D. Granting such other and further relief as the Court may deem just and proper.

JURY TRIAL DEMANDED

Plaintiff demands a jury trial of all issues so triable.

Date: February 6, 2001

Respectfully submitted,

BERMAN DEVALERIO PEASE & TABACCO, P.C.
Counsel for Plaintiff Gregory D. Callender and the Class

APPENDIX 15: THE SECURITIES LITIGATION REFORM ACT

SECTION 1. SHORT TITLE; TABLE OF CONTENTS.

(a) SHORT TITLE—This Act may be cited as the 'Securities Litigation Reform Act'.

(b) TABLE OF CONTENTS—The table of contents for this Act is as follows:

SECTION 2. PREVENTION OF LAWYER-DRIVEN LITIGATION.

(a) PLAINTIFF STEERING COMMITTEES TO ENSURE CLIENT CONTROL OF LAWSUITS—The Securities Exchange Act of 1934 (15 U.S.C. 78a et seq.) is amended by adding at the end the following new section:

'SEC. 36. CLASS ACTION STEERING COMMITTEES.

'(a) CLASS ACTION STEERING COMMITTEE-In any private action arising under this title seeking to recover damages on behalf of a class, the court shall, at the earliest practicable time, appoint a committee of class members to direct counsel for the class (hereafter in this section referred to as the 'plaintiff steering committee') and to perform such other functions as the court may specify. Court appointment of a plaintiff steering committee shall not be subject to interlocutory review.

'(b) MEMBERSHIP OF PLAINTIFF STEERING COMMITTEE-

'(1) QUALIFICATIONS-

'(A) NUMBER—A plaintiff steering committee shall consist of not fewer than 5 class members, willing to serve, who the court believes will fairly represent the class.

'(B) OWNERSHIP INTERESTS—Members of the plaintiff steering committee shall have cumulatively held during the class period not less than-

'(i) the lesser of 5 percent of the securities which are the subject matter of the litigation or $10,000,000 in market value of the securities which are the subject matter of the litigation; or

'(ii) such smaller percentage or dollar amount as the court finds appropriate under the circumstances.

'(2) NAMED PLAINTIFFS—Class plaintiffs serving as the representative parties in the litigation may serve on the plaintiff steering committee, but shall not comprise a majority of the committee.

'(3) NONCOMPENSATION OF MEMBERS—Members of the plaintiff steering committee shall serve without compensation, except that any member may apply to the court for reimbursement of reasonable out-of-pocket expenses from any common fund established for the class.

'(4) MEETINGS—The plaintiff steering committee shall conduct its business at one or more previously scheduled meetings of the committee, of which prior notice shall have been given and at which a majority of its members are present in person or by electronic communication. The plaintiff steering committee shall decide all matters within its authority by a majority vote of all members, except that the committee may determine that decisions other than to accept or reject a settlement offer or to employ or dismiss counsel for the class may be delegated to one or more members of the committee, or may be voted upon by committee members seriatim, without a meeting.

'(5) RIGHT OF NONMEMBERS TO BE HEARD—A class member who is not a member of the plaintiff steering committee may appear and be heard by the court on any issue relating to the organization or actions of the plaintiff steering committee.

'(c) FUNCTIONS OF PLAINTIFF STEERING COMMITTEE—The authority of the plaintiff steering committee to direct counsel for the class shall include all powers normally permitted to an attorney's client in litigation, including the authority to retain or dismiss counsel and to reject offers of settlement, and the authority to accept an offer of settlement subject to final approval by the court. Dismissal of counsel other than for cause shall not limit the ability of counsel to enforce any contractual fee agreement or to apply to the court for a fee award from any common fund established for the class.

'(d) IMMUNITY FROM CIVIL LIABILITY; REMOVAL—Any person serving as a member of a plaintiff steering committee shall be immune from any civil liability for any negligence in performing such service, but shall not be immune from liability for intentional misconduct or from the assessment of costs pursuant to section 20B(c). The court may remove a member of a plaintiff steering committee for good cause shown.

'(e) EFFECT ON OTHER LAW—This section does not affect any other provision of law concerning class actions or the authority of the court to give final approval to any offer of settlement.'.

(b) PROHIBITION ON ATTORNEYS' FEES PAID FROM COMMISSION DISGORGEMENT FUNDS—Section 21(d) of the Securities Exchange Act of 1934 (15 U.S.C. 78u(d)) is amended by adding at the end the following new paragraph:

'(4) PROHIBITION ON ATTORNEYS' FEES PAID FROM COMMISSION DISGORGEMENT FUNDS—Except as otherwise ordered by the court, funds disgorged as the result of an action brought by the Commission, or of any Commission proceeding, shall not be distributed as payment for attorneys' fees or expenses incurred by private parties seeking distribution of the disgorged funds.'.

SECTION 3. PREVENTION OF ABUSIVE PRACTICES THAT FOMENT LITIGATION.

(a) ADDITIONAL PROVISIONS APPLICABLE TO PRIVATE ACTIONS—The Securities Exchange Act of 1934 is amended by inserting after section 20A (15 U.S.C. 78t-1) the following new section:

'PROCEDURES APPLICABLE TO PRIVATE ACTIONS

'SEC. 20B. (a) ELIMINATION OF BONUS PAYMENTS TO NAMED PLAINTIFFS IN CLASS ACTIONS—In any private action under this title that is certified as a class action pursuant to the Federal Rules of Civil Procedure, the portion of any final judgment or of any settlement that is awarded to class plaintiffs serving as the representative parties shall be equal, on a per share basis, to the portion of the final judgment or settlement awarded to all other members of the class. Nothing in this subsection shall be construed to limit the award to any representative parties of actual expenses (including lost wages) relating to the representation of the class.

'(b) RESTRICTIONS ON PROFESSIONAL PLAINTIFFS—Except as the court may otherwise permit for good cause, a person may be a named plaintiff, or an officer, director, or fiduciary of a named plaintiff, in no more than 5 class actions filed during any 3-year period.

'(c) AWARDS OF FEES AND EXPENSES—

'(1) AUTHORITY TO AWARD FEES AND EXPENSES—If the court in any private action arising under this title enters a final judgment against a party litigant on the basis of a motion to dismiss, motion for summary judgment, or a trial on the merits, the court shall, upon motion by the prevailing party, determine whether (A) the position of the losing party was not substantially justified, (B) imposing fees and expenses on the losing party or the losing party's attorney would be just, and (C) the cost of such fees and expenses to the prevailing party is substantially burdensome or unjust. If the court makes the determinations described in clauses (A), (B), and (C), the court shall award the prevailing party reasonable fees and other expenses incurred by that party. The determination of whether the position of the losing party was substantially justified shall be made on the basis of the record in the action for which fees and other expenses are sought, but the burden of persuasion shall be on the prevailing party.

'(2) SECURITY FOR PAYMENT OF COSTS IN CLASS ACTIONS—In any private action arising under this title that is certified as a class action pursuant to the Federal Rules of Civil Procedure, the court shall require an undertaking from the attorneys for the plaintiff class, the plaintiff class, or both, in such proportions and at such times as the court determines are just and equitable, for the payment of the fees and expenses that may be awarded under paragraph (1).

'(3) APPLICATION FOR FEES—A party seeking an award of fees and other expenses shall, within 30 days of a final, nonappealable judgment in the action, submit to the court an application for fees and other expenses that certifies that the party is entitled to such an award under paragraph (1) and the amount sought, including an itemized statement from any attorney or expert witness representing or appearing on behalf of the party stating the actual time expended and the rate at which fees and other expenses are computed.

'(4) ALLOCATION AND SIZE OF AWARD—The court, in its discretion, may—

'(A) determine whether the amount to be awarded pursuant to this section shall be awarded against the losing party, its attorney, or both; and

'(B) reduce the amount to be awarded pursuant to this section, or deny an award, to the extent that the prevailing party during the course of the proceedings engaged in conduct that unduly and unreasonably protracted the final resolution of the action.

'(5) AWARDS IN DISCOVERY PROCEEDINGS—In adjudicating any motion for an order compelling discovery or any motion for a protective order made in any private action arising under this title, the court shall award the prevailing party reasonable fees and other expenses incurred by the party in bringing or defending against the motion, including reasonable attorneys' fees, unless the court finds that special circumstances make an award unjust.

'(6) RULE OF CONSTRUCTION—Nothing in this subsection shall be construed to limit or impair the discretion of the court to award costs pursuant to other provisions of law.

'(7) PROTECTION AGAINST ABUSE OF PROCESS—In any action to which this subsection applies, a court shall not permit a plaintiff to withdraw from or voluntarily dismiss such action if the court determines that such withdrawal or dismissal is taken for purposes of evasion of the requirements of this subsection.

'(8) DEFINITIONS—For purposes of this subsection—

'(A) The term 'fees and other expenses' includes the reasonable expenses of expert witnesses, the reasonable cost of any study, analysis, report, test, or project which is found by the court to be necessary for the preparation of the party's case, and reasonable attorneys' fees and expenses. The amount of fees awarded under this section shall be based upon prevailing market rates for the kind and quality of services furnished.

'(B) The term 'substantially justified' shall have the same meaning as in section 2412(d)(1) of title 28, United States Code.

'(d) PREVENTION OF ABUSIVE CONFLICTS OF INTEREST—In any private action under this title pursuant to a complaint seeking damages on behalf of a class, if the class is represented by an attorney who directly owns or otherwise has a beneficial interest in the securities that are the subject of the litigation, the court shall, on motion by any party, make a determination of whether such interest constitutes a conflict of interest sufficient to disqualify the attorney from representing the class.

'(e) DISCLOSURE OF SETTLEMENT TERMS TO CLASS MEMBERS—In any private action under this title that is certified as a class action pursuant to the Federal Rules of Civil Procedure, any proposed or final settlement agreement that is published or otherwise disseminated to the class shall include the following statements:

'(1) STATEMENT OF POTENTIAL OUTCOME OF CASE-

'(A) AGREEMENT ON AMOUNT OF DAMAGES AND LIKELIHOOD OF PREVAILING—If the settling parties agree on the amount of damages per share that would be recoverable if the plaintiff prevailed on each claim alleged under this title and the likelihood that the plaintiff would prevail—

'(i) a statement concerning the amount of such potential damages per share; and

'(ii) a statement concerning the likelihood that the plaintiff would prevail on the claims alleged under this title and a brief explanation of the reasons for that conclusion.

'(B) DISAGREEMENT ON AMOUNT OF DAMAGES OR LIKELIHOOD OF PREVAILING—If the parties do not agree on the amount of damages per share that would be recoverable if the plaintiff prevailed on each claim alleged under this title or on the likelihood that the plaintiff would prevail on those claims, or both, a statement from each settling party concerning the issue or issues on which the parties disagree.

'(C) INADMISSIBILITY FOR CERTAIN PURPOSES—Statements made in accordance with subparagraphs (A) and (B) concerning the amount of damages and the likelihood of prevailing shall not be admissible for purposes of any Federal or State judicial action or administrative proceeding.

'(2) STATEMENT OF ATTORNEYS' FEES OR COSTS SOUGHT—If any of the settling parties or their counsel intend to apply to the court for an award of attorneys' fees or costs from any fund established as part of the settlement, a statement indicating which parties or counsel intend to make such an application, the amount of fees and costs that will be sought (including the amount of such fees and costs determined on a per-share basis, together with the amount of the settlement proposed to be distributed to the parties to suit, determined on a per-share basis),

and a brief explanation of the basis for the application. Such information shall be clearly summarized on the cover page of any notice to a party of any proposed or final settlement agreement.

'(3) IDENTIFICATION OF LAWYERS' REPRESENTATIVES—The name and address of one or more representatives of counsel for the class who will be reasonably available to answer written questions from class members concerning any matter contained in any notice of settlement published or otherwise disseminated to the class.

'(4) OTHER INFORMATION—Such other information as may be required by the court, or by any plaintiff steering committee appointed by the court pursuant to section 36.

'(f) ENCOURAGEMENT OF FINALITY IN SETTLEMENT DISCHARGES-

'(1) DISCHARGE—A defendant who settles any private action arising under this title at any time before verdict or judgment shall be discharged from all claims for contribution brought by other persons with respect to the matters that are the subject of such action. Upon entry of the settlement by the court, the court shall enter a bar order constituting the final discharge of all obligations to the plaintiff of the settling defendant arising out of the action. The order shall bar all future claims for contribution arising out of the action—

'(A) by any person against the settling defendant; and

'(B) by the settling defendant against any person other than a person whose liability has been extinguished by the settling defendant's settlement.

'(2) REDUCTION—If a person enters into a settlement with the plaintiff prior to verdict or judgment, the verdict or judgment shall be reduced by the greater of—

'(A) an amount that corresponds to the percentage of responsibility of that person; or

'(B) the amount paid to the plaintiff by that person.

'(g) CONTRIBUTION FROM NON-PARTIES IN INTERESTS OF FAIRNESS-

'(1) RIGHT OF CONTRIBUTION—A person who becomes liable for damages in any private action under this title (other than an action under section 9(e) or 18(a)) may recover contribution from any other person who, if joined in the original suit, would have been liable for the same damages.

'(2) STATUTE OF LIMITATIONS FOR CONTRIBUTION—Once judgment has been entered in any such private action determining liability, an action for contribution must be brought not later than 6 months after the entry of a final, nonappealable judgment in the action.

'(h) DEFENDANT'S RIGHT TO WRITTEN INTERROGATORIES ESTABLISHING SCIENTER—In any private action under this title in which the plaintiff may recover money damages, the court shall, when requested by a defendant, submit to the jury a written interrogatory on the issue of each such defendant's state of mind at the time the alleged violation occurred.'.

(b) PROHIBITION OF REFERRAL FEES THAT FOMENT LITIGATION—Section 15(c) of the Securities Exchange Act of 1934 (15 U.S.C. 78o(c)) is amended by adding at the end the following new paragraph:

'(8) RECEIPT OF REFERRAL FEES—No broker or dealer, or person associated with a broker or dealer, may solicit or accept remuneration for assisting an attorney in obtaining the representation of any customer in any private action under this title.'.

SECTION 4. PREVENTION OF 'FISHING EXPEDITION' LAWSUITS.

The Securities Exchange Act of 1934 (15 U.S.C. 78a et seq.) is amended by inserting after section 10 the following new section:

'SEC. 10A. REQUIREMENTS FOR SECURITIES FRAUD ACTIONS.

'(a) SCIENTER—

'(1) IN GENERAL—In any private action arising under section 10(b) of this title based on a fraudulent statement, liability may be established only on proof that—

'(A) the defendant directly or indirectly made a fraudulent statement;

'(B) the defendant possessed the intention to deceive, manipulate, or defraud; and

'(C) the defendant made such fraudulent statement knowingly or recklessly.

'(2) FRAUDULENT STATEMENT—For purposes of this section, a fraudulent statement is a statement that contains an untrue statement of a material fact, or omits to state a material fact necessary in order to make the statements made, in the light of the circumstances in which they were made, not misleading.

'(3) KNOWINGLY—For purposes of paragraph (1), a defendant makes a fraudulent statement knowingly if the defendant knew that the statement of a material fact was untrue at the time it was made, or knew that an omitted fact was necessary in order to make the statements made, in the light of the circumstances in which they were made, not misleading.

'(4) RECKLESSNESS—For purposes of paragraph (1), a defendant makes a fraudulent statement recklessly if the defendant, in making such statement, is guilty of highly unreasonable conduct that (A) involves not merely simple or even gross negligence, but an extreme departure from standards of ordinary care, and (B) presents a danger of misleading buyers, sellers, or security holders that was either known to the defendant or so obvious that the defendant must have been aware of it. Deliberately refraining from taking steps to discover whether one's statements are false or misleading constitutes recklessness, but if the failure to investigate was not deliberate, such conduct shall not be considered to be reckless.

'(b) REQUIREMENT FOR EXPLICIT PLEADING OF SCIENTER—In any private action to which subsection (a) applies, the complaint shall specify each statement or omission alleged to have been misleading, and the reasons the statement or omission was misleading. The complaint shall also make specific allegations which, if true, would be sufficient to establish scienter as to each defendant at the time the alleged violation occurred. It shall not be sufficient for this purpose to plead the mere presence of facts inconsistent with a statement or omission alleged to have been misleading. If an allegation is made on information and belief, the complaint shall set forth with specificity all information on which that belief is formed.

'(c) DISMISSAL FOR FAILURE TO MEET PLEADING REQUIREMENTS; STAY OF DISCOVERY; SUMMARY JUDGMENT—In any private action to which subsection (a) applies, the court shall, on the motion of any defendant, dismiss the complaint if the requirements of subsection (b) are not met, except that the court may, in its discretion, permit a single amended complaint to be filed. During the pendency of any such motion to dismiss, all discovery and other proceedings shall be stayed unless the court finds upon the motion of any party that particularized discovery is necessary to preserve evidence or to prevent undue prejudice to that party. If a complaint satisfies the requirements of subsection (b), the plaintiff shall be entitled to conduct discovery limited to the facts concerning the allegedly misleading statement or omission. Upon completion of such discovery, the parties may move for summary judgment.

'(d) RELIANCE AND CAUSATION—

'(1) IN GENERAL—In any private action to which subsection (a) applies, the plaintiff shall prove that—

'(A) he or she had knowledge of, and relied (in connection with the purchase or sale of a security) on, the statement that contained the misstatement or omission described in subsection (a)(1); and

'(B) that the statement containing such misstatement or omission proximately caused (through both transaction causation and loss causation) any loss incurred by the plaintiff.

'(2) FRAUD ON THE MARKET—For purposes of paragraph (1), knowledge and reliance may be proven by establishing that the market as a whole considered the fraudulent statement, that the price at which the security was purchased or sold reflected the market's estimation of the fraudulent statement, and that the plaintiff relied on that market price. Proof that the market as a whole considered the fraudulent statement may consist of evidence that the statement—

'(A) was published in publicly available research reports by analysts of such security;

'(B) was the subject of news articles;

'(C) was delivered orally at public meetings by officers of the issuer, or its agents;

'(D) was specifically considered by rating agencies in their published reports; or

'(E) was otherwise made publicly available to the market in a manner that was likely to bring it to the attention of, and to be considered as credible by, other active participants in the market for such security.

Nonpublic information may not be used as proof that the market as a whole considered the fraudulent statement.

'(3) PRESUMPTION OF RELIANCE—Upon proof that the market as a whole considered the fraudulent statement pursuant to paragraph (2), the plaintiff is entitled to a rebuttable presumption that the price at which the security was purchased or sold reflected the market's estimation of the fraudulent statement and that the plaintiff relied on such market price. This presumption may be rebutted by evidence that—

'(A) the market as a whole considered other information that corrected the allegedly fraudulent statement; or

'(B) the plaintiff possessed such corrective information prior to the purchase or sale of the security.

'(4) REASONABLE EXPECTATION OF INTEGRITY OF MARKET PRICE—A plaintiff who buys or sells a security for which it is unreasonable to rely on market price to reflect all current information may not establish reliance pursuant to paragraph (2). For purposes of paragraph (2), the following factors shall be considered in determining whether it was reasonable for a party to expect the market price of the security to reflect substantially all publicly available information regarding the issuer of the security:

'(A) The weekly trading volume of any class of securities of the issuer of the security.

'(B) The existence of public reports by securities analysts concerning any class of securities of the issuer of the security.

'(C) The eligibility of the issuer of the security, under the rules and regulations of the Commission, to incorporate by reference its reports made pursuant to section 13 of this title in a registration statement filed under the Securities Act of 1933 in connection with the sale of equity securities.

'(D) A history of immediate movement of the price of any class of securities of the issuer of the security caused by the public dissemination of information regarding unexpected corporate events or financial releases.

In no event shall it be considered reasonable for a party to expect the market price of the security to reflect substantially all publicly available information regarding the issuer of the security unless the issuer of the security has a class of securities listed and registered on a national securities exchange or quoted on the automated quotation system of a national securities association.

'(E) ALLOCATION OF LIABILITY—

'(1) JOINT AND SEVERAL LIABILITY FOR KNOWING FRAUD—A defendant who is found liable for damages in a private action to which subsection (a) applies may be liable jointly and severally only if the trier of fact specifically determines that the defendant acted knowingly (as defined in subsection (a)(3)).

'(2) PROPORTIONATE LIABILITY FOR RECKLESSNESS—If the trier of fact does not make the findings required by paragraph (1) for joint and several liability, a defendant's liability in a private action to which subsection (a) applies shall be determined under paragraph (3) of this subsection only if the trier of fact specifically determines that the defendant acted recklessly (as defined in subsection (a)(4)).

'(3) DETERMINATION OF PROPORTIONATE LIABILITY—If the trier of fact makes the findings required by paragraph (2), the defendant's liability shall be determined as follows:

'(A) The trier of fact shall determine the percentage of responsibility of the plaintiff, of each of the defendants, and of each of the other persons or entities alleged by the parties to have caused or contributed to the harm alleged by the plaintiff. In determining the percentages of responsibility, the trier of fact shall consider both the nature of the conduct of each person and the nature and extent of the causal relationship between that conduct and the damage claimed by the plaintiff.

'(B) For each defendant, the trier of fact shall then multiply the defendant's percentage of responsibility by the total amount of damage suffered by the plaintiff that was caused in whole or in part by that defendant and the court shall enter a verdict or judgment against the defendant in that amount. No defendant whose liability is determined under this subsection shall be jointly liable on any judgment entered against any other party to the action.

'(C) Except where contractual relationship permits, no defendant whose liability is determined under this paragraph shall have a right to recover any portion of the judgment entered against such defendant from another defendant.

'(4) EFFECT OF PROVISION—This subsection relates only to the allocation of damages among defendants. Nothing in this subsection shall affect the standards for liability under any private action arising under this title.

'(f) DAMAGES—In any private action to which subsection (a) applies, and in which the plaintiff claims to have bought or sold the security based on a reasonable belief that the market value of the security reflected all publicly available information, the plaintiff's damages shall not exceed the lesser of—

'(1) the difference between the price paid by the plaintiff for the security and the market value of the security immediately after dissemination to the market of information which corrects the fraudulent statement; and

'(2) the difference between the price paid by the plaintiff for the security and the price at which the plaintiff sold the security after dissemination of information correcting the fraudulent statement.'.

SECTION 5. ESTABLISHMENT OF 'SAFE HARBOR' FOR PREDICTIVE STATEMENTS.

The Securities Exchange Act of 1934 (15 U.S.C. 78a et seq.) is amended by adding at the end the following new section:

'SEC. 37. APPLICATION OF SAFE HARBOR FOR FORWARD-LOOKING STATEMENTS.

'(a) SAFE HARBOR IN GENERAL—In any private action arising under this title based on a fraudulent statement (as defined in section 10A), a person shall not be liable with respect to any forward-looking statement if and to the extent that the statement-

'(1) contains a projection, estimate, or description of future events; and

'(2) refers clearly (or is understood by the recipient to refer) to-

'(A) such projections, estimates, or descriptions as forward-looking statements; and

'(B) the risk that such projections, estimates, or descriptions may not be realized.

The safe harbor for forward-looking statements established under this subsection shall be in addition to any safe harbor the Commission may establish by rule or regulation.

'(b) DEFINITION OF FORWARD-LOOKING STATEMENT—For the purpose of this section, the term 'forward-looking statement' shall include (but not be limited to) projections, estimates, and descriptions of future events, whether made orally or in writing, voluntarily or otherwise.

'(c) NO DUTY TO MAKE CONTINUING PROJECTIONS—In any private action arising under this title, no person shall be deemed to have any obligation to update a forward-looking statement made by such person unless such person has expressly and substantially contemporaneously undertaken to update such statement.

'(d) AUTOMATIC PROCEDURE FOR STAYING DISCOVERY; EXPEDITED PROCEDURE FOR CONSIDERATION OF MOTION ON APPLICABILITY OF SAFE HARBOR-

'(1) STAY PENDING DECISION ON MOTION—Upon motion by a defendant to dismiss on the ground that the statement or omission upon which the complaint is based is a forward-looking statement within the meaning of this section and that the safe harbor provisions of this section preclude a claim for relief, the court shall stay discovery until such motion is decided.

'(2) PROTECTIVE ORDERS—If the court denies a motion to dismiss to which paragraph (1) is applicable, or if no such motion is made and a party makes a motion for a protective order, at any time beginning after the filing of the complaint and ending 10 days after the filing of such party's answer to the complaint, asserting that the safe harbor provisions of this section apply to the action, a protective order shall issue forthwith to stay all discovery as to any party to whom the safe harbor provisions of this section may apply, except that which is directed to the specific issue of the applicability of the safe harbor. A hearing on the applicability of the safe harbor shall be conducted within 45 days of the issuance of the protective order. At the conclusion of the hearing, the court shall either dismiss the portion of the action based upon the use of the forward-looking information or determine that the safe harbor is unavailable in the circumstances.

'(e) REGULATORY AUTHORITY—The Commission shall exercise its authority to describe conduct with respect to the making of forward-looking statements that will be deemed not to provide a basis for liability in private actions under this title. Such rules and regulations shall—

'(1) include clear and objective guidance that the Commission finds sufficient for the protection of investors;

'(2) prescribe such guidance with sufficient particularity that compliance shall be readily ascertainable by issuers prior to issuance of securities; and

'(3) provide that forward-looking statements that are in compliance with such guidance and that concern the future economic performance of an issuer of securities registered under section 12 of this title will be deemed not to be in violation of this title.

Nothing in this section shall be deemed to limit, either expressly or by implication, the authority of the Commission to exercise similar authority or to adopt similar rules and regulations with respect to forward-looking statements under other statutes under which the Commission exercises rulemaking authority.'.

SECTION 6. AMENDMENT TO RACKETEER INFLUENCED AND CORRUPT ORGANIZATIONS ACT.

Section 1964(c) of title 18, United States Code, is amended by inserting ', except that no person may bring an action under this provision if the racketeering activity, as defined in section 1961(1)(D), involves conduct actionable as fraud in the purchase or sale of securities' before the period.

SECTION 7. FINANCIAL FRAUD DETECTION AND DISCLOSURE.

(a) AMENDMENTS TO THE SECURITIES EXCHANGE ACT OF 1934—The Securities Exchange Act of 1934 is amended by inserting after section 13 (15 U.S.C. 78m) the following new section:

'SEC. 13A. FRAUD DETECTION AND DISCLOSURE.

'(a) AUDIT REQUIREMENTS—Each audit required pursuant to this title of an issuer's financial statements by an independent public accountant shall include, in accordance with generally accepted auditing standards, as may be modified or supplemented from time to time by the Commission, the following:

'(1) procedures designed to provide reasonable assurance of detecting illegal acts that would have a direct and material effect on the determination of financial statement amounts;

'(2) procedures designed to identify related party transactions which are material to the financial statements or otherwise require disclosure therein; and

'(3) an evaluation of whether there is substantial doubt about the issuer's ability to continue as a going concern over the ensuing fiscal year.

'(b) REQUIRED RESPONSE TO AUDIT DISCOVERIES—

'(1) INVESTIGATION AND REPORT TO MANAGEMENT—If, in the course of conducting any audit pursuant to this title to which subsection (a) applies, the independent public accountant detects or otherwise becomes aware of information indicating that an illegal act (whether or not perceived to have a material effect on the issuer's financial statements) has or may have occurred, the accountant shall, in accordance with generally accepted auditing standards, as may be modified or supplemented from time to time by the Commission—

'(A)(i) determine whether it is likely that an illegal act has occurred, and (ii) if so, determine and consider the possible effect of the illegal act on the financial statements of the issuer, including any contingent monetary effects, such as fines, penalties, and damages; and

'(B) as soon as practicable inform the appropriate level of the issuer's management and assure that the issuer's audit committee, or the issuer's board of directors in the absence of such a committee, is adequately informed with respect to illegal acts that have been detected or otherwise come to the attention of such accountant in the course of the audit, unless the illegal act is clearly inconsequential.

'(2) RESPONSE TO FAILURE TO TAKE REMEDIAL ACTION—If, having first assured itself that the audit committee of the board of directors of the issuer or the board (in the absence of an audit committee) is adequately informed with respect to illegal acts that have been detected or otherwise come to the accountant's attention in the course of such accountant's audit, the independent public accountant concludes that—

'(A) any such illegal act has a material effect on the financial statements of the issuer,

'(B) senior management has not taken, and the board of directors has not caused senior management to take, timely and appropriate remedial actions with respect to such illegal act, and

'(C) the failure to take remedial action is reasonably expected to warrant departure from a standard auditor's report, when made, or warrant resignation from the audit engagement, the independent public accountant shall, as soon as practicable, directly report its conclusions to the board of directors.

'(3) NOTICE TO COMMISSION; RESPONSE TO FAILURE TO NOTIFY—An issuer whose board of directors has received a report pursuant to paragraph (2) shall inform the Commission by notice within one business day of receipt of such report and shall furnish the independent public accountant making such report with a copy of the notice furnished the Commission. If the independent public accountant making such report shall fail to receive a copy of such notice within the required one-business-day period, the independent public accountant shall—

'(A) resign from the engagement; or

'(B) furnish to the Commission a copy of its report (or the documentation of any oral report given) within the next business day following such failure to receive notice.

'(4) REPORT AFTER RESIGNATION—An independent public accountant electing resignation shall, within the one business day following a failure by an issuer to notify the Commission under paragraph (3), furnish to the Commission a copy of the accountant's report (or the documentation of any oral report given).

'(c) AUDITOR LIABILITY LIMITATION—No independent public accountant shall be liable in a private action for any finding, conclusion, or statement expressed in a report made pursuant to paragraph (3) or (4) of subsection (b), including any rules promulgated pursuant thereto.

'(d) CIVIL PENALTIES IN CEASE-AND-DESIST PROCEEDINGS—If the Commission finds, after notice and opportunity for hearing in a proceeding instituted pursuant to section 21C of this title, that an independent public accountant has willfully violated paragraph (3) or (4) of subsection (b) of this section, then the Commission may, in addition to entering an order under section 21C, impose a civil penalty against the independent public accountant and any other person that the Commission finds was a cause of such violation. The determination whether to impose a civil penalty, and the amount of any such penalty, shall be governed by the standards set forth in section 21B of this title.

'(e) PRESERVATION OF EXISTING AUTHORITY—Except for subsection (d), nothing in this section limits or otherwise affects the authority of the Commission under this title.

'(f) DEFINITIONS—As used in this section, the term 'illegal act' means any action or omission to act that violates any law, or any rule or regulation having the force of law.'.

(b) EFFECTIVE DATES—As to any registrant that is required to file selected quarterly financial data pursuant to item 302(a) of Regulation S-K (17 CFR 229.302(a)) of the Securities and Exchange Commission, the amendments made by subsection (a) of this section shall apply to any annual report for any period beginning on or after January 1, 1996. As to any other registrant, such amendment shall apply for any period beginning on or after January 1, 1997.

SECTION 8. RULE OF CONSTRUCTION.

Nothing in the amendments made by this Act shall be deemed to create or ratify any implied private right of action, or to prevent the Commission by rule from restricting or otherwise regulating private actions under the Securities Exchange Act of 1934.

SECTION 9. EFFECTIVE DATE.

This Act and the amendments made by this Act are effective on the date of enactment of this Act and shall apply to cases commenced after such date of enactment.

APPENDIX 16: EMPLOYMENT DISCRIMINATION CLASS ACTION COMPLAINT

UNITED STATES DISTRICT COURT
NORTHERN DISTRICT OF CALIFORNIA

BETTY DUKES, PATRICIA SURGESON, SANDRA STEVENSON, STEPHANIE ODLE, KIMBERLY MILLER and MICKI EARWOOD on behalf of themselves and all other similarly situated,	No. C-01-2252 MJJ FIRST AMENDED COMPLAINT
Plaintiffs,	[CLASS ACTION]
vs.	DEMAND FOR JURY TRIAL
WAL-MART STORES, INC.	
Defendant.	

INTRODUCTION

1. Wal-Mart is the largest retailer in the world and the largest private employer in the United States. Through its Wal-Mart and Sam's Club divisions, it is the industry leader not only in size, but also in its failure to advance its female employees. There are two workforces at Wal-Mart. By far the largest workforce is female, which comprises over 72% of the hourly sales employees, yet only one-third of management positions. This workforce is predominantly assigned to the lowest paying positions with the least chance of advancement. The other workforce is male. This workforce is the reverse image of the female workforce—it comprises less than 28% of the hourly sales workers, yet

holds two-thirds of all store management positions and over 90% of the top Store Manager positions. This disparate distribution of the genders is the result of purposeful discrimination and of practices that serve no reasonable business purpose yet have a disproportionate impact on women.

2. This class action is accordingly brought by present and former Wal-Mart employees on behalf of themselves and all other similarly situated women who have been subjected to Wal-Mart's continuing policies and practices of gender discrimination. Plaintiffs, and the class that they represent, charge that Wal-Mart discriminates against its female employees by advancing male employees more quickly than female employees, by denying female employees equal job assignments, promotions, training and compensation, and by retaliating against those who oppose its unlawful practices.

3. This action seeks an end to Wal-Mart's discriminatory practices, make whole relief for the class, and punitive damages.

JURISDICTION AND VENUE

4. Plaintiffs' claims arise under Title VII of the Civil Rights Act of 1964, 42 U.S.C. §§ 2000e, et seq. This Court has jurisdiction over this matter pursuant to 42 U.S.C. § 2000e5(f), 28 U.S.C. §§ 1331 and 1343(a)(4). The Court has supplemental jurisdiction pursuant to 28 U.S.C. 1367 over claims under the California Fair Employment & Housing Act, Government Code § 12920, et. seq.

5. Venue is proper in this district pursuant to 42 U.S.C. § 2000e5(f) and 28 U.S.C. § 1391(b) & (c). Lead plaintiff's claims arose in the Northern District of California. Members of the plaintiffs' class reside throughout the United States, including the Northern District of California. Many of the acts complained of herein occurred in this District and gave rise to the claims alleged. Wal-Mart operates over 140 stores and Sam's Clubs in California where it employs more than 40,000 workers. It operates at least 18 stores in the Northern District of California.

PARTIES

6. Plaintiff, Betty Dukes, is an African American woman and a resident of Contra Costa County, California. She is currently employed by Wal-Mart Stores, Inc.

7. Plaintiff, Patricia Surgeson, is a woman and a resident of Solano County, California. She was employed by Wal-Mart Stores, Inc. from August 1997 to March 2001. Plaintiffs are informed and believe she is eligible for rehire.

8. Plaintiff, Sandra Stevenson, is a woman and a resident of Lake County, Illinois. She was employed by Wal-Mart Stores, Inc. from November 1996 to June 2000.

9. Plaintiff, Stephanie Odle, is a woman and a resident of Norman, Oklahoma. She was employed by Wal-Mart Stores, Inc. from November 1991 to October 1999.

10. Plaintiff, Kimberly Miller, is a woman and a resident of Marion County, Florida. She was employed by Wal-Mart Stores, Inc. from November 1991 to February 2000.

11. Plaintiff Micki Earwood is a woman and a resident of Springfield, Ohio. She was employed by Wal-Mart Stores, Inc. from 1989 until September 28, 2000.

12. Defendant Wal-Mart Stores Inc. is a Delaware corporation with stores throughout California. Its corporate headquarters are located in Arkansas. Wal-Mart Stores, Inc. operates retail stores doing business as Wal-Mart, Wal-Mart Supercenters and Sam's Club Stores.

CLASS ALLEGATIONS

13. Plaintiffs bring this action pursuant to Rule 23 of the Federal Rules of Civil Procedure on behalf of a class of all past, present and future female employees of Wal-Mart's retail stores (including Wal-Mart discount, supercenter and neighborhood markets and Sam's Club stores, hereinafter collectively referred to as "Wal-Mart") in the United States. Plaintiffs are members of the class they seek to represent.

14. The members of the class are sufficiently numerous that joinder of all members is impracticable. Plaintiffs are informed and believe that the class exceeds 700,000 present and former female employees of Wal-Mart.

15. There are questions of law and fact common to the class, and these questions predominate over individual questions. Such questions include, without limitation, whether defendant's common operating practices and procedures discriminate against its female employees; whether defendant's policies have an adverse impact upon the class and, if so, whether said impact

can be justified by business necessity; whether defendant has a policy and practice of retaliating against class-members who object to or oppose unlawful employment practices; and whether injunctive and other equitable remedies and punitive damage relief for the class is warranted.

16. The claims alleged by the plaintiffs are typical of the claims of the class.

17. The named plaintiffs will fairly and adequately represent and protect the interests of the class.

18. This action is properly maintainable under both Fed. R. Civ. Proc. Rule 23(b)(2) and (3) because defendant has acted or refused to act on grounds generally applicable to the class, thereby making appropriate final injunctive relief or corresponding declarative relief with respect to the class as a whole; and because questions of law and fact common to the class predominate over any questions affecting only individual members, and a class action is superior to other available methods for the fair and efficient adjudication of this case. This action is also properly maintainable under Rule 23(c)(4)(A) for all class issues alleged herein.

WAL-MART'S OPERATION AND ITS GENERAL PRACTICE OF DISCRIMINATION

19. Wal-Mart is the largest private employer in the United States and the world's largest retailer. Through its Wal-Mart and Sam's Club divisions, it operates over 3000 stores across the country, encompassing every state. There are so many Wal-Mart locations in the United States that, according to Wal-Mart, the average store is within 30 miles of the next Wal-Mart store. In the United States, Wal-Mart employs nearly one million "associates," Wal-Mart's term for its hourly employees. In its last fiscal year, it had sales exceeding $191 billion. It claims that it has 100 million customers each week.

20. Wal-Mart employs uniform employment and personnel policies throughout the United States. All of its stores are linked by state-of-the-art electronic and video communications, through which all stores regularly report payroll, labor and other employment data. Regardless of division, there are uniform policies for employees, uniform "orientation" procedures, uniform salary, assignment, pay, training, and promotion policies. All stores are regularly audited for compliance with these uniform, company-wide policies and procedures.

21. The vast majority of Wal-Mart store employees are hourly paid sales associates, who report to department heads. Each store has a number of assistant managers who have different functional responsibilities, one or more "co-managers" and a store manager. District and regional managers supervise the stores.

22. Few objective requirements or qualifications for specific store assignments, promotions, or raises exist. Salaries are supposed to con-

form to general company guidelines, but store management has substantial discretion in setting salary levels within salary ranges for each employee. Salaries are also adjusted based on performance reviews, which are largely based on subjective judgments of performance. Plaintiffs are informed and believe that Wal-Mart policy prohibits employees from exchanging information about their salary levels.

23. The hourly sales workforce at Wal-Mart is predominantly female, representing over 72% of all hourly employees. Yet, male and female employees are not evenly distributed among the departments in the store. In some departments and positions, such as furniture, garden, electronics, hardware, sporting goods, guns, produce, and stocking, males are disproportionately assigned. In other departments, such as front-end cashier, customer service, health and beauty aids, cosmetics, house wares, stationary, toys, layaway, fabrics and clothes, women are disproportionately assigned.

Plaintiffs are informed and believe that the male-dominated departments and jobs are better paid and offer greater opportunities for advancement than the female-dominated positions and departments.

24. Male employees are more likely than female employees to obtain "cross-training" in other departments or to receive training and support to enter into departments that would aid their advancement.

25. Plaintiffs are informed and believe that female employees are paid less than male employees who perform substantially similar work, with similar or lesser skills and experience. Plaintiffs are further informed and believe that segregated assignment patterns exacerbate such unequal pay, because men are more likely to be assigned to departments that pay better than departments to which women are assigned.

26. Although women comprise the substantial majority of all hourly employees, the source from which most managers are drawn, their representation in management is the polar opposite. Women hold only about one-third of the positions that Wal-Mart identifies as management. However, even this figure overstates the proportion of female managers in true management positions. Thus the "one third" of management positions held by women includes traditionally "female" positions, such as assistant managers whose primary responsibility is supervising cashiers, and the lowest level of managers. Plaintiffs are informed and believe that women comprise less than 10% of all Store Managers and approximately 4% of all District Managers. There are few, if any female Regional Managers. There is only one woman among the 20 executive officers of the company. Plaintiffs are informed and

believe that even when women are promoted, on average they are advanced later, and then more slowly, than similarly situated male employees.

27. The workforce profile of Wal-Mart does not reflect the industry or the profile of its largest competitors. In fact, although it is the largest discount retailer in the country, it lags far behind its competitors in the promotion of women. Thus, while Wal-Mart's store management is only about one-third female, among its 20 top competitors women comprise over 56% of management, even though the proportion of hourly workers that are female at these companies is comparable to Wal-Mart. These differences are consistently found around the country. Moreover, these differences are longstanding. In fact, female representation among managers at Wal-Mart is at a substantially lower level today than the level of representation among Wal-Mart's competitors in 1975.

28. This pattern of unequal assignments, pay, training, and advancement opportunities is not the result of random or non-discriminatory factors. Rather, it is the result of an on-going and continuous pattern and practice of intentional sex discrimination in assignments, pay, training and promotions, and reliance on policies and practices that have an adverse impact on female employees that cannot be justified by business necessity, and for which alternative policies and practices with less discriminatory impact could be utilized that equally serve any asserted justification. Plaintiffs are informed and believe that such policies and practices include, without limitation:

a. Failure to consistently post job and promotional openings to ensure that all employees have notice of and an opportunity to seek advancement or more desirable assignments and training.

b. Reliance upon unweighted, arbitrary and subjective criteria utilized by a nearly all male managerial workforce in making assignments, training, pay, performance review and promotional decisions. Even where Wal-Mart policy states objective requirements, these requirements are often applied in an inconsistent manner and ignored at the discretion of management.

c. Reliance on gender stereotypes in making employment decisions such as assignments, promotions, pay and training.

d. Pre-selection and "grooming" of male employees for advancement, favorable assignments and training.

e. Maintenance of largely sex-segregated job categories and departments.

f. Deterrence and discouragement of female employees from seeking advancement, training, and favorable assignments and pay.

g. Paying female employees lower compensation than similarly situated men.

h. Assigning women to lower paying positions, and positions with lesser advancement potential than those given to men, and advancing women more slowly than similarly situated male employees.

i. Providing less training and support to female employees and managers than that given to male employees and managers.

j. Harassing female employees interested in advancement and subjecting them to a hostile work environment.

k. Requiring, as a condition of promotion to management jobs, that employees be willing to relocate, often to significantly distant stores, and applying this policy to require frequent and substantial relocations of its managers without any reasonable business justification. Plaintiffs are further informed and believe that the relocation policy is applied disparately between male and female employees, to the disadvantage of female employees.

l. Retaliating against female employees who have complained either internally or externally about Wal-Mart's treatment of its female employees. Wal-Mart maintains a company-wide, toll free telephone number, which it encourages employees to use if they have a problem or complaint in their store or with store management. Plaintiffs are informed and believe that Wal-Mart retaliates against women who use this number to report discrimination, sexual harassment or other unfair working conditions.

ALLEGATIONS OF NAMED PLAINTIFFS

BETTY DUKES

29. Betty Dukes is an African American woman currently employed in Wal-Mart store #1615, located in Pittsburg, California. She was hired as a part-time front-end cashier at the Pittsburg store in May 1994. Within one year after her hire date, Ms. Dukes received an excellent 90-day review, a promotion to full-time status and a merit pay raise. She was promoted to Customer Service Manager in June 1997, which also included an increase in salary.

30. In September 1997, Ms. Dukes began to experience harsh and discriminatory treatment from head Customer Service Manager Leilani (Lonnie) Barrett and male Store Manager Ken Cagle.

In November 1997, she complained to male District Manager Chuck Salby about the discriminatory treatment.

31. After she complained, Ms. Dukes experienced retaliation from Wal-Mart store management, beginning with a disciplinary write-up on February 13, 1998, for returning late from her breaks, even though male and/or Caucasian employees returned late from their breaks or failed to clock out for breaks and were not disciplined. Ms. Dukes was also written up on March 31, 1998, for having a front-end cashier cover her lunch break, even though she had used this procedure many times before without incident and Caucasian employees used this procedure without being reprimanded. Ms. Dukes complained to male District Manager Jay King but he simply referred her back to the store manager.

32. On June 29, 1999, Ms. Dukes called in sick. Store Manager Cagle reacted in a highly negative and unprofessional way towards her request, even though she was entitled to use sick leave. Ms. Dukes called the district management office about Cagle and, ultimately, she spoke with the male Loss Prevention District Manager Charles Chibante. Only after she threatened to make a complaint to the Wal-Mart home office in Arkansas did she receive a reluctant apology from Store Manager Cagle. However, Cagle's apology only served to escalate the retaliation.

33. In July of 1999, Ms. Dukes expressed interest in becoming a department manager by requesting of Ken Cagle that she receive training for that position, but she was never given the opportunity to be trained. Rather, shortly thereafter on August 14, 1999, Plaintiff was demoted from Customer Service Manager to cashier and falsely accused of violating company policy while performing a transaction that had been performed many times by Plaintiff and other employees without incident. The demotion was Wal-Mart's retaliation for Plaintiff's numerous complaints of discrimination.

34. On August 18, 1999, Ms. Dukes traveled to the Wal-Mart District Office in Livermore and made a complaint to male Wal-Mart District Manager John Scatlin about her demotion and her concerns about employment discrimination at the Pittsburg Wal-Mart store. Wal-Mart took no steps to address Dukes' concerns.

35. As a result of the demotion, Plaintiff became ineligible for several promotions to positions that she was qualified to perform from August 1999 to August 2000, the year following the demotion. For example, a support manager position was filled in July or August 2000 by Rosa Trevino (Hispanic female). Between July and September 2000, the position of Domestics Department Manager was open and filled by Joseph

Topasna (Filipino male). As a result of the demotion, Ms. Dukes' hours and hourly wage were reduced.

36. After August 14, 2000, when Ms. Dukes once again became eligible for promotion, at least four department manager and/or support manager positions at the Pittsburg store were filled by men. None of these positions was posted. Between October and December 2000, Richard Morales (Hispanic male) was promoted from night receiving stocker to night support manager. In November 2000, Joseph Topasna (Filipino male) was promoted to support manager. Between October and December 2000 Robert (Aaron) Mendez (Hispanic male) was promoted to support manager. In December 2000 or January 2001, Will Martines (Caucasian male) filled the position of Department Manager for Tire Lube Express (TLE).

37. After the demotion, Ms. Dukes was discouraged from seeking other positions because of the way she and other women had been treated by Wal-Mart. Dukes did not apply for three department manager positions open after August 14, 2000 (Hardware, Over The Counter Pharmacy and Stationery) because she was discouraged after the discriminatory treatment she and other women received from Wal-Mart managers.

38. Furthermore, Ms. Dukes' knowledge of Wal-Mart's discriminatory practices against other women at the Pittsburg store also discouraged her from seeking a promotion. In June of 2000, Brooke Terrell (African American female) was demoted from department manager to a sales floor position, although she continued to fulfill the responsibilities of a department manager until a replacement was found. The department manager position vacated by Terrell was filled by Kevin Sims (African American male). In 2000, Trina Wallace (African American female) was demoted from a department manager position to a sales floor position and later terminated. The department manager position vacated by Wallace was ultimately filled by Kendall Dimery (African American male). In 1999, Darla Harper (Caucasian woman) was denied a department manager job in which she had expressed an interest. Without posting this position, Wal-Mart selected Spencer Ostrom (Caucasian male) to fill this position.

39. On or about June 1, 2000, Dukes filed a charge of discrimination with the California Department of Fair Employment & Housing (DFEH), a copy of which is attached hereto as Exhibit 1 and incorporated by reference. On June 15, 2000, she received a right to sue letter, and commenced this action in a timely manner.

40. On or about May 2, 2001, Dukes filed a charge of discrimination with the United States Equal Opportunity Commission (EEOC), a copy of which is attached as Exhibit 2 and incorporated by reference. She re-

ceived a right to sue letter on or about May 22, 2001 and commenced this action in a timely manner.

STEPHANIE ODLE

41. Stephanie Odle was hired by Wal-Mart on November 21, 1991, as an hourly associate to work at the Sam's Club in Lubbock, Texas. She was successively transferred to Sam's Clubs in Dallas, Texas; Yuba City, California; and Vacaville, California.

42. On September 3, 1994, while employed at the Vacaville, California, Sam's Club, Ms. Odle was promoted to Assistant Manager and was assigned to the Sam's Club in Roseville, California, as a Manager-in-Training. Ms. Odle was then assigned to the Sam's Club in Sacramento, California, where she worked as an Assistant Manager. Ms. Odle was subsequently transferred in succession to the Sam's Clubs in Riverside, California; Las Vegas, Nevada; and back to Sacramento, California.

43. In October 1998, Ms. Odle was transferred to the Sam's Club in Sherman, Texas. While at this Sam's Club, she was led to believe by the Regional Director of Operations that she would be promoted to the position of Co-Manager of the Sam's Club store in Tulsa, Oklahoma.

44. On May 14, 1999, to insure that Ms. Odle was not promoted to the Co- Manager position at the Tulsa, Oklahoma, Sam's Club, she was discriminated against by management by being wrongfully suspended for five days concerning a legitimate refund she had made to a customer. On or about May 19, 1999, Ms. Odle was informed by management that she would not be promoted to the position of Co-Manager of the Tulsa, Oklahoma, Sam's Club, and that said position was being given to a male manager from Florida.

45. On May 20, 1999, Ms. Odle was given the most severe form of discipline at Sam's Club short of termination, even though management knew that she did not do anything to warrant such discipline, and management never disciplined male employees in this fashion.

46. Also on May 20, 1999, the Store's male managers wrongfully denied Ms. Odle access to the Store or to the Store's employees and ordered her against her will to transfer from the Sam's Club in Sherman, Texas, to the Sam's Club in Lubbock, Texas.

47. On or about October 6, 1999, Ms. Odle complained to management that she was being denied an opportunity to take a skills assessment test critical for future promotion that was being administered to three male managers.

48. On October 16, 1999, Ms. Odle was training three hourly Sam's Club employees with respect to a new store procedure. During the training, a $13.74 accounting adjustment occurred. Ms. Odle notified accounting and the acting store manager of the adjustment, and neither expressed any concern. Two days later, even though management knew that the cash register discrepancy was a harmless training adjustment causing no loss to the company, management, in order to make available a managerial position for a male manager from Arizona, wrongfully suspended Ms. Odle and placed her on administrative leave.

49. On October 19, 1999, Ms. Odle was wrongfully terminated by the General Manager of the store, and by the Regional Director of Operations for Sam's Club.

50. On October 22, 1999, Ms. Odle's attorney filed a charge of discrimination against Sam's Club with the El Paso Area Office of the United States Equal Employment Opportunity Commission and tele-faxed a copy of this Charge of Discrimination to Sam's Club headquarters in Bentonville, Arkansas, regarding the gender discrimination perpetrated against her by Sam's Club. A copy of this charge is attached hereto as Exhibit 3 and incorporated by reference. Despite being briefly reinstated pending further "investigation," in retaliation for filing a Charge of Discrimination with the EEOC. Ms. Odle was again wrongfully discharged on October 29, 1999, and was replaced by the male manager who was transferred to the Lubbock, Texas store from a Sam's Club in Arizona.

51. Ms. Odle filed amended EEOC charges on January 4, 2000, and April 4, 2000, copies of which are attached hereto as Exhibits 4 and 5 and incorporated by reference. On or about May 31, 2001, the EEOC issued a notice of right to sue on these charges, and this action was timely commenced thereafter.

SANDRA STEVENSON

52. Sandra Stevenson began working at the Gurnee, Illinois Sam's Club in November, 1996 as a cashier. She later transferred to the night shift as a receiver, and then as a stocker. In December 1997, she was promoted to night supervisor. Ms. Stevenson understood that she had a better chance of being promoted to area manager if she worked as a team leader during the day shift. Accordingly, on numerous occasions throughout her employment, Ms. Stevenson informed her supervisors and managers that she wished to work as a supervisor during the day shift and that she wished to be promoted to a manager. In approximately 1999, Wal-Mart promoted Randy Walker, a male employee that

Ms. Stevenson had supervised, to a team leader position during the day shift. Despite their knowledge that Ms. Stevenson was interested in being promoted, at no time did Wal-Mart inform Ms. Stevenson about this opening or give her the opportunity to apply for this team leader position.

53. In January 2000, after Ms. Stevenson threatened to quit her job, Wal-Mart made her a team leader of the produce department during the day shift. Todd Christian, the store General Manager informed her that this position would lead to her being promoted to Area Manager in Produce, which was an open position. Thereafter, Ms. Stevenson made numerous requests to various supervisors and managers to promote her to Area Manager of Produce. Each time she asked one of her supervisors about the promotion, she was informed that it was up to someone else to decide whether or not to promote her.

54. Throughout her employment, Ms. Stevenson worked extremely hard in an effort to be promoted to a manager. She often worked without pay to make up for the lack of support from management and lack of training that she received as a night supervisor and as a team leader. As a team leader in produce, she performed the work and had the responsibilities of an area manager, which was a vacant position, but was never compensated as a manager, given the proper training, or given the title of manager.

55. Despite her numerous requests and her hard work, Ms. Stevenson was never promoted to Area Manager of Produce or any other area management position. Wal-Mart also failed to offer her any training to become a manager, nor offer her any opportunity to apply for a management position.

56. Moreover, Wal-Mart also discriminated against Ms. Stevenson on the basis of her sex, by denying her pay equal to that of a male employee, Kelly Walker, who held a similar position as Ms. Stevenson. Defendant also groomed Walker for management and placed him in the Manager-in-Training program. Subsequently, in or about 1999, Wal-Mart promoted Kelly Walker to area manager.

57. During the time that Stevenson was an employee, Wal-Mart promoted an atmosphere of a "Boy's Club" where men were treated better than female employees. Chester Roberts, a co-general manager at the Sam's Club in Gurnee, made derogatory comments about women including stating that women are not competent to be managers and are unable to drive forklifts as well as men. Defendant also did not post available manager positions or otherwise make these opportunities known to the male and female employees on an equal basis.

58. After being denied training to become a manager and promotion to an area manager position, and having been subjected to unequal treatment from management, Ms. Stevenson resigned in June 2000.

59. On or about March 15, 2001, Stevenson filed a charge of discrimination with the EEOC, a copy of which is attached hereto as Exhibit 6 and incorporated by reference. On or about May 15, 2001, the EEOC issued a right to sue notice on this charge. This action was timely commenced thereafter.

PATRICIA SURGESON

60. Patricia Surgeson was hired by Wal-Mart in Vacaville, California in August 1997 as a sales associate. She was assigned to the Tire and Lube Express department and, within two weeks of her hire, was subjected to sexually harassing remarks and touching by a co-worker. After reporting the harassment, she was transferred to the health and beauty aids department. She repeatedly applied to transfer to other positions but was denied.

61. In November 1998, Surgeson was assigned to the Lay-Away Department. In approximately May 1999, she was made the Lay-Away Department manager. Because she was assuming additional responsibilities, her Store Manager promised her a raise. Despite repeated requests, Surgeson was never given the promised raise.

62. In late 1999, the Store Manager decided that the Lay-Away Department no longer needed a manager. Ms. Surgeson's department manager title was taken away but she was expected to continue performing manager responsibilities. When she left the department, a male employee who was given the position and title of Lay-Away Department Manager replaced her. He was paid more than Ms. Surgeson had been paid for working in the same position with the same responsibilities.

63. In June or July 2000, Ms. Surgeson was moved to a position in the Cash Office. Although she assumed greater responsibilities, she again did not receive a raise. She was expected to work overtime without lunches or breaks, locked in the cash office. In her position, she became aware that many male employees were being paid more than she was, although they had worked at Wal-Mart for less time and had less responsibility.

64. In January 2001, she requested a merit increase. Her request was ignored for two months.

65. Ms. Surgeson was interested in attending the assistant manager training program and in being promoted to assistant manager. She asked one of her managers for information about how to qualify for the

program, as she had not seen any information posted about such opportunities. The manager provided only a vague response.

66. As a result of the discriminatory pay and working conditions, Ms. Surgeson resigned in March 2001.

67. On or about May 14, 2001, Surgeson filed a charge of discrimination with the EEOC, a copy of which is attached hereto as Exhibit 7 and incorporated by reference. The EEOC issued a notice of right to sue on May 31, 2001, and this action was timely commenced thereafter.

KIMBERLY MILLER

68. Plaintiff Kimberly Miller was employed by Defendant Wal-Mart Stores, Inc. from November 1991 until February 2000 as an hourly associate at a Sam's Club located in Ocala, Florida, except for a brief period in 1998 when she was assigned to Wal-Mart's Ocoee, Florida store.

69. During her tenure at Wal-Mart, Ms. Miller worked in a wide variety of areas of the store, gaining valuable exposure to the full range of activities in which the store was engaged.

70. Ms.Miller began her employment at Wal-Mart as a cashier. Shortly after her employment began, Wal-Mart was sufficiently impressed with Ms. Miller to assign her to the Accounting Office where she was entrusted with responsibility for handling cash and opening the jewelry department.

71. In April 1993, Ms. Miller was assigned to the Membership Desk where she again handled cash and sensitive company documents such as membership and sales reports. In April 1994, Ms. Miller became assigned to the MPU Desk where her duties again included handling cash as well as refunds and film. About one year later, in April 1995, Ms. Miller was assigned to the Cigarette area where she again handled cash and responding to cigarette orders. Later that year, Ms. Miller was assigned to the Information Desk where she responded to member requests and inquiries and preparing reports for all areas of the store.

72. Still later in 1995, Ms. Miller was assigned to the Tire Mounting Area ("TMA") where, except for several brief assignments to other departments, she remained until she resigned in February 2000. In the TMA area, Ms. Miller filled work orders, handled cash and responded to the full range of member inquiries.

73. Throughout her tenure at Wal-Mart, Ms. Miller received performance evaluations that were well above average. She also received many letters of commendation submitted by customers who received outstanding service from Ms. Miller.

74. Notwithstanding the breadth of Ms. Miller's experience and her distinguished performance, she failed to receive any promotions during her nearly nine years of service at Wal-Mart.

75. For most of Ms. Miller's tenure at Wal-Mart, the company failed to publicize vacancies for supervisory and managerial positions. In order to express her interest in advancement to Team Leader and other supervisory positions, therefore, Ms. Miller regularly informed her immediate supervisor as well as the Assistant Manager with responsibility for her work area and the General Manager of the store of her interest in, and ample qualifications for, supervisory positions.

76. Ms. Miller was never granted an interview, much less selected, for several vacant supervisory positions for which she was qualified. Instead, male employees were selected who lacked the breadth of experience and distinguished performance that Ms. Miller possessed.

77. Ms. Miller was compensated at levels lower than those paid to men with comparable experience and records of performance.

78. Initially, the positions to which Ms. Miller was assigned were in Departments or Areas in which the overwhelming majority of employees were women. Those areas included the Membership, Cashier, Refunds and Accounting Areas and Departments. The employees in the Tire Mounting Area to which Ms. Miller was assigned for the most part from 1995 until her departure in 2000 were all men except for her.

79. During her tenure in the Tire Mounting Area, Ms.Miller was exposed to sexual taunts and statements disparaging of women, undermining her authority in the workplace and subjecting her to a working environment hostile to women. Ms. Miller was regularly called "Bitch" by her male supervisors, including her Assistant Manager. In front of her co-workers, Ms. Miller's male Team Leader offered to make her pregnant when she was encountering difficulties in conceiving a child. In 1999, Ms. Miller entered the waiting area of the Tire Mounting Area and encountered her co-workers watching a pornographic video during working hours. Ms. Miller's co-workers made other sexual comments about female customers and Ms. Miller on nearly a daily basis.

80. Ms. Miller complained on more than a dozen occasions to supervisors at all levels of the Wal-Mart hierarchy about the sexually polluted working environment in which she worked and about the repeated denial of promotions.

81. Ms. Miller complained to the male General Manager of the store about sexual comments directed at her by her male Assistant Manager. There was no promise that the conditions would improve and no improvement occurred.

82. At one point, Ms. Miller even complained to the male District Manager, who supervised the General Manager of her store, about the sexual comments made in the workplace and about the denial of promotions. His response was to attribute her concerns to a difference in personality styles and to offer Ms. Miller a story about baseball.

83. On or about November 13, 2000, Miller filed a charge of discrimination with the EEOC, a copy of which is attached hereto as exhibit 8 and incorporated by reference. On or about March 29, 2001, the EEOC issued a notice of right to sue on this charge, and this action was timely commenced thereafter.

MICKI EARWOOD

84. Ms. Earwood was hired by Wal-Mart on January 12, 1989, at the Urbana, Ohio, store as an unloader in the receiving department. In 1991, she became a sales clerk and later in 1991 became a department supervisor. In 1993, she transferred to the Wal-Mart store in Mentor, Ohio, where she was a department supervisor. In 1994, she was transferred to the Bellefontaine, Ohio Wal-Mart store where she was a department supervisor. In 1995, she was transferred back to the Urbana, Ohio, Wal-Mart as a support supervisor and, in August of 1999, was assigned the position of personnel manager/training coordinator. All of Ms. Earwood's employment with Wal-Mart was as an hourly employee.

85. In 1998, Ms. Earwood applied for promotion to the position of assistant manager but was told by Wal-Mart management that she could not be the assistant manager unless she was willing to move to New York State, which condition was not imposed on male applicants for the position of assistant manager. At the time of her application, Ms. Earwood was a single mother with a four-year- old daughter, and it would have been impossible for her to afford to transfer to New York State. Subsequent to management's constructive denial of her application for promotion to assistant manager in 1998, through approximately July of 2000, Ms. Earwood became aware of other assistant manager positions coming open, yet she was deterred from applying for them because she knew that management would require her to transfer and because she knew that Mr. Jim Phelps, the Urbana, Ohio, Wal-Mart Store Manager, had blocked the promotion of other women to assistant manager throughout this period.

86. While performing her job as personnel manager at the Urbana Wal-Mart, Ms. Earwood had access to the promotion and pay records of the store. While reviewing these records during the normal course of her regular job duties, it became apparent to her that the male employees were given many more opportunities for promotion and better pay

than the female employees. On one occasion, Mr. Phelps told Ms. Earwood that no one could be promoted to support manager, which required evening and weekend work, if "they had kids", which essentially eliminated working mothers from consideration for the position.

87. When hiring and authorizing increases in pay for employees of the Urbana Wal-Mart, Wal-Mart authorized more pay for male employees than for female employees hired for the same or similar positions.

88. In approximately September of 2000, Ms. Miller complained to Mr. Fetrow, Wal-Mart's District Manager and Mr. Phelps' supervisor, about, among other things, the disparate treatment of women in the Urbana Wal-Mart store.

89. Within two weeks of Ms. Earwood's complaint to Mr. Fetrow about the disparate treatment of women, Ms. Earwood was suspended for allegedly having a tape recorder in her office and taping private conversations with Mr. Fetrow and Mr. Phelps, which allegations were untrue and fabricated by management as a pretext for retaliating against Ms. Earwood for complaining to Mr. Fetrow about the disparate treatment of women.

90. On September 28, 2000, Ms. Earwood was wrongfully terminated from her employment at Wal-Mart because Ms. Earwood was a female and because she had made complaints to management about gender discrimination in the workplace. No similarly situated male employees were ever mistreated by Wal-Mart management in a like manner.

91. After Ms. Earwood was terminated, she received a threatening letter, dated October 24, 2000, from the senior corporate counsel of Wal-Mart, making false and slanderous allegations against Ms. Earwood, telling her that she could no longer shop at Wal-Mart and threatening her with legal action, in direct retaliation for Ms. Earwood's protected activity and because she is female.

92. On or about May 17, 2001, Ms. Earwood filed a charge of discrimination with the EEOC, a copy of which is attached hereto as Exhibit 9 and incorporated by reference. Ms. Earwood has requested a right to sue notice on these charges.

FIRST CLAIM FOR RELIEF
Violation of Title VII

93. Plaintiffs incorporate Paragraphs 1 through 92.

94. This claim is brought on behalf of all Plaintiffs and the class they represent.

95. The foregoing conduct violates Title VII of the Civil Rights Act of 1964, 42 U.S.C. §§ 2000(e), et. seq.

96. Wal-Mart has maintained a system for making decisions about promotions, assignments, transfers and compensation which is excessively subjective and which has had a disparate impact on female employees, and which is not justified by business necessity, or, if it could be so justified, less discriminatory alternatives exist that could equally serve said necessity.

97. Wal-Mart has maintained a 'willingness to relocate' prerequisite for promotion to management which has had a disparate impact on plaintiffs and the class they represent, and which is not justified by business necessity, or, if it could be so justified, less discriminatory alternatives exist which could equally serve said necessity.

98. Wal-Mart has intentionally discriminated against the class and maintained a system for making decisions about promotions, transfers, assignments and compensation that is excessively subjective and through which Wal-Mart discriminates against female employees by denying them for job assignments, upward mobility and compensation afforded to similarly situated male employees.

99. The defendant's discriminatory practices described above have denied female employees promotional opportunities, transfers, assignments and compensation to which they are entitled, which has resulted in the loss of past and future wages and other job benefits.

100. Wal-Mart has systematically retaliated against women who have complained about discrimination and unfair treatment.

101. Defendant's retaliatory practices have resulted in the loss of past and future wages and other job benefits for class members.

102. Plaintiffs request relief as provided in the Prayer for Relief below.

SECOND CLAIM FOR RELIEF
Violation of Title VII

103. Paragraphs 1-92 are incorporated by reference. This claim is brought on behalf of the named plaintiffs individually for their non-class claims.

104. Defendant discriminated against named plaintiffs on the basis of their gender by demoting, terminating, and/or by retaliating against them and by subjecting them to a hostile work environment.

105. Defendant's discriminatory and retaliatory practices have resulted in the loss of past and future wages and other job benefits, and

have caused plaintiffs to suffer humiliation, embarrassment and emotional distress.

106. Plaintiffs request relief as provided in the Prayer for Relief below.

THIRD CLAIM FOR RELIEF
Violation of California Fair Employment and Housing Act-Race Discrimination

107. Plaintiffs incorporate by reference Paragraphs 29 through 39.

108. This claim for relief is brought on behalf of Plaintiff Dukes only.

109. Defendant discriminated against plaintiff Dukes on the basis of her race, African American. The foregoing conduct violates the California Fair Employment and Housing Act, Government Code §§ 12940, et. seq.

110. Defendant's discriminatory and retaliatory practices have resulted in the loss of past and future wages and other job benefits, and have caused plaintiff to suffer humiliation, embarrassment and emotional distress.

111. Plaintiff Dukes requests relief as provided in the Prayer for Relief below.

RELIEF ALLEGATIONS

112. Plaintiffs and the class they represent have no plain, adequate or complete remedy at law to redress the wrongs alleged herein, and the injunctive relief sought in this action is the only means of securing complete and adequate relief. Plaintiffs and the class they represent are now suffering and will continue to suffer irreparable injury from Defendant's discriminatory acts and omissions.

113. The actions on the part of Defendant have caused and continue to cause Plaintiffs and all class members substantial losses in earnings, promotional opportunities and other employment benefits, in an amount to be determined according to proof.

114. Defendant acted or failed to act as herein alleged with malice or reckless indifference to the protected rights of Plaintiffs' and class members. Plaintiffs and class members are thus entitled to recover punitive damages in an amount to be determined according to proof.

PRAYER FOR RELIEF

WHEREFORE, Plaintiffs and the class pray for relief as follows:

1) Certification of the case as a class action on behalf of the proposed Plaintiff class and designation of Plaintiffs as representatives of the class and their counsel of record as Class Counsel;

2) All damages which individual Plaintiffs and the class have sustained as a result of Defendant's conduct, including back pay, front pay, general and special damages for lost compensation and job benefits that they would have received but for the discriminatory practices of Defendant;

3) For Plaintiffs' individual, non-class claims, all damages they have sustained as a result of defendant's conduct, including back pay, front pay, general and specific damages for lost compensation and job benefits they would have received but for the discriminatory practices of defendant, damages for emotional distress, and punitive damages, according to proof;

4) Exemplary and punitive damages in an amount commensurate with Defendant's ability to pay and to deter future conduct;

5) A preliminary and permanent injunction against Defendant and its directors, officers, owners, agents, successors, employees and representatives, and any and all persons acting in concert with them, from engaging in each of the unlawful practices, policies, customs and usages set forth herein;

6) A declaratory judgment that the practices complained of in this first amended complaint are unlawful and violate 42 U.S.C. § 2000(e), et. seq., Title VII of the Civil Rights Act of 1964;

7) An order restoring class members to their rightful positions at Wal-Mart;

8) An assignment of Plaintiffs and the class to those jobs they would now be occupying but for Defendant's discriminatory practices;

9) An adjustment of the wage rates and benefits for Plaintiffs and the class to that level which Plaintiffs and the class would be enjoying but for Defendant's discriminatory practices;

10) Costs incurred, including reasonable attorneys' fees, to the extent allowable by law;

11) Pre-Judgment and Post-Judgment interest, as provided by law; and

12) Such other and further legal and equitable relief as this Court deems necessary, just and proper.

DATED: June 19, 2001 Respectfully submitted,

By:________________________________

Brad Seligman

THE IMPACT FUND

SHEILA THOMAS
DORIS NG
EQUAL RIGHTS ADVOCATES

STEVE STEMERMAN
ELIZABETH LAWRENCE
DAVIS, COWELL & BOWE

JOSEPH SELLERS
DEBORAH VAGINS
COHEN, MILSTEIN, HAUSFELD & TOLL

STEPHEN TINKLER
MERIT BENNETT
TINKLER & BENNETT

JONATHAN SMITH
DEBRA GARDNER
PUBLIC JUSTICE CENTER

Attorneys for Plaintiffs BETTY DUKES, PATRICIA SURGESON, SANDRA STEVENSON, STEPHANIE ODLE, KIMBERLY MILLER and MICKI EARWOOD

DEMAND FOR JURY TRIAL

Plaintiffs hereby demand a jury trial as provided by Rule 38(a) of the Federal Rules of Civil Procedure.

By________________________________

Brad Seligman

APPENDIX 17: BREACH OF CONTRACT CLASS ACTION COMPLAINT

IN THE CIRCUIT COURT FOR THE FIRST JUDICIAL CIRCUIT
WILLIAMSON COUNTY, ILLINOIS

TAMMY SNIDER and MICHAEL AVERY,
On Behalf of Themselves and All Others
Similarly Situated,

Plaintiffs,

CLASS ACTION

No. 97-L-114

vs.

STATE FARM MUTUAL AUTOMOBILE
INSURANCE COMPANY,

Defendant.

CLASS ACTION COMPLAINT

JEANNE M. TETER, individually and not as a class representative, TAMMY SNIDER and MICHAEL E. AVERY, Plaintiffs, on behalf of themselves and all others similarly situated, by Don Barrett, G. Patrick Murphy, Thomas P. Thrash, Elizabeth J. Cabraser, Morris A. Ratner, and other named counsel, their attorneys, state their and the class' complaint against Defendant, STATE FARM MUTUAL AUTOMOBILE INSURANCE COMPANY, as follows:

1. Plaintiff Teter resides in Marion, Williamson County, Illinois. Plaintiff Teter holds a "State Farm car policy" or a vehicle casualty insurance policy issued by Defendant State Farm ("State Farm Policy" and/or "State Farm Policies").

2a. Plaintiff Snider resides in Williamson County, Illinois. Plaintiff Snider holds a "State Farm car policy" or a vehicle casualty insurance policy issued by Defendant State Farm ("State Farm Policy" and/or "State Farm Policies").

2b. Plaintiff Avery resides in Caddo Parish, Louisiana. Plaintiff Avery holds a "State Farm car policy" or a vehicle casualty insurance policy issued by Defendant State Farm ("State Farm Policy" and/or "State Farm Policies").

3. State Farm Mutual Automobile Insurance Company is an Illinois insurance company transacting business in the State of Illinois and in all states throughout the United States, sometimes by or through its subsidiaries or affiliates.

4. This Court has jurisdiction over the subject matter hereto and the parties hereof.

5. Venue is proper in this Court.

6. Plaintiffs and the class assert no federal question. Plaintiffs' state law claim cannot be federally preempted on any grounds, and this case must be heard in a state forum.

7. Defendant State Farm advertised, solicited and sold the State Farm Policy to Plaintiffs. Under the terms of Defendant State Farm's Policy, in consideration for the premiums paid, Defendant State Farm agreed to restore Plaintiffs' vehicles to their pre-loss condition using parts of like kind and quality. The State Farm Policy specifically provides that Defendant State Farm will "pay to repair or replace the property with like kind and quality." Defendant State Farm endorsements to the policy provide that Defendant State Farm "will include in the estimate parts sufficient to restore the vehicle to its pre-loss condition. You agree with us that such parts may include either parts furnished by the vehicle's manufacturer or parts from other sources including non-original equipment manufacturers." A copy of the Vehicle Casualty Insurance Policy, including the endorsements, and collectively called "the State Farm Car Policy," is attached as Exhibit 1. The "Declaration Pages" are attached as Exhibit 2. Defendant State Farm has acknowledged that a similar endorsement to the policy did not change Defendant State Farm's obligations, but simply clarified its practices concerning vehicle repairs. Defendant State Farm acknowledges that pursuant to the terms of the Defendant State Farm Policy and endorsement, Defendant State Farm is obligated to restore a vehicle to its pre-loss condition and represents that "parts are of 'like kind and quality' when they are sufficient to restore a vehicle to its pre-loss condition." A copy of Defendant State Farm's representations in the form of responses to interrogatories in similar cases based upon a similar endorsement (also attached) are attached as Exhibit 7. Thus, based upon the State Farm Car Policy, a contract, Plaintiffs reasonably expected

that their vehicles would be repaired with crash parts that were of like kind and quality and would restore their vehicles to their pre-loss condition. After Plaintiffs wrecked their vehicles, Defendant State Farm's practice and policy is to use inferior, substandard imitation crash parts (whenever possible and practicable) in the repair of Plaintiffs' vehicles.

8. Plaintiffs bring this class action to secure redress for Defendant State Farm's uniform and common practice of using inferior, imitation parts. At all times material hereto, Defendant State Farm was obligated to all its policy holders to make repairs pursuant to the same or common general terms set forth in Plaintiffs' State Farm Policy, (which includes the Endorsement Booklet) which is attached as Exhibit 1. Specifically, Defendant State Farm was obligated to undertake repairs on damaged vehicles using only parts of like kind and quality sufficient to restore the vehicles to their pre-loss condition. As a practical matter, this obligation could be met only by requiring the exclusive use in repairs of factory-authorized or OEM parts. Defendant State Farm's common practice of using inferior, imitation parts in repairs constitutes a breach of its obligation to all insureds who either received such parts in repairs or were obligated to pay the difference in price between imitation parts and the OEM parts actually installed. Exhibit 8 is a collective exhibit of affidavits from experts attesting, *inter alia*, that imitation parts that Defendant State Farm authorizes do not restore vehicles to their pre-loss condition. (Affidavits of Paul Tatman, Peter W. Bartlett, and Alan E. Hildebrand).

9. Plaintiffs' insured vehicles were involved in accidents causing damage to Plaintiffs' vehicles. Plaintiffs' damaged vehicles were presented to Defendant State Farm for repair. Defendant State Farm inspected Plaintiffs' vehicles and prepared estimates of repair costs. A copy of certain of these estimates is attached as Exhibit 3.

10. Upon presenting Defendant State Farm's estimate of repair costs to Plaintiffs, Defendant State Farm failed to disclose to Plaintiffs that the estimate was prepared based on the use of inferior imitation crash parts supplied by a source other than the manufacturer of the vehicle.

11. Defendant State Farm requires the use of inferior copies of vehicle crash parts, which are not authorized or sanctioned by the vehicle manufacturer, commonly referred to as "imitation crash parts," "after market crash parts," and/or "non-original equipment manufacturer's parts/non-OEM crash parts," hereinafter referred to as imitation parts. Since many of these imitation parts are manufactured in Taiwan, in the trade they are commonly referred to as "Taiwan tin," which reflects their inferior quality and craftsmanship. These inferior imitation parts are not authorized for use by vehicle manufacturers, and their incorpo-

ration into an insured vehicle will not restore the vehicle to its pre-loss condition.

12. The imitation parts are inferior in quality to the factory-authorized parts made by or for the original equipment manufacturer, in that the imitation parts have, among other defects:

a. substandard fit and appearance;

b. substandard finish;

c. substandard structural integrity and mechanical operation;

d. substandard corrosion resistance; and

e. substandard dent resistance.

13. These defects make the imitation parts inferior in quality to the parts made by or for the original equipment manufacturer, and the imitation parts are not of "like kind and quality" as the parts originally installed in the vehicle nor will use of the imitation parts restore the insured vehicle to its pre-loss condition.

14. Use of the imitation parts does the following to Plaintiffs and members of the class: (i) diminishes the vehicle's value, (ii) jeopardizes the effectiveness of the manufacturer's vehicle warranty, (iii) impairs the vehicle's structural integrity and impacts passenger safety, (iv) may detrimentally affect the vehicle's performance, (v) reduces the vehicle's resale value, and (vi) does not restore the vehicle to its pre-loss condition.

15. Defendant State Farm refused to authorize the repair of Plaintiffs' vehicles with factory-authorized parts made by or for the original equipment manufacturer. Defendant State Farm directed certain of the Plaintiffs to either (a) accept repairs to Plaintiffs' vehicles utilizing inferior imitation parts, or (b) pay the difference between the cost of the inferior imitation parts and the cost of the factory-authorized parts made by or for the original equipment manufacturer. In a common variation on this theme, the body shop repairing another plaintiff's vehicle installed OEM parts, even though State Farm only authorized and paid for inferior imitation parts, because the body shop technicians knew that imitation parts were categorically inferior and would not restore the vehicle back to its pre-loss condition. In this and numerous similar instances, the body shop absorbed the cost difference between the non-OEM parts for which State Farm paid and the OEM parts that were actually installed. Copies of certain Plaintiffs' invoices reflecting the cost of repair with the nonfactory authorized or non-OEM parts are attached. Plaintiffs' affidavits are attached.

16. Defendant State Farm entered into a common course of conduct using or paying the cost of inferior imitation parts to satisfy its repair obligations wherever such parts were available, thereby reducing its coverage obligations under its policies, all at the expense and loss to policy holders, but Defendant State Farm did not disclose these practices to its policy holders.

17. Defendant State Farm did not disclose to Plaintiffs prior to their purchase of the State Farm Policy, that Defendant State Farm would use and pay for only unauthorized inferior imitation parts (whenever possible and practicable) rather than factory-authorized parts made by or for the original equipment manufacturer, and that use of unauthorized imitation parts would not restore Plaintiffs' vehicles to their pre-loss condition.

18. Defendant State Farm was aware of its obligation to repair vehicles using "like kind and quality" parts and its obligation to restore the vehicles to their pre-loss condition. At all times material hereto, Defendant State Farm knew or should have known that the unauthorized imitation parts were not of "like kind and quality" as parts originally installed in Plaintiffs' vehicles, and the use of the inferior imitation parts would not restore the vehicles to their pre-loss condition or their pre-loss value.

19. At all times material hereto, Defendant State Farm avoided its obligations under these insurance policies, which policies used common language by only authorizing repairs by using inferior imitation parts.

20. Defendant State Farm has refused to pay or not paid to Plaintiffs or Class Members an amount equal to the difference in value of Plaintiffs' vehicles before the accident and their value after the accident, once repaired, restored, and returned to Plaintiffs. Plaintiffs are aware of other class actions suits filed against Defendant State Farm in concerning the same general practice at issue here in the states of Arkansas and Tennessee on behalf of citizens of those states, and certain suits elsewhere. Copies of certain of those complaints are attached hereto as Collective Exhibit 6.

21. Plaintiffs bring this action on behalf of themselves, and all others similarly situated, pursuant to 735 ILCS 5/2 -801, as representatives of the following class:

> All persons in the United States, except those residing in Arkansas and Tennessee, who (1) were insured by a vehicle casualty insurance policy issued by Defendant State Farm and (2) made a claim for vehicle repairs pursuant to their policy and had imitation that is, non factory-authorized and/or non-OEM parts installed in their vehicles or

else received monetary compensation determined in relation to the cost of imitation parts.

Excluded from the class are employees of Defendant State Farm, its officers, its directors, its subsidiaries or its affiliates.

In addition, the following persons are excluded from the class: (1) persons who resided in Illinois and whose policies were issued/executed prior to April 16, 1994, and (2) persons who resided in California and whose policies were issued/executed prior to September 26, 1996.

22. The requirements of 735 ILCS 5/2-801, *et seq.*, as explicated in applicable Illinois case law, have been met. The class is so numerous that joinder of all members is impracticable. 735 ILCS 5/2-801(1). Plaintiffs do not know the exact size of the class, since such information is in the exclusive control of Defendant State Farm. However, the exact number may be determined by appropriate discovery. Published reports state that State Farm has over 22 million auto policy holders nationwide, insures one out of every four motorists nationwide, and insures one out of every three motorists in Illinois.

23. There are questions of fact and law common to the class, which common questions predominate over any questions affecting only individual members. Those common questions include:

a. whether imitation parts of the kind utilized by Defendant State Farm are of a "like kind and quality" as the original equipment parts made by or for the original equipment manufacturer;

b. whether the use of imitation parts in the repair of Class Members' vehicles restores the vehicles to their pre-loss condition;

c. whether the use of imitation parts in the repair of Class Members' vehicles restores the vehicles to their pre-loss value; and

d. whether Defendant State Farm breached its duties and obligations owed to class members or breached the standard form provisions of its contracts (policies) with class members by its common practice of repairing class members' vehicles with imitation parts and/or paying class members or repair shops the cost of imitation, rather than original equipment, parts.

24. As per 735 ILCS 5/2-801(3), Plaintiffs can and will fairly and adequately represent and protect the interests of the class and have no interests that conflict with or are antagonistic to the interests of the class. Plaintiffs have retained attorneys who are among the most experienced

and competent in the United States in class action litigation. No conflict exists between Plaintiffs and class members because:

a. all of the questions of law and fact regarding the liability of Defendant State Farm are common to the class and predominate over any individual issues that may exist, such that by prevailing on their own claims, Plaintiffs necessarily will establish Defendant State Farm's liability to all class members;

b. without the representation provided by Plaintiffs, virtually no class member would receive legal redress or representation for his/her damages; and

c. Plaintiffs and their counsel have the necessary financial resources to adequately and vigorously litigate this class action, and Plaintiffs and counsel are aware of their fiduciary responsibilities to the class members and are determined to diligently discharge those duties by vigorously seeking the maximum possible recovery for the class.

25. All class members have the same legal rights to, and interests in, the fair treatment by State Farm, the proper interpretation and implementation of the Policy, and the restoration of their vehicles to their pre-loss condition when they are damaged. Defendant State Farm engaged in a uniform or common practice regarding repairs to its insured vehicles. When Plaintiffs' or a Class Member's car needed repairs it paid for imitation parts, as set forth herein, and not "like kind and quality" as set forth in its vehicle casualty insurance policies. Plaintiffs, thus, by proving their own claims presumptively prove the claims of the class.

26. The class action is an appropriate method for the fair and efficient adjudication of the controversy given the following:

a. Common questions of law and/or fact predominate over any individual questions that may arise, such that there would be enormous economies to the courts and the parties in litigating the common issues on a classwide instead of a repetitive individual basis, 735 ILCS 5/2-801(2);

b. Class members' individual damage claims are too small to make individual litigation an economically viable alternative;

c. Class treatment is required for optimal deterrence and compensation and for limiting the court-awarded reasonable legal expenses incurred by class members;

d. Despite the relatively small size of individual class members' claims, their aggregate volume, coupled with the economies of scale inherent in litigating similar claims on a common basis, will enable this case to be litigated as a class action on a cost-effective basis, especially when compared with repetitive individual litigation; and

e. No unusual difficulties are likely to be encountered in the management of this class action in that all questions of law or fact to be litigated at the liability stage are common to the class.

27. Class certification is fair and efficient as well because prosecution of separate actions would create a risk of adjudications with respect to individual members of the class, which as a practical matter, may be dispositive of the interests of other members not parties to the adjudication or substantially impair or impede their ability to protect their interests.

28. Class certification is appropriate under Illinois law because Defendant State Farm has acted on grounds generally applicable to the class.

Count 1
Breach of Contract

29. Defendant State Farm's common practice regarding the use of inferior imitation parts to its insureds, Plaintiffs and Class Members, constitutes a breach of contract. The uniform insurance policy is a contract. Plaintiffs and Class Members entered these contracts with Defendant State Farm and undertook obligations, paying premiums; the use of inferior imitation parts breaches that contract to Plaintiffs and Class Members.

30. Plaintiffs and Class Members were injured or damaged as a result. The courts in Illinois and the other states enforce contracts and provide remedies for breach.

31. Therefore, Plaintiffs and Class Members are entitled to lawful remedies attendant with the breach of contract by Defendant State Farm.

Count 2
Illinois Consumer Fraud and Deceptive Business Practices Act

32. Paragraphs 1-31 are re-alleged and restated, as if fully set forth herein.

33. This Count is brought pursuant to the Illinois Consumer Fraud and Deceptive Business Practices Act, 815 ILCS 505/1 *et seq*.

34. At all times material hereto, Plaintiffs, the class, and State Farm were persons within the meaning of 815 ILCS 505/1(c).

35. At all times material hereto, Plaintiffs and the class were consumers within the meaning of 815 ILCS 505/1(e).

36. At all times material hereto, State Farm conducted trade and commerce within the meaning of 815 ILCS 505/1(f).

37. Section 2 of the Illinois Consumer Fraud and Deceptive Business Practices Act, 815 ILCS 505/2, provides:

> [U]nfair or deceptive acts or practices, including but not limited to the use or employment of any deception, fraud, false pretense, false promise, misrepresentation, or the concealment, suppression, or omission of any material fact . . . in the conduct of any trade or commerce are hereby declared unlawful . . ..

38. Defendant engaged in unfair or deceptive acts or practices in the conduct of trade or commerce within the meaning of 815 ILCS 505/2. Among the unlawful practices that Defendant engaged in was the practice of installing non-OEM crash parts in its insureds' vehicles that were inferior, substandard parts, when State Farm had promised and was obligated to undertake repairs on damaged vehicles using only parts of like kind and quality, so as to restore the vehicles to their pre-loss condition.

39. By way of false or deceptive pretenses, acts, or practices, defendant did not disclose to Plaintiffs that they were: a) using inferior, imitation parts that diminished the value of their vehicles; and/or b) paying the cost of cheaper imitation parts when available and refusing to pay for OEM parts, thereby causing class members and/or their repair shops to absorb the cost difference.

40. By using these unfair or deceptive acts or practices, State Farm reduced its coverage obligations under Plaintiffs' and class members' policies, to the continuing detriment of Plaintiffs and the class.

41. Defendant engaged in the unfair or deceptive practices described herein for the purpose of inducing reliance and with the intent of to deceive or mislead Plaintiffs and class members.

42. Defendant's actions were wilful and wanton, knowing, or at least reckless, and constitute violations of the Act.

43. As a result of these acts and practices, Plaintiffs and the class suffered damages or are threatened with damage when their vehicles are repaired using inferior, imitation parts.

Count 3
Injunctive/Equitable Relief

44. Paragraphs 1-43 are re-alleged and restated, as if fully set forth herein.

45. State Farm's practice and policy, whenever possible under the circumstances, is to authorize or use inferior, imitation (non-OEM) parts to repair Plaintiffs' and the class' vehicles.

46. Each time that their vehicles may be or actually are wrecked and inferior imitation parts are available, because of State Farm's policy and practice, Plaintiffs and class members' vehicles will not be restored to their pre-loss condition at State Farm's cost.

47. As such, State Farm consistently and repeatedly violated its contracts (insurance policies).

48. Because of this policy and practice, Plaintiffs and class members will not receive the benefit of the common or similar terms of contracts entered with State Farm. Plaintiffs and class members are subject to defendant's policy and practice with each contract that they enter with State Farm.

49. State Farm does not meaningfully or effectively disclose the policy of using inferior imitation parts.

50. Unless a declaration of rights and a permanent injunction are issued requiring State Farm to comply with these provisions of these contracts with Plaintiffs and class members' contracts, class members will not receive the benefit of the bargain, will have no effective means to learn about the practice and policy of defendant not to honor the terms of its policies (set forth herein), State Farm will continue not to restore Plaintiffs' and class members' vehicles to their pre-loss condition, and will otherwise continue to avoid its contractual obligations.

Relief Requested

1. An order confirming that this conditionally certified class action is properly maintainable as a class action, and appointing Plaintiffs and their undersigned counsel to represent the class;

2. An award of compensatory damages and all monetary relief authorized by law or referenced in the Complaint, including punitive, exemplary, or special damages;

3. An Order declaring the rights of the class and the obligations of State Farm under the standard contractual provisions at issue in this action;

4. An Order enjoining State Farm from using inferior, imitation non-OEM parts, from refusing to pay for original equipment parts, and from engaging in unfair or deceptive acts or practices set forth in or related to the policy and practice in the amended complaint;

5. An Order requiring State Farm to restore Plaintiffs' and class members' vehicles to their pre-loss condition, to meaningfully and effectively disclose its past policy and practice of using inferior, imitation parts and to fully remedy these past acts or practices, and to cease and desist from making any false, deceptive, or misleading representations about its practices in authorizing or repair and restoration to Plaintiffs and class members;

6. An award of prejudgment and post judgment interest;

7. An award providing for payment of costs of suit, including payment of experts' fees and expenses;

8. An award of reasonable attorneys' fees; and

9. Such other and further relief as this Court may deem proper and just.

Respectfully submitted,

____
G. PATRICK MURPHY, #1994484

____
DON BARRETT

OF COUNSEL:

G. PATRICK MURPHY
Attorney at Law
104 West Calvert
Post Office Box 907
Marion, IL 62959
Telephone No. (618) 993-8420

DON BARRETT
BRIAN HERRINGTON
BARRETT LAW OFFICES
404 Court Square North
Post Office Box 987
Lexington, Mississippi 39095
Telephone No. (601) 834-2376
Telephone No. (601) 834-2409

THOMAS P. THRASH
Rose Law Firm
120 East Fourth Street
Little Rock, Arkansas
Telephone No. (501) 375-9131
Telecopier No. (501) 375-1309

ELIZABETH J. CABRASER
MORRIS A. RATNER
Lieff, Cabraser, Heimann & Bernstein, LLP
Embarcadero Center West
275 Battery Street, 30th Floor
San Francisco, California 94111-3339
Telephone: (415) 956-1000
Telecopier: (415) 956-1008

MICHAEL B. HYMAN
Much Shelist Freed Denenberg Ament
Bell & Rubenstein
200 N. La Salle Street, Suite 2100
Chicago, Illinois 60601-1095
Telephone: (312) 346-3100
Telecopier: (312) 621-1484

PATRICK W. PENDLEY
Attorney at Law
58005 Meriam Street
Plaquemine, Louisiana 70764
Telephone No. (504) 687-6396

GORDON BALL
750 Nations Bank Center
550 West Main Avenue, Suite 750
Knoxville, Tennessee 37902
Telephone No. (423) 525-7028

STEVEN L. MARTINO
Jackson, Taylor & Martino, P.C.
Southtrust Bank Building, Suite 1600
61 St. Joseph Street
Post Office Box 894
Mobile, Alabama 36602
Telephone No. (334) 433-3131

APPENDIX 18: PHARMACEUTICAL CLASS ACTION COMPLAINT

Karen A. Barth, Esq. (Bar No. 180234)
BAUM, HEDLUND, ARISTEI, GUILFORD & SCHIAVO
12100 Wilshire Blvd., Suite 950
Los Angeles, CA 90025
Phone: (310) 207-3233

Donald J. Farber, Esq. (Bar No. 168837)
LAW OFFICES OF DONALD J. FARBER
1907 Las Gallinas
San Rafael, CA 94903

Attorneys for Plaintiffs

SUPERIOR COURT OF THE STATE OF CALIFORNIA IN AND FOR THE COUNTY OF LOS ANGELES

KATHERINE KEITH; LESLI HAMILTON; MARILYN S. ATWOOD; JONNA NIELSEN; ADRIENNE L. BRANSKY; JOHN ALLEN; ANTHONY S. AMES; SUSAN K. AYERS; SANDRA F. CLARK; LUCYANN COSENTINO; DANIEL C. DENNISON; PAUL DOMB; JOSEPHINE GOGUEN-TREMBLAY; MARY FRANCES HALPIN; JEFF HERMSEN; DIANE HILL; CATHERINE HURLOCK-DICK; DAN KABIC; JANET KARCHER; KEVIN M. MURPHY, as Guardian Ad Litem for KELLY MURPHY, a Minor; KELLY J. OWEN; JENNIFER PARKER; KEVIN RIDER; ALLEN CHRISTOPHER SAENZ; SHANNON SCHOEFFEL; FRANCES L. SMITH; TRISHA SPINELLI; MARIANNE STERLING; FRANK W. STREICHER; LAURA J. STUCKEY; KATRINA TURNER; BENARD WAGNER; KIMBERLY WINGER; SUE KENNAN WORSTELL; LAURA S. ZIMMERMAN; on behalf of themselves and all other persons similarly situated,

Plaintiffs,

vs.

GLAXOSMITHKLINE, INC., a North Carolina Corporation; and DOES 1-100, Defendants.

Case No.:

CLASS ACTION COMPLAINT FOR:

1. FRAUD AND DECEIT;

2. NEGLIGENCE;

3. STRICT LIABILITY;

4. BREACH OF EXPRESS WARRANTY;

5. BREACH OF IMPLIED WARRANTY

DEMAND FOR JURY TRIAL

Plaintiffs, KATHERINE KEITH; LESLI HAMILTON; MARILYN S. ATWOOD; JONNA NIELSEN; ADRIENNE L. BRANSKY; JOHN ALLEN; ANTHONY S. AMES; SUSAN K. AYERS; SANDRA F. CLARK; LUCYANN COSENTINO; DANIEL C. DENNISON; PAUL DOMB; JOSEPHINE GOGUEN-TREMBLAY; MARY FRANCES HALPIN; JEFF HERMSEN; DIANE HILL; CATHERINE HURLOCK-DICK; DAN KABIC; JANET KARCHER; KEVIN M. MURPHY, as Guardian Ad Litem for KELLY MURPHY, a Minor; KELLY J. OWEN; JENNIFER PARKER; KEVIN RIDER; ALLEN CHRISTOPHER SAENZ; SHANNON SCHOEFFEL; FRANCES L. SMITH; TRISHA SPINELLI; MARIANNE STERLING; FRANK W. STREICHER; LAURA J. STUCKEY; KATRINA TURNER; BENARD WAGNER; KIMBERLY WINGER; SUE KENNAN WORSTELL; LAURA S. ZIMMERMAN (hereinafter "Plaintiffs"), by their attorneys, bring this action on behalf of themselves and all other persons similarly situated, demanding a trial by jury and on information and belief, except as to those allegations which pertain to

Plaintiffs, which allegations are based upon Plaintiffs' personal knowledge, and allege as follows:

I. JURISDICTION AND VENUE

1. Jurisdiction over this proceeding in California State court is based on Defendant's activities in the State of California, and in this County, and misconduct alleged herein which was intentionally directed at residents of the State of California. Accordingly, this Court has jurisdiction of this action under Article VI, section 10 of the California Constitution and section 410.10 of the Code of Civil Procedure.[1]

2. Pursuant to Code of Civil Procedure section 395, venue is proper in this judicial district, as this action concerns acts occurring within this County.

3. Furthermore, Plaintiff alleges on information and belief that Defendant GLAXOSMITHKLINE CORPORATION has purposefully availed itself of the benefits and protections of the State of California and/or have had sufficient contact with this County such that maintenance of the action in this locale would be consistent with traditional notions of fair play and substantial justice.

II. NATURE OF THE CASE

4. This is a class action on behalf of all individuals in the United States who were prescribed and took the drug Paxil (generically known as **paroxetine**) which is, and at all times relevant herein was, manufactured, marketed and distributed by Defendant GLAXOSMITHKLINE CORPORATION, formerly known as SmithKline Beecham, and who experienced dependency/withdrawal syndrome. Plaintiff and members of the plaintiff class seek damages, as well as injunctive and other relief.

5. Thousands of Paxil users suffer dependency/withdrawal syndrome. Currently, on one website alone there are 1,359 electronic signatures of persons complaining to GLAXOSMITHKLINE CORPORATION about withdrawal reactions they have suffered from Paxil. Given that the signatures provide the full name of each person, many of whom provided their E-mail addresses and lengthy commentary, this is a reliable example of the numerosity of the persons suffering from Paxil withdrawal. Over the past two (2) years, plaintiffs' attorneys have been individually contacted by approximately 500 Paxil withdrawal victims. The pain and suffering experienced by each of these individuals is the direct result of GLAXOSMITHKLINE CORPORATION's failure to warn users of Paxil's addictive nature, the drug's inducement of physical or

1 All statutory references herein are to California law.

psychologic dependency, and its infliction of dependency/withdrawal syndrome when the patient's Paxil dosage is reduced or terminated.

6. Since its introduction into the U.S. market on December 29, 1992, Paxil has been an antidepressant medication of the selective serotonin reuptake inhibitor ("SSRI") class (which class includes Zoloft and Prozac).

7. Paxil has caused some people who take it to experience serious and unexpected withdrawal reactions. These reactions are "unexpected" to the victims and even their physicians because the manufacturer has deliberately failed to properly warn of this. Both physician and patient unwittingly use Paxil without knowing the drug's addictive traits. Plaintiffs were never informed before starting Paxil that it was addictive, induced dependency, or caused withdrawal reactions when dosage was reduced or terminated.

8. Paxil creates both physical and psychological dependency and, because GLAXOSMITHKLINE CORPORATION has suppressed the information about the severe withdrawal reactions caused by its drug, many patients and their physicians are fooled into thinking that the withdrawal reactions the patients are experiencing are caused by another condition (such as relapse), thus prompting further incorrect and unnecessary medical treatment, including increased dosages of Paxil. Some of the class members remain on Paxil today because they have become dependant and feel they cannot get off the drug.

9. GLAXOSMITHKLINE CORPORATION has known for years the distinct characteristics of Paxil which make it prone to cause withdrawal reactions and dependency/withdrawal syndrome after its use is discontinued. While the medical community has acknowledged the potential for all SSRIs to cause withdrawal reactions, Paxil is, by far, the worst. According to World Health Organization ("WHO") data obtained by the plaintiff class members, Paxil has the highest incidence rate of withdrawal adverse experiences of any antidepressant drug in the world.

10. Plaintiffs in their individual and representative capacities for the proposed Class, respectfully ask the Court to: (a) require Defendant GLAXOSMITHKLINE CORPORATION to provide class notice; (b) award damages, including punitive damages; and (c) award all costs, including attorneys* fees.

III. THE PARTIES

11. Plaintiff Katherine Keith resides in North Hollywood, California. Ms. Keith was originally prescribed Paxil in September, 1999, by her OB GYN. In the year 2000, Ms. Keith attempted to discontinue use of the drug with her doctor's approval. Upon initial termination of dosage

and continuing thereafter until February 2001, she experienced severe withdrawal reactions including, but not limited to, restlessness and pain which severely impaired her ability to perform activities of daily living. She did not know she was experiencing Paxil withdrawal.

12. Plaintiff, Lesli Hamilton resides in Hollywood, California. She is a website designer who was prescribed Paxil by her doctor for "panic attacks." Soon after taking the drug, Ms. Hamilton's ability to eat and sleep were severely impaired, and she was "nerved out all the time." When Ms. Hamilton decided to stop taking the drug, her physician instructed her to lower her dose to 10mg. After about a month and shortly after her last pill was consumed, she experienced frightening physical sensations, including the sensation of being shocked with electrical charges, uncontrollable shaking and unwanted intrusive thoughts. She did not know this was caused by Paxil. As of February 25, 2001, she was taking a daily dosage of 3 mg daily, and attempting to wean off completely.

13. Plaintiff Marilyn Atwood lives in San Diego, California. She first took Paxil in July, 2000, which was prescribed by her internist and allergist. When Ms. Atwood tried to discontinue use of Paxil, she experienced unwanted sensations of sharp, intermittent stabbing pain in her head, severe headaches, dizziness, nausea, weakness in her body and legs, shakiness, and severely impaired ability to perform mental functions. As time passed, the reactions got worse and she became bedridden. Ms. Atwood thought she was losing her mind and that she had a brain tumor. She was hospitalized and had a CT scan. It was not until later that she discovered her reactions were caused by Paxil withdrawal. As of April 30, 2001, Ms. Atwood continues to suffer the injurious effects of Paxil withdrawal.

14. Plaintiff Jonna Nielsen resides in El Cajon, California. She was prescribed Paxil in June, 2000. Because she quickly gained 25 pounds on the drug, she was prescribed to discontinue the use of Paxil. She was prescribed a tapering regime which was extremely painful and suffered painful reactions. At the time, she did not know these reactions were due to Paxil. From October, 2000 to January 22, 2001, Ms. Nielsen kept taking Paxil to combat her withdrawal reactions. As of February 27, 2001, Ms. Nielsen was still suffering shocks from Paxil withdrawal.

15. Plaintiff Jeff Hermsen lives in San Diego, California. He is a Texas Tech University graduate, an ex Marine, and a veteran of Desert Storm. In the Spring of 1995, Jeff was first prescribed Paxil. Initially his physician told him that Paxil's side effects were mild, and specifically that there were no problems stopping the drug if it was done gradually over a few weeks. After 5 years on the drug, while discontinuing use of Paxil, he suffered debilitating physical and psychological reactions,

and became at times disabled. Unbeknownst to him, the reactions were Paxil withdrawal. On August 25, 2000, still suffering as he tried to reduce his Paxil usage, he saw the television program "20/20" regarding Paxil withdrawal. It was at that time he became determined to wean himself off of Paxil once and for all. Mr. Hermsen continued to suffer Paxil withdrawal reactions until the end of the year 2000.

16. The remaining named plaintiffs come from all walks of life and reside throughout the United States. Each has experienced similar withdrawal reactions and dependency/withdrawal syndrome. In fact, the withdrawal reactions are nearly universal in phenomenology and can summed up as one or more of the following complaints:

> jolting electric "zaps," dizziness, light headedness, vertigo, incoordination, gait disturbances, sweating, extreme nausea, vomiting, high fever, abdominal discomfort, flu symptoms, anorexia, diarrhea, agitation, tremulousness, irritability, aggression, sleep disturbance, nightmares, tremor, confusion, memory and concentration difficulties, lethargy, malaise, weakness, fatigue, paraesthesias, ataxia, and/or myalgia.

17. None of the named plaintiffs were ever informed before starting Paxil that it was addictive, induced dependency, or caused withdrawal reactions when dosage was reduced or terminated, nor what the reactions were.

18. Plaintiffs are informed and believe and based thereon allege that Defendant GLAXOSMITHKLINE CORPORATION ("GSK") is a North Carolina corporation that is, and at all relevant times was, doing business throughout the United States, California and in this County. GSK manufactures, markets and distributes Paxil.

19. The true names and capacities, whether individual, corporate, associate, or otherwise, of the defendants named herein under the fictitious names of Does 1 through 100, inclusive, are unknown to Plaintiffs, who, therefore, sue said defendants by such fictitious names. Plaintiffs will ask leave of Court to amend this complaint and insert the true names and capacities of said defendants when the same have been ascertained. Plaintiffs allege on information and belief that each of the defendants designated herein as a "Doe" is legally responsible in some manner for the events and happenings herein alleged, and that plaintiffs', the class', and members of the general public's damages as alleged herein were proximately caused by such defendants. Unless otherwise specified, references herein to "defendants" refer to the entities GLAXOSMITHKLINE CORPORATION, and Does 1 through 100, inclusive.

IV. CLASS ACTION ALLEGATIONS

20. Plaintiffs bring this action on behalf of themselves and all others similarly situated, as members of the proposed Class, defined as follows:

> "All former or present Paxil patients who, after December 29, 1992, suffered or continue to suffer from withdrawal reactions following reduction or termination of their Paxil dosage."

As used herein, "withdrawal reactions" are medically defined and include physical and psychological symptoms.

21. Specifically excluded from the proposed class are defendants, their officers, directors, agents, trustees, parents, children, corporations, trusts, representatives, employees, principals, servants, partners, joint venturers, or entities controlled by defendants, and their heirs, successors, assigns, or other persons or entities related to or affiliated with defendants and/or their officers and/or directors, or any of them; the Judge assigned to this action, any member of the Judge's immediate family, and all governmental entities.

22. This action is brought and may properly be maintained as a class action pursuant to California Code of Civil Procedure section 382. The proposed class satisfies the ascertainability, numerosity and community of interest requirements of section 382, and all other applicable statutory and jurisprudential criteria for class certification.

23. The members of the proposed Class number in at least the thousands. As a result, the Class is so numerous that joinder in a single action is impracticable. However, each Class member should be readily identifiable from information and records available to defendants. The disposition of these claims in a class action will provide substantial benefits to the Class, the public, and the Court.

24. Separate actions by individual members of the class would create adjudications that would be identical with each other, thus adding to judicial backlog in many state and federal courts. Moreover, Paxil "labeling" is identical in each jurisdiction within the U.S. because it was approved by the Food & Drug Administration. Total uniformity in this respect is consistent with class action principles. There is one labeling scheme for a prescription drug, not fifty, and thus singular legal focus is achieved. Denial of class action would effectively compel some plaintiffs with modest means to relinquish their rights. Individual Paxil "withdrawal" cases with merit have not been taken by the plaintiffs' bar because of the economic calculus. Drug product liability cases are too complicated and the resources of the pharmaceutical companies too substantial for a plaintiffs' law firm to take a random plaintiff's case wherein damages are limited to pain and suffering. Thus denial of class action in this instance would substantially impair the ability of

the other Paxil withdrawal sufferers to obtain attorneys and protect their interests.

25. Individual members of the Class do not have a significant interest in individually controlling the prosecution of separate actions, and individualized litigation would also present the potential for varying, inconsistent, or contradictory judgments and would magnify the delay and expense to all parties and to the court system resulting from multiple trials of the same factual issues. Plaintiffs know of no difficulty to be encountered in the management of this action that would preclude its maintenance as a class action. Relief concerning Plaintiffs' rights under the laws herein alleged and with respect to the Class would be proper.

26. There is a well-defined community of interest and common questions of law and fact which predominate over any questions affecting only individual members of the Class. These common legal and factual questions do not vary from one class member to another, and may be determined without reference to the individual circumstances of any Class member. These include, but are not limited to, the following:

a. Whether Paxil causes withdrawal reactions;

b. Whether Plaintiffs took Paxil and experienced withdrawal reactions;

c. Whether defendants properly and adequately warned Plaintiffs and class members that Paxil can cause withdrawal reactions;

d. Whether defendants properly and adequately warned physicians in the United States that Paxil can cause withdrawal reactions;

e. Whether defendants over-promoted its drug Paxil to such an extent that any warnings it may have given regarding withdrawal reactions were nullified;

f. Whether defendants, due to their direct to consumer advertising and marketing, owed a duty to warn consumers directly of the withdrawal reactions caused by Paxil.

g. Whether defendants are liable for fraud and misrepresentation.

h. Whether defendants are liable for negligence.

i. Whether defendants are liable for breach of express warranty.

j. Whether defendants are liable for breach of implied warranty.

k. Whether defendants' wrongful conduct resulted in damages to Plaintiffs and the Class.

l. Whether punitive damages should be imposed against defendants and if so, the amount of such damages.

27. The claims of Plaintiffs are typical of the class. The named Plaintiffs are typical of Paxil withdrawal victims. Each of the Plaintiffs and class members was uninformed of the hazards in reducing or terminating their Paxil dosage. Each of them did, in fact, reduce or terminate their daily Paxil intake. Within one or two days thereafter, severe withdrawal reactions appeared. As stated above, all Plaintiffs and class members suffered one or more of the following:

> jolting electric "zaps," dizziness, light headedness, vertigo, incoordination, gait disturbances, sweating, extreme nausea, vomiting, high fever, abdominal discomfort, flu symptoms, anorexia, diarrhea, agitation, tremulousness, irritability, aggression, sleep disturbance, nightmares, tremor, confusion, memory and concentration difficulties, lethargy, malaise, weakness, fatigue, paraesthesias, ataxia, and/or myalgia.

Each patient victim and class member had no idea what was occurring, other than knowing that he/she was very sick. Severe physical and psychological anguish developed and persisted. Typically, the patient went to see his/her physician, who, ignorant of Paxil's withdrawal inducing traits, started down an erroneous path to diagnose the problem. This included suggesting unnecessary tests and diagnoses, including "relapse," which in the physicians' mind warranted an increase of Paxil dosage—thus compounding the problem. The physician, in many instances, was the last person to acknowledge that Paxil withdrawal was in fact the culprit behind the patient's suffering. As a result, the patient's pain and suffering and resulting disabilities were prolonged, often lasting weeks, even months. Some plaintiff patients, after a lengthy regimen of gradually tapering down their Paxil dosage, were successful in completely weaning themselves off of the drug. Some plaintiff patients remain on Paxil today because they are "hooked" on the drug and feel they cannot get off of it. The only difference among Class members is the amount of damages sustained, which can be readily determined, and does not bar class certification.

28. Plaintiffs will fully and adequately protect the interests of the Class, and have retained class counsel who are experienced and qualified in prosecuting class actions and complex pharmaceutical litigation. Neither Plaintiffs, nor their attorneys, have interests which are contrary to, or conflicting with, those of the Class. Plaintiffs are informed and believe and based thereon allege that the number and identity of the members of the Class are determinable from records in the possession, custody and/or control of defendants and/or third parties, and that Class members may be easily and quickly notified of the pendency of this class action by mail or publication notice.

V. PLAINTIFFS' TRANSACTIONS WITH DEFENDANTS

29. Each of the named Plaintiffs was prescribed and took Paxil as recommended by Defendant to their treating physicians. Each of the named Plaintiffs suffered withdrawal reactions caused by Paxil. Each of the named Plaintiffs adequately represent the entire nationwide class of Paxil withdrawal Plaintiffs. They come from all regions, are of all ages, have suffered through the range of withdrawal reactions, and through such representation will fairly and adequately protect the interests of the class. Each of the named Plaintiffs continues to suffer Paxil withdrawal and/or suffered Paxil withdrawal on January 1, 2001.

VI. DEFENDANTS' COMMON COURSE OF MISCONDUCT

30. Paxil is a short "half life" drug which means it leaves the body at a relatively fast rate. GSK uses this feature to distinguish it from its competitors alleging that, as a result, it has a shorter duration of adverse events, decreased drug accumulation over time, better management of sexual dysfunction, and reduction of time to establish steady state drug regimen. The great disadvantage of a short half life substance, however, is that it is more addictive, has a greater tendency to induce physical and psychological dependency, and causes withdrawal reactions. While these characteristics of "half life" substances have been well known among Defendant and psychopharmacologists, such information is not generally known by general practice physicians or even psychiatrists.

31. The habit-forming nature of Paxil has not been fully divulged to physicians in the United States, hence neither physician nor patient has had sufficient information to weigh the benefits/risks associated with Paxil. Serious habit forming characteristics affect the patient, and he/she is unable to wean himself/herself off of the drug after therapeutic use is no longer needed. Physical and psychological dependency on Paxil is the result. When withdrawal problems arise, the patient often feels entrapped, in despair, and desolate.

32. From 1992 to the present, patients attempting to taper down or discontinue use of Paxil have suffered withdrawal reactions and dependency/withdrawal syndrome, as noted above. In addition to the physical reactions mentioned above, patients can also experience psychiatric reactions such as anxiety, agitation, lability of mood, nervousness, hypersexuality, crying spells, irritability and despair. The result of these combined reactions is that many patients continue to take Paxil because they are unable to endure the withdrawal reactions.

33. "Relapse" is not "withdrawal." Relapse occurs when a patient who has improved his/her depressive state, then reverts back to a more seriously depressed state.

Symptoms exhibited during relapse are frequently comparable to reactions exhibited during withdrawal. As indicated elsewhere in this complaint, it is alleged on information and belief that GSK, over the years, categorized numerous patients' withdrawal reactions as relapse symptoms. GSK did this in order to gain FDA approval for Paxil and avoid revealing the drug's withdrawal problems.

34. After representing to FDA that Paxil had been systematically tested for withdrawal and that the tests were successful, Paxil was approved for marketing in the United States. However, at that time and prior thereto, GSK knew of the withdrawal problems with Paxil (particularly from its clinical trials, including those held in Yugoslavia). Contrary to obtaining its marketing approval from the FDA based on its "systematic testing," GSK's label for Paxil stated:

> **DRUG ABUSE AND DEPENDENCE. Physical and Psychologic Dependence:**
>
> "Paxil *has not been systematically studied in animals or human for its potential for abuse, tolerance, or physical dependence*. While the clinical trials did not reveal any tendency for any drug seeking behavior, these observations were not *systematic* and it is not possible to predict on the basis of this limited experience the extent to which a . . . (central nervous system) . . . active drug will be misused, diverted and/or abused once marketed. Consequently, patients should be evaluated carefully for history of drug abuse, and such patients should be observed closely for signs of Paxil misuse or abuse (e.g., development of tolerance, incrementations *of dose, drug seeking behavior*).

35. The above prescribing information and labeling is false and misleading on its face.

36. Evidence of GSK's knowledge of the withdrawal reactions its drug was causing can also be found in a report to Dr. Martin Brecher of the FDA which disclosed subjective reporting gathered from patients by clinical investigators who told GSK management that Paxil was dangerously addictive. A group of 108 patients ending their participation in a trial told GSK that Paxil had caused them to suffer "withdrawal" reactions ("Group of 108 Complaining Patients' Study"). Out of the 1293 patients in that trial, the 108 complaining patients constituted 8.3% of the participants. GSK improperly reclassified these patients' withdrawal reactions as "relapse" symptoms.

37. Notwithstanding GSK's knowledge of the withdrawal reactions associated with Paxil from its pre-FDA approval clinical trials and its post-marketing seven and a half (7 ½) years of Paxil experience with the general patient population, GSK has done nothing about it. GSK

has been consciously indifferent to the problem in order to preserve its profits of nearly $2 billion a year, and to further increase its market share.

38. GSK's continuing advertising on print, radio, and television regarding Paxil's short "half life" induces both physicians and patients to believe that Paxil has no withdrawal reactions. In public promotion programs, GSK asserts that Paxil's short "half life" does not affect the therapeutic process and reduces side effects. As a result, more and more patients are being prescribed Paxil and are getting "hooked" on the drug. The list of patients addicted to Paxil grows daily.

39. For example, in a "question and answer" pamphlet published by GSK that is available at doctors' offices and disseminated to patients, GSK asks the question: "Is *Paxil* addictive?" The pamphlet then answers the question as follows:

> *Paxil* has been studied both in short- and long-term use and is not associated with dependence or addiction. The class of drugs called *benzodiazepines* (which are used to treat certain anxiety disorders) have been associated with physical dependence in some patients. *Paxil* does not belong to this class of drugs.

40. GSK has also known for years from clinical studies conducted by prominent scientists that Paxil causes withdrawal reactions, in addition to learning of the complaints of thousands of individuals who have used Paxil.

41. In 1993 Stoker and Eric reported paroxetine withdrawal at the American Psychiatric Association's annual meeting in San Francisco, May 22-27, 1993. The authors conducted 2 week tapering regimes for 186 patients in 6 to 12 week doubled blinded comparative studies. Paroxetine patients fared badly. Low dose and high dose groups were both studied. Paxil's low dose group actually fared worse than the high dose group, suffering 42% withdrawal rate, as opposed to 38% in the high dose group. Both occurred notwithstanding the fact that a tapering regime was initiated during reduction of dosage. An imipramine patient group was also studied. The imipramine group had a lower incidence of withdrawal than either paroxetine group. This report occurred 5 months after Paxil entered the U.S. market. Plaintiffs allege GSK did nothing in response to this information.

42. In 1993, D'Arcy reported that paroxetine was reported to cause withdrawal reactions more often than other SSRI's, and that paroxetine appeared to cause dystonia in the reported instance; (Int Pharm J 7:140).

43. In 1993, the Committee on Safety of Medicines ("CSM"), Great Britain's counterpart to the FDA, reported 78 cases of withdrawal after dis-

continuation of paroxetine, reporting that "such reactions have been reported more often with paroxetine than with other SSRI's." ("Current Problems in Pharmacovigilance" (1993; 19:1). GSK refused to react to this warning.

44. In 1994, Barr and colleagues reported 50% of paroxetine patients suffered withdrawal syndrome despite the fact that the suffering patients tapered dosage over a 7-10 day period; (Am J Psychiatry 151:2, February, 1994).

45. In 1994, Keuthen and colleagues reported Paxil withdrawal, indicating that paroxetine "has been reported to cause such reactions more often than other SSRI's." The percentage of Paxil patients with obsessive compulsive disorder ("OCD") adverse affects was 38.5%, and such reactions appeared notwithstanding a tapering down dosage. Patients affected reported dizziness, ranging from "mild to severe." (J Clin Psychopharmacol 1994; 14:206-7).

46. In 1995, Debattista & Schatzberg reported paroxetine withdrawal, reporting that a patient who had been on Paxil 4 months and discontinued suffered severe fatigue, nausea, dizziness, and malaise 2 days after discontinuing a small daily dosage of 10 mg; (Am J Psychiatry 1995;152(8):1235-1244.

47. In 1995, Block and colleagues reported very severe paroxetine withdrawal involving two previously healthy men, ages 36 and 48. They were given Paxil, not for mental disorders, but to treat stuttering. Both men, without a history of major psychiatric disorder, developed severe behavioral symptoms when paroxetine was withdrawn. After being treated for six (6) weeks on Paxil, both men were taken off the drug. One of the men, 2 days after stopping Paxil, developed hypomanic like symptoms, including hyperactivity, decreased need for sleep, and irritability that developed into agitation, aggressiveness, and volatility. After 2 weeks of fluctuating withdrawal reactions, he experienced ego-dystonic impulsive behavior such as shoplifting and suicidal impulses and gestures. These adverse withdrawal reactions lasted 2 ½ weeks. The second man tapered his Paxil use downward over a 12 day period. The first week of withdrawal was occasioned by an uncharacteristic feeling of confidence and optimism, talkativeness, and a subjective feeling of sharpened and quickened thought processes. During the second week, the patient developed physical symptoms of dizziness, blurred vision, nausea, lethargy, and insomnia. He became angry, irritable, and short tempered, with some highly atypical explosive vocal outbursts and tantrums. He then became preoccupied with homicidal thoughts and plans. These were initially directed towards acquaintances and later towards his own children. They became so intense and ego-dystonic that he contemplated suicide. These phys-

ical and behavioral symptoms lasted 9 days, then remitted spontaneously over the next 2-3 days. The four (4) medical professionals who reported these cases all stated "we believe that the serious behavioral symptoms seen in these cases were adverse effects of paroxetine withdrawal." They further stated "clinicians should be aware of a possible serious withdrawal syndrome with prominent psychiatric symptoms consequent to paroxetine discontinuation." (Lancet, Volume 346(8966), July 1, 1995.57) Despite the compelling evidence of this report, it is alleged on information and belief that GSK did absolutely nothing of substance in response. These two incidents reflected both serious and unexpected adverse drug experiences, and required GSK to fully investigate them and report within 15 days to the FDA. The report, likewise, should have spurred additional proposed labeling to be included with Paxil.

48. In 1995, Dominguez and colleagues reported 3 severe cases of adverse events after abrupt discontinuation of paroxetine. The authors outlined their "dechallenge" testing methods to verify causation, and thus claimed a "probable" association to paroxetine. (Pharmacotherapy 1995 Nov-Dec;15(6):778-80.) GSK refused to respond to this information.

49. In 1995, Frost and Lal reported paroxetine withdrawal notwithstanding that the patient tapered his dose over 3 weeks. Two (2) days after his final 10mg dose, the patient experienced electric-like waves that ran from his forehead to his chest and stopped in the abdomen. The attacks lasted 5 seconds and occurred 3 to 5 times every evening for 3 weeks. In addition, the patient experienced nausea, light headedness, insomnia, inner shakiness, and dizziness that forced him to hold on to the wall to walk, all lasting one week. The authors concluded "tapering of such drugs over many weeks may be required for some patients." (Am J Psychiatry 152:5, May 1995.) GSK refused to react to this report.

50. In 1995, Koopowitz and Berk reported additional paroxetine withdrawal problems in patients, and indicated that paroxetine "has been reported to cause such . . . (withdrawal). . . reactions more often than other SSRI's." (Hum Psychopharmacol, 1995, 10: 147-8.)

51. In 1995, Lazowick and Levin reported on potential withdrawal syndrome associated with SSRI discontinuation. The drugs reported upon were paroxetine, sertraline, and fluvoxamine. (Ann Pharmacother 1995 Dec;29(12):1284-85.) GSK did nothing in response.

52. In 1995, Oehrberg and colleagues reported that 34.5% of paroxetine patients reported adverse events on discontinuation, most commonly dizziness—compared to only 13.5% of placebo patients. (British Jour-

nal of Psychiatry 1995; 167: 374-379.) GSK did not respond to this report.

53. In 1995, R.E. Pyke reported on serious paroxetine withdrawal syndrome. The reactions were unlike prior symptoms of the patient and were incapacitating for the 2nd through 4th days of reactions. On the 11th day, the reactions improved, but dizziness and diarrhea recurred intermittently through the 23rd day. Dr. Pyke specifically mentioned the disparity between the reactions he observed and GSK's "package insert" in which "withdrawal syndrome" was listed as a "rare" occurrence. Dr. Pyke also reported that his patient's 3 week- long dilemma was greater than the "5-15 days" indicated by the manufacturer. (Am J Psychiatry 152:1, January, 1995.) GSK did nothing in response.

54. In 1995, S.D. Phillips reported a possible paroxetine withdrawal syndrome. The patient had been taking a daily 20mg Paxil dosage for 5 weeks, but suffered adverse effects. She then immediately switched to Zoloft. Three days later, she suffered withdrawal, consisting of headaches, nausea, vomiting, abdominal discomfort, and agitation. (Amer J Psychiat 152:645-646 (Apr) 1995.) GSK took no action on this report.

55. In 1995, Fava and Grandi reported withdrawal syndrome after discontinuation of paroxetine. It was noteworthy that withdrawal occurred notwithstanding the fact that the patient immediately shifted to desipramine after discontinuing paroxetine. (J Clin Psychopharmacol 1995 Oct;15(5):374-4.) GSK refused to respond to this article.

56. In 1996 Bhaumik & Wildgust reported on Paxil withdrawal, indicating that paroxetine "has been reported to cause such reactions more often than other SSRI's."

57. Dr. Arya reported withdrawal in a patient after discontinuation of paroxetine in Aust N Z J Psychiatry 1996 Oct;30(5):702.

58. In 1996, Coupland and colleagues reported that withdrawal occurred on SSRI reduction of dosage "despite slowly tapered withdrawal." The authors warned that SSRI withdrawal occurs more frequently with short-half-life SSRI's such as paroxetine and fluvoxamine than with Zoloft or Prozac. Paxil patients suffered tremendous withdrawal reactions in these studies. Of Paxil's 50 patients suffering withdrawal, 16% suffered dizziness, 12% suffered paresthesia, 12% suffered lethargy, 6% suffered nausea, 2% dysphoria, 4% anxiety, 4% vivid dreams, 4% insomnia, 16% movement related adverse symptoms, and 20% suffered more than one adverse event. (J Clin Psychopharmacol 1996 Oct;16(5):356-62.)

59. In 1996, Nuss and Kinkaid, studied serotonin discontinuation syndrome, and paroxetine patients in particular. The authors concluded

that "with the advent of the..(SSRI), there is now growing evidence to support a 'discontinuation syndrome' associated with withdrawal of therapy." (W V Med J 2000 Mar-Apr;96(2):405-7.) GSK failed to act on this report.

60. In 1996, Pacheco and colleagues reported five (5) cases of paroxetine withdrawal, all despite gradual tapering of the Paxil dosage. Three patients tapered for 29 days, two for 2 weeks. Two of the five were treated in urgent care due to the severity of the reactions. The authors indicated "what is striking from a clinical point of view is the fact that a conservative tapering regime was unable to prevent symptoms appearing. As a result of this experience we are now applying a dosage reduction of 5 mg per week in an attempt to avoid this withdrawal syndrome." GSK failed to offer any assistance or guidance in resolving this dilemma, much less proposing more detailed labeling instructions for Paxil.

61. In 1996, Price and colleagues reported on the British data base of adverse effects on withdrawal for SSRI medications. By far, paroxetine was the largest inducer of withdrawal. The most prevalent reactions cited were dizziness, paraesthesia, tremor, anxiety, nausea, and palpitation. The authors stated that while the overall safety profiles of the SSRI's were similar, "withdrawal reactions with paroxetine constitute a greater (5.1%) proportion of reports than with the other SSRI's (0.06% to 0.09%). (Br J Clin Pharmacol 1996 Dlec;42(6):757-63.) GSK failed to act on this report.

62. In 1996, Reeves and Pinkofsky reported that their patient's paroxetine withdrawal was so severe that she had to be taken to the emergency room. The authors reported that their patient's reactions were unlike those previously documented. The patient ran out of her paroxetine while on vacation, and 30 hours after her last dose, she experienced nausea, headache, lightheadedness, and hot and cold flashes. She experienced "electric shock like feelings through her back and limbs." The reactions appeared as the patient moved about, and increased markedly over the next 2 days. The physician conducted "dechallenge" and "rechallenge" test procedures, and concluded it was "certain" that paroxetine caused the reactions. (J Clin Psychopharmacol 1996 Oct;16(5):411-2.) Per their standard procedure, GSK did nothing on this information.

63. In February, 1996, Australia's "Adverse Drug Reactions Advisory Committee" ("ADRAC") published results of a study showing that Paxil had the highest rate of SSRI withdrawal adverse events in that country. Even though Zoloft outsells Paxil in Australia, the latter had more than three (3) times the number of adverse complaints as Zoloft. Complaints on Paxil exceeded Prozac by a rate of greater than 4 to 1.

64. In 1997, Dr. Haddad reported that the highest incidence of discontinuation reactions among the SSRI's was paroxetine. (J Clin Psychiatry 1997; 58Suppl7:17-1; discussion 220.) GSK refused to act on this report.

65. In 1997, Landry and Roy reported withdrawal hypomania associated with paroxetine. The acute reactions lasted 4 days and residual reactions lasted another 5 days. Depressive symptoms reappeared 1 week after complete resolutions of hypomanic symptoms. (J Clin Psychopharmacol 1997 Feb;17(1):60-1.) GSK did nothing in response.

66. In 1997, Lejoyeux and colleagues provided extensive review of the literature on antidepressant discontinuation, concluding that "they . . . (withdrawal symptoms) . . . are much more common with the shorter acting SSRI such as paroxetine, than with the longer acting agent fluoxetine. Because the symptoms of antidepressant discontinuation include changes in mood, affect, appetite, and sleep, they are sometimes mistaken for sign of a relapse into depression." (J Clin Psychiatry 1997;58Suppl7:11-5.) GSK did nothing in response to this article.

67. In 1997, Mackay and colleagues reported on British experience with SSRI's, reporting on a study done by the Drug Safety Research Unit, Bursledon Hall, Southhampton. A patient population of 13,741 was screened. It was concluded "*Withdrawal symptoms were significantly more frequent with paroxetine than the other three SSRI's." The* report indicated "agitation, anxiety, tremor, dizziness, loss of balance nausea, vomiting, paraesthesia, and restlessness are all associated with withdrawal." (Pharmacoepidemiology & Drug Safety, 1997; 6:No.4. 235-46.) In late 1997, GSK falsified the results of this study. In an internal document, GSK's corporate leadership fabricated the results of this British study and told GSK sales representatives in the United States that the British study showed that all of the SSRI's were the same as to withdrawal. This false message was sent to the sales representatives for the express purpose of conveying this misrepresentation to all physicians in the United States. On information and belief, Plaintiffs allege that this false message was, in fact, delivered to U.S. physicians from late 1997 to the present.

68. In 1997, Rosenbaum and colleagues reported on the clinical management of antidepressant discontinuation. They indicated that antidepressant agents with shorter half lives should be tapered gradually, and cited paroxetine in that category. Moreover the authors recognized the serious diagnostic problem: "symptoms of discontinuation may be mistaken for physical illness or relapse into depression . . . misdiagnosing the symptoms may lead to unnecessary, costly

tests and treatment." (Biol Psychiatry 1998 Jul 15;44(2):77-87.) GSK declined to take any action on this report.

69. In 1997, Stahl and seven (7) colleagues documented Paxil's leading withdrawal status in the world. The authors investigated and reported upon the World Health Organization ("WHO") database. From the year of introduction for each of the SSRI's, all case reports for Paxil, Prozac, and Zoloft were retrieved. Sales figures were also retrieved. Paxil's rate of withdrawal reactions were higher than Prozac and Zoloft for each of the 16 countries surveyed, and also for those countries for which a detailed analysis was conducted (U.S., U.K., and Australia). (Eur J Clin Pharmacol 1997;53(3-4):163-9.) GSK showed no sensitivity to this report, taking no action.

70. In 1997, Walker-Kinnear and colleagues reported paroxetine discontinuation syndrome in association with sertindole therapy. (Br J Psychiatry 1997 Apr;170:389.) Again, GSK took no action.

71. In 1997, Young and Currie of Newcastle reported on their survey indicating that a sizeable minority of physicians were aware of the existence of antidepressant withdrawal reactions. This included psychiatrists, 28% of whom expressed no awareness that antidepressant medications could induce discontinuation reactions. The conclusion of the authors was that "education about discontinuation reactions . . . is needed for both psychiatrists and family practice physicians." (J Clin Psychiatry 1997;58 Suppl &:28-30.) GSK disregarded this study by insisting that all physicians understand "discontinuation" and that no further labeling on Paxil withdrawal was needed.

72. In 1997, Zajecka and colleagues reported on discontinuation reactions suffered by SSRI patients. The authors proposed a definition for antidepressant discontinuation syndrome, indicating it should indicate the "onset of a cluster of somatic and psychic symptoms following the discontinuation of an SRI (sic) and not attributable to other causes (e.g. concomitant medication, illness)." The authors further advised that the reactions include dizziness, light headedness, insomnia, fatigue, anxiety, agitation, nausea, headache, and sensory disturbance. The authors indicated that the syndrome may last up to 3 weeks and may be improved by restarting the antidepressant or starting an antidepressant with a similar pharmacologic profile. (J Clin Psychiatry 1997 Jul;58(7i):291-7.) GSK continued to ignore outside advice as it disregarded this report.

73. In 1997, Dahl and colleagues reported paroxetine withdrawal syndrome in a neonate. (Br J Psychiatry 1997 Oct;171:391-2.)

74. In 1998, Bryois and colleagues reported several cases of withdrawal syndrome, and further reported that paroxetine is the most fre-

quently cited antidepressant in the literature for such syndrome. The authors further recommended that SSRI treatment be stopped, as applicable, "progressively...over a period of several weeks." GSK refused to implement the required labeling instructions which would reflect this guidance.

75. In 1998, B.G. Pollock reported discontinuation reactions on Paxil patients. (J Clin Psychiatry 1998 Oct;59(10):535-7.) GSK took no action.

76. In 1998 Dr. Thompson of Southhampton reported on withdrawal reactions in antidepressant medications, citing paroxetine, fluoxetine, and sertraline. He discussed emerging complications in this medical area and their relevance. (J Clin Psychiatry 1998 Oct;59(10):541-8.)

77. In 1998, M.Z. Wincor of U.S.C. (Los Angeles) School of Pharmacy reported withdrawal syndrome associated with abrupt discontinuation of paroxetine; (J Am Pharm Assoc (Wash) 1998 Jul-Aug;38(4):500-1.) GSK took no action.

78. In 1998, Milliken and Cooper reported on 3 case studies of paroxetine patients suffering withdrawal including, in 2 cases, akathisia. 72 hours after discontinuation, withdrawal set in, including restlessness, palpitations, irritability and anxiety. One suffered increased anxiety, restlessness, muscle twitching and paresthesia. Withdrawal occurred in one patient notwithstanding that the patient had commenced lofepramine dosage.

79. In 1999, Bakker and colleagues reported severe withdrawal reactions with fever upon a patient discontinuing paroxetine treatment. (Ned Tijdschar Geneeskd 1999 Aug 28;143(35):1795.)

80. In 1999, Peeters and colleagues reported severe withdrawal reactions with fever during paroxetine tapering. The authors reported in regard to SSRI withdrawal, "such withdrawal symptoms are most prevalent after discontinuation of paroxetine, but can occur after use of all . . . (SSRI's) . . . ." (Ned Tijdsche Geneeskd 1999 Jul 3;143(27):1429-31.) GSK did nothing in response.

81. In 1999, Vergouwen and colleagues reported severe withdrawal reactions with fever by a patient upon stopping paroxetine. (Ned Tijdschr Geneeskd 1999 Aug 28; 143(35):1794-5, discussion 1995-6.) GSK failed to act on this report.

82. In 2000, Belloeuf and colleagues reported paroxetine withdrawal syndrome on their patient population. (Ann Med Interne (Paris) 2000 Apr;151SupplA:A52-3.)

83. Black and colleagues reported on SSRI discontinuation syndrome and proposed diagnostic criteria, further indicating that "paroxetine was the most frequently implicated" of the SSRI's.

84. In 2000, Dr. Fagan reported withdrawal syndrome on 2 patients who discontinued paroxetine. The author called such symptoms "numerous" and indicated that the syndrome is "not well known" and that it differs from the withdrawal syndrome caused by tricyclic antidepressants. (Tidsskr Nor Laegeforen 2000 Mar 20:120(8):913-4.) Dr. Fagan's comments amply demonstrate that Paxil's labeling is grossly inadequate. GSK refused to respond in any manner to this well reasoned analysis.

85. In 2000, Diler and colleagues reported withdrawal reactions associated with paroxetine discontinuation in a 9 year old boy. (J Clin Psychopharmacol 2000 Oct;20(5):586-7.) GSK refused to respond to this information.

86. In 2000, Dr. Haddad sounded the alarm on professional unawareness of the serious withdrawal problem, stating that there is widespread "misdiagnosis of antidepressant discontinuation symptoms" and that "increased professional awareness of discontinuation symptoms is necessary to prevent misdiagnosis and inappropriate treatment." (Acta Psychiatri Scand 2000 Dec; 102(6):466-7; discussion 467-8.) GSK likewise refused to heed this report, continuing to withhold needed labeling changes regarding Paxil withdrawal.

87. In 2000, Hindmarch and colleagues concluded, with respect to a study involving four SSRIs, that cognitive and psychomotor performance was adversely affected after treatment was interrupted over 4-7 days. Particularly cited was paroxetine, in which it was stated abrupt discontinuation of treatment with paroxetine leads to deterioration in various aspects of health and functioning. The authors made clear their opinion that Paxil was the worst of all, stating that these effects "are not evident in patients receiving (Prozac), (Zoloft), and (Celexa), suggesting they are not an SSRI class phenomenon." (Int Clin Psychopharmacol 2000 Nov;15(6):305-18.) GSK refused to act on this report.

88. In 2001, Nijhuis and colleagues reported withdrawal reactions of a premature neonate after maternal use of paroxetine. (Arch Dis Child Fetal Neonatal Ed 2001 Jan;84(1):F77.) GSK took no action after this report.

89. In response to this extensive documented history of withdrawal reactions and dependency/withdrawal syndrome associated with Paxil and an ever increasing number of Paxil withdrawal complaints, GSK adopted a policy of strategic ambiguity. The policy is a public relations

ploy. The strategy recognizes that certain code words must be placed in the public arena to make it appear that GSK is confronting Paxil safety issues forthrightly. One tactic in that strategy is labeling "withdrawal" as "discontinuation." In this, GSK, attempts to nullify the negative connotation of "withdrawal" and redefines it with misleading terminology. This strategy is a fraud on its face. There is no word "discontinuation" in the medical dictionary. All medical dictionaries properly define "withdrawal" as the operative word to describe the condition. The American Psychiatric Association, the official authority on diagnosing such symptoms, likewise specifies "withdrawal" as the proper word.

90. The strategy of ambiguity extends to Paxil's labeling. Only the slightest hint of the withdrawal problem was noted in Paxil's initial labeling. GSK's proposal and its wording reflect an SSRI "class" warning and what FDA had earlier approved for Prozac and Zoloft. In that labeling, first issued on December 29, 1992, there was a great dispersal of adverse event data into various minute categories. There were over 60 central nervous system adverse symptoms listed, most dispersed into categories which were inaccurately classified as "rare" occurrences. "Drug dependence" and "withdrawal syndrome" were two (2) such "rare" symptoms.

91. On December 12, 1994, at the FDA's direction, GSK added the following label change in the "post marketing" section of the label. Notwithstanding, it was inadequate:

> "There have been spontaneous reports *that abrupt discontinuation* may lead to symptoms such as dizziness, sensory disturbances, agitation or anxiety, nausea and sweating; these events are generally self limiting."

92. In 2001, there was a minor change to the above warning in the "post marketing section" which read:

> "There have been spontaneous reports that *discontinuation (particularly when abrupt)* may lead to symptoms such as dizziness, sensory disturbances, agitation or anxiety, nausea and sweating; these events are generally self-limiting."

93. The above is woefully inadequate in light of what GSK has learned over the past 10 years, particularly since the drug has been on the market.

FIRST CLAIM FOR RELIEF
(Against All Defendants for Fraud and Deceit)

94. The allegations of each of the preceding and subsequent paragraphs are incorporated by reference as if fully set forth herein.

95. Defendant GSK, has since December 29, 1992, defrauded the medical profession in general and Plaintiffs' physicians in particular, and

the Paxil patient population in general and Plaintiffs in particular, in that it, among other acts:

(a) Knowingly mischaracterized and miscoded withdrawal syndrome occurring during the clinical trials so as to reduce the number of recorded occurrences of withdrawal reactions;

(b) Failed to inform the medical community that a significant number of individuals taking Paxil during foreign clinical trials experienced dependency/withdrawal syndrome;

(c) Knowingly misrepresented and continues to misrepresent that its clinical trials and investigations adequately tested for withdrawal syndrome;

(d) Knowingly claimed that Paxil's withdrawal problems were a relapse, when in fact they were not;

(e) Actively deceived Plaintiffs and class members by representations in written labeling and oral communications suggesting that Paxil is not addictive, that it does not cause physical or psychologic dependency, and that it would not cause withdrawal reactions if dosage were reduced or terminated.

(f) Answering the question: "Is *Paxil* addictive?" with the response: "*Paxil* has been studied both in short- and long-term use and is not associated with dependence or addiction."

(g) Implementing false and misleading techniques to hide the linkage between dependency/withdrawal syndrome on one hand, and Paxil on the other. After censoring the word "withdrawal" from company files and instructing its agents similarly, defendant, GSK,

began to dilute the medical vocabulary by using misleading medical terms to substitute for withdrawal such as "discontinuation syndrome."

(h) Over-promoting Paxil in order to increase its sale at the expense of revealing the truth about the addictive/dependency nature of Paxil.

(i) Fraudulently conveyed to all health care providers in the U.S. that Paxil's side effects were only "mild," when in fact GSK knew many of the drug's withdrawal side effects were severe.

(j) Fraudulently conveyed to all health care providers in the U.S. that a British study involving 13,741 patients illustrated that all of the SSRI's exhibited a similar rate of withdrawal reactions, when in fact GSK knew that study illustrated Paxil to have the highest rate of withdrawal reactions among SSRI's as recorded and reported by the authors.

96. As a result of GSK's fraudulent acts and omissions as set forth herein, GSK has deceived the medical community, including Plaintiffs' physicians, into believing Paxil does not have the addictive qualities and does not cause dependency/withdrawal syndrome which defendant GSK knows it in fact does.

97. When said representations were made by defendant GSK, it knew those representations to be false, or in the alternative, willfully and wantonly and recklessly disregarded whether the representations were true. These representations were made by said defendant, GSK, with the intent of defrauding and deceiving the public in general and the medical community and to induce the medical community to recommend, prescribe, and dispense Paxil and for the public to take it.

98. At the time the aforesaid representations were made by the defendant, GSK, and at the time that Plaintiffs ingested Paxil, both Plaintiffs and their prescribing physicians were unaware of the falsity of said representations and reasonably relied on GSK's assertions, promulgated through its aggressive sales force to Plaintiffs' physicians as set forth herein, that the drug was safe. In reliance upon said representations, Plaintiffs' physicians did prescribe Paxil and Plaintiffs were induced to and did take Paxil. Had Plaintiffs known of the actual dangers of Paxil, through their physicians or otherwise, they would not have ingested Paxil.

99. GSK's motive of deliberately failing to advise physicians and the public of the adverse effects that can lead to withdrawal problems (and that it knew a percentage of users of the drug inevitably would experience) was for financial gain and its fear that, if properly labeled the drug, Paxil would lose its share of the SSRI market through the efforts of competing manufacturers who would adversely compare GSK's half-life to their own. GSK's goal, at the expense of those who took its drug Paxil, was for Paxil to become the dominant SSRI on the market.

100. At all times relevant herein, the conduct of defendant GSK, as set forth hereinabove, was malicious, fraudulent and oppressive toward Plaintiffs and the public generally, and said defendant, GSK, conducted itself in a willful, wanton and reckless manner as set forth hereinabove. Despite its specific knowledge as set forth above, defendant GSK deliberately recommended, manufactured, produced, marketed, sold, distributed, merchandized, packaged, promoted and advertised the dangerous and defective drug Paxil. All of the foregoing constitute an utter, wanton and conscious disregard of the rights and safety of a large segment of the public, and by reason thereof, defendant GSK, is guilty of reckless, willful and wanton acts and omissions which evidence a total and conscious disregard for the safety of Plain-

tiffs and class members which proximately caused the injuries as set forth herein.

101. As a proximate result of defendant GSK's fraudulent and deceitful conduct and representations and due to Paxil's addictive qualities, inducement of physical and psychological dependency, and inducement of dependency/withdrawal syndrome, all Plaintiffs and class members unexpectedly suffered prolonged physical and mental anguish, harm, and suffering and have sustained damages and other losses in an amount to be proven at trial.

WHEREFORE, Plaintiffs pray judgment against defendants, and each of them, as hereinafter set forth.

SECOND CLAIM FOR RELIEF
(Against All Defendants for Negligence)

102. The allegations of each of the preceding and subsequent paragraphs are incorporated by reference as if fully set forth herein.

103. GSK owed Plaintiffs and class members a standard of care to ensure that they and their physicians were adequately warned of Paxil's addictive qualities and dependency/withdrawal characteristics before any were prescribed the drug. GSK violated that standard of care through active misrepresentations and failure to warn when it was GSK's duty to do so.

104. As a proximate result of defendant GSK's breach of its duty and due to Paxil's addictive qualities, inducement of physical and psychological dependency, and inducement of withdrawal syndrome, all Plaintiffs and class members proximately suffered prolonged physical and mental anguish, harm, and suffering. have sustained damages and other losses in an amount to be proven at trial.

WHEREFORE, Plaintiffs pray judgment against defendants, and each of them, as hereinafter set forth.

THIRD CLAIM FOR RELIEF
[Against All Defendants for Strict Liability Per § 402 Restatement (Torts)]

105. The allegations of each of the preceding and subsequent paragraphs are incorporated by reference as if fully set forth herein.

106. At all times herein mentioned, defendants knew or should have known that Paxil was and is addictive and causes withdrawal syndrome.

107. At all times hereinafter mentioned, neither members of the general medical community nor members of the general public knew of the withdrawal dangers existing with respect to the administration of Paxil.

108. Paxil was used by Plaintiffs and class members in the manner and amounts in which the defendants intended it to be used.

109. At all times material hereto, in the United States, Paxil was not properly labeled by defendants; in fact it was mislabeled and was not accompanied by proper warnings that Paxil can cause withdrawal reactions and dependency/withdrawal syndrome.

110. Defendants promoted and maintained Paxil on the market both to physicians and directly to patients/consumers with the knowledge of Paxil's unreasonable risk to the public in general, and specifically to Plaintiffs and class members.

111. Paxil, as used by Plaintiffs and class members, was defective and unreasonably dangerous when sold by defendants, and defendants are strictly liable for the injuries arising from its manufacture and Plaintiffs and class members' use.

112. As a direct and proximate result of the foregoing, Plaintiffs and class members sustained damages and other losses according to proof.

WHEREFORE, Plaintiffs pray judgment against defendants, and each of them, as hereinafter set forth.

FOURTH CLAIM FOR RELIEF
(Against All Defendants for Breach of Express Warranty)

113. The allegations of each of the preceding and subsequent paragraphs are incorporated by reference as if fully set forth herein.

114. At all times herein mentioned, Defendant GSK, utilized FDA proceedings, packaging, promotional materials and activities, and the advertising media to urge doctors, such as Plaintiffs' doctors, to prescribe Paxil, and patients, such as Plaintiffs, to purchase and use Paxil. GSK expressly warranted to physicians, to Plaintiffs, class members and the general public, that Paxil's association with "drug dependency" and "withdrawal syndrome" were "rare." As a result, Plaintiffs' physicians prescribed Paxil without any warning to the patients that Paxil could cause drug dependency and withdrawal syndrome.

115. GSK represented to the consumers who would use Paxil and to the physicians who would prescribe it—without full and complete disclosure of the risks of Paxil's side effects—that Paxil would not create

drug dependency and that "withdrawal syndrome" was "rare." This amounts to an express warranty.

116. GSK, knew, or in the exercise of reasonable diligence should have known, that Paxil has serious side effects and can cause serious withdrawal reactions and dependency/withdrawal syndrome and that the occurrences are not "rare," but rather frequent.

117. Plaintiffs and their physicians relied on the express warranty representations of GSK, in the use of Paxil, but GSK breached its warranty because Paxil can and frequently does cause severe withdrawal reactions and dependency/withdrawal syndrome.

118. As a direct and proximate result of the breach of express warranty by GSK, Plaintiffs and class members sustained damages and other losses according to proof.

WHEREFORE, Plaintiffs pray judgment against defendants, and each of them, as hereinafter set forth.

FIFTH CLAIM FOR RELIEF
(Against All Defendants for Breach of Implied Warranty)

119. The allegations of each of the preceding and subsequent paragraphs are incorporated by reference as if fully set forth herein.

120. GSK, through Paxil's labeling, implied that Paxil was at least fit for the ordinary purposes as stated in its labeling. It was not because the promises and affirmations on the labeling stated that drug dependency and withdrawal syndrome were "rare." That was false. They were frequent, thus victimizing Plaintiffs and class members. Accordingly, the implied warranty was breached.

121. As a direct and proximate result of the breach of implied warranty by GSK, Plaintiffs and class members sustained damages and other losses according to proof.

WHEREFORE, Plaintiffs pray judgment against defendants, and each of them, as hereinafter set forth.

PRAYER

WHEREFORE, Plaintiffs pray judgment against defendants, and each of them, as follows:

1. For an order certifying that this action may be maintained as a class action against defendants, appointing Plaintiff and her counsel to represent the Class, and directing that reasonable notice of this action be given by defendants to the members of the Class;

2. For damages in an amount to be determined at trial, and awarding prejudgment interest at the maximum rate allowable by law;

3. For punitive damages, according to proof;

4. For prejudgment interest as allowed by law;

5. For reasonable attorneys' fees, accountants' fees, and other experts' fees;

6. For the costs of their suit; and

7. For such other and further relief as this Court may deem just and proper.

Dated: August 23, 2001 ______________________________

Karen A. Barth, Esq.
BAUM, HEDLUND, ARISTEI, GUILFORD & SCHIAVO
and
Donald J. Farber, Esq.
LAW OFFICES OF DONALD J. FARBER

Attorneys for Plaintiffs

DEMAND FOR JURY TRIAL

The above Plaintiffs hereby demand a trial by jury in this action.

Dated: August 23, 2001 ______________________________

Karen A. Barth, Esq.
BAUM, HEDLUND, ARISTEI, GUILFORD & SCHIAVO
and
Donald J. Farber, Esq.
LAW OFFICES OF DONALD J. FARBER

Attorneys for Plaintiffs

GLOSSARY

Abstract of Judgment—A document issued by the clerk of the court. When recorded at the county recorder, it places a lien on any real property owned by the judgment debtor in that county.

Abuse of Process—The improper and malicious use of the criminal or civil process.

Accord and Satisfaction—Accord and satisfaction refers to the payment of money, or other thing of value, which is usually less than the amount owed or demanded, in exchange for extinguishment of the debt.

Acknowledgment of Satisfaction of Judgment—A form that the judgment creditor must complete, sign, and file with the court when the judgment is fully paid.

Action at Law—A judicial proceeding whereby one party prosecutes another for a wrong done.

Actionable—Giving rise to a cause of action.

Actual Damages—Actual damages are those damages directly referable to the breach or tortious act, and which can be readily proven to have been sustained, and for which the injured party should be compensated as a matter of right.

Adjournment—To put off a court hearing until another time or place.

Adjudicate—When a judge hears and decides a case.

Adjudication—The judge's decision in a case or action.

Admissible Evidence—Evidence that can legally and properly be used in court.

Admission—A statement that certain facts are true.

Adversary System—The system of trial practice in the United States and some other countries in which each of the opposing parties has the opportunity to present and establish opposing positions before the court.

Adverse Witness—A person called to testify for the other side.

Affidavit—A written statement that someone swears to under oath in front of someone that is legally authorized, like a judge or notary public.

Affirm—To make a solemn statement.

Affirmative Defense—In a pleading, a matter constituting a defense.

Allegation—A statement or claim that is made and hasn't been proved to be true or false.

Allege—To state that something is true even though it hasn't yet been proven.

Alternative Dispute Resolution (ADR)—Methods of resolving disputes without official court proceedings, including mediation and arbitration.

Amend—To add to or change a claim that has been filed in court.

American Arbitration Association (AAA)—National organization of arbitrators from whose panel arbitrators are selected for labor and civil disputes.

Answer—In a civil proceeding, the principal pleading on the part of the defendant in response to the plaintiff's complaint.

Appeal—New hearing of all of the claims by a higher court.

Appearance—To come into court, personally or through an attorney, after being summoned.

Appellant—Someone that appeals a court's decision.

Appellate Court—A court that can review the decisions of a lower court.

Appellee—A person that answers an appeal in higher court.

Application for Waiver of Court Fees and Costs—A form to be completed by a party who desires the court to waive a filing fee or court costs.

Arbitration—The reference of a dispute to an impartial person chosen by the parties to the dispute who agree in advance to abide by the arbitrator's award issued after a hearing at which both parties have an opportunity to be heard.

Arbitration Clause—A clause inserted in a contract providing for compulsory arbitration in case of a dispute as to the rights or liabilities under such contract.

Arbitrator—A private, disinterested person, chosen by the parties to a disputed question, for the purpose of hearing their contention, and awarding judgment to the prevailing party.

Asset—The entirety of a person's property, either real or personal.

Assignee—A person or business that stands in the place of the original creditor, such as a collection agency.

Attachment—The act or process of taking, apprehending, or seizing persons or property, by virtue of a writ, summons, or other judicial order, and bringing the same into the custody of the court for the purpose of securing satisfaction of the judgment ultimately to be entered in the action.

Attachment Execution—A name given in some states to a process of garnishment for the satisfaction of a judgment.

Bad Faith—A willful failure to comply with one's statutory or contractual obligations.

Bank Levy—Enforcement of a judgment against the judgment debtor's checking or savings account at a bank, savings association, or credit union, or other financial institution.

Breach of Contract—The failure, without any legal excuse, to perform any promise which forms the whole or the part of a contract.

Burden of Proof—The duty of a party to substantiate an allegation or issue to convince the trier of fact as to the truth of their claim.

Calendar—A list of all the cases in each courtroom every day.

Caption—The title of the case which appears at the top of all papers given to the court, including the name of the case, the court, and the case file or index number.

Cause of Action—The charges that make up the case or lawsuit.

Capacity—Capacity is the legal qualification concerning the ability of one to understand the nature and effects of one's acts.

Cause of Action—The factual basis for bringing a lawsuit.

Chambers—The judge's office.

Civil Action—An action maintained to protect a private, civil right as opposed to a criminal action.

Civil Court—The court designed to resolve disputes arising under the common law and civil statutes.

Civil Law—Law which applies to noncriminal actions.

Circumstantial Evidence—Indirect evidence not based on actual personal knowledge or observation of the facts in dispute.

Claim of Exemption—A document filed by the judgment debtor that lists the property that the judgment debtor claims is exempt and therefore can't be taken to pay the judgment.

Class Action—A means by which, where a large group of persons are interested in a matter, one or more may sue or be sued as representatives of the class without needing to join every member of the class.

Clean Hands Doctrine—The concept that claimants who seek equitable relief must not themselves have indulged in any impropriety in relation to the transaction upon which relief is sought.

Collateral—Property which is pledged as additional security for a debt, such as a loan.

Complaint—The legal document setting for the plaintiff's allegations against the defendant and a request for damages.

Confession of Judgment—An admission of a debt by the debtor which may be entered as a judgment without the necessity of a formal legal proceeding.

Consequential Damages—Consequential damages are those damages which are caused by an injury, but which are not a necessary result of the injury, and must be specially pleaded and proven in order to be awarded.

Costs—Certain fees and charges a party pays to file and present a case or to enforce a judgment.

Counterclaim—The part of the response that says why the Plaintiff owes the Defendant money or property.

Court—The branch of government responsible for the resolution of disputes arising under the laws of the government.

Creditor—A person to whom a debt is owing by a debtor.

Cross-claim—A demand by the defendant against the plaintiff. The cross-claim is usually heard at the same hearing as the plaintiff's claim. It need not relate to the plaintiff's claim.

Cross-examination—The testimony a witness gives when the opposing side is asking the questions at a trial.

Damages—In general, damages refers to monetary compensation which the law awards to one who has been injured by the actions of another, such as in the case of tortious conduct or breach of contractual obligations.

Debt—A sum of money due by a certain or express agreement.

Debtor—One who owes a debt, payment or other performance of the obligation secured, whether or not he owns or has rights in the collateral.

Default—Failure of a party to the lawsuit who was properly notified of the action to attend the court hearing.

Default Judgment—A decision entered when one party doesn't attend the court hearing.

Defendant—In a civil proceeding, the party responding to the complaint.

Defense—Opposition to the truth or validity of the plaintiff's claims.

Demand for Arbitration—A unilateral filing of a claim in arbitration based on the filer's contractual or statutory right to do so.

Deposition—Written or oral testimony given under oath in front of an authorized third person like a court reporter.

Discovery—The gathering of information before a case goes to trial through the use of depositions, interrogatories, or requests for admissions.

Dismiss With Prejudice—To set aside the present action and deny the right to file another suit on that claim.

Dismiss Without Prejudice—To set aside the present action but leave open the possibility of another suit on the same claim.

Docket—A record with the complete chronological history of each case a court hears.

Due Process—The individual's right to notice and opportunity to be heard and to defend oneself in an orderly proceeding adapted to the nature of the case, and the guarantee that every man have protection of day in court and benefit of general law.

Enforce—To put the judgment into effect by taking legal steps to bring about compliance.

Execution—Carrying out some act or course of conduct to its completion. Execution upon a money judgment is the legal process of enforcing the judgment, usually by seizing and selling property of the debtor.

Exempt Assets—Property of a judgment debtor that is legally protected.

Exemption—A privilege allowed by law to a judgment debtor, by which he may hold property to a certain amount or certain classes of property, free from all liability to levy and sale on execution or attachment.

Federal Rules of Civil Procedure—Body of procedural rules which govern all civil actions in U.S. District Courts and after which most of the states have modeled their own rules of procedure.

File—When a person officially gives a paper to a court clerk and that paper becomes part of the record of a case.

Filing Fees—Money paid to the court clerk to file court papers and start a civil case.

Fraud—A false representation of a matter of fact, whether by words or by conduct, by false or misleading allegations, or by concealment of that which should have been disclosed, which deceives and is intended to deceive another, and thereby causes injury to that person.

Fraudulent Conveyance—The transfer of property for the purpose of delaying or defrauding creditors.

Garnish—To attach the wages or property of an individual.

Garnishee—A person who receives notice to hold the assets of another, which are in his or her possession, until such time as a court orders the disposition of the property.

Garnishment—A legal process that allows part of a person's wages and/or assets to be withheld for payment of a debt.

General Damages—General damages are those damages directly referable to the breach or tortious act and which can be readily proven to have been sustained, and for which the injured party should be compensated as a matter of right.

Grace Period—In contract law, a period specified in a contract which is beyond the due date but during which time payment will be accepted without penalty.

Good Cause—A sufficient reason.

Guardian ad litem—A person appointed by the court to represent a minor or incompetent adult.

Guarantor—An individual or company that has agreed to be responsible for the acts or omissions of another.

Guaranty—An agreement to perform in the place of another if that person reneges on a promise contained in an underlying agreement.

Homestead—The house, outbuilding, and land owned and used as a dwelling by the head of the family.

Homestead Exemption—Laws passed in most of the states allowing a householder or head of a family to designate a house and land as his homestead and exempt the same homestead from execution for his general debts.

Impound—To place property in the custody of an official.

In Rem—Refers to actions that are against property, and concerned with the disposition of that property, rather than against the person.

Indemnification Clause—An indemnification clause in a contract refers to the agreement by one party to secure the other party against loss or damage which may occur in the future in connection with performance of the contract.

Indemnify—To hold another harmless for loss or damage which has already occurred, or which may occur in the future.

Injunction—A judicial remedy either requiring a party to perform an act, or restricting a party from continuing a particular act.

Injury—Any damage done to another's person, rights, reputation or property.

Judge—The individual who presides over a court, and whose function it is to determine controversies.

Judgment—A judgment is a final determination by a court of law concerning the rights of the parties to a lawsuit.

Judgment Creditor—A creditor who has obtained a judgment against a debtor, which judgment may be enforced to obtain payment of the amount due.

Judgment Debtor—An individual who owes a sum of money, and against whom a judgment has been awarded for that debt.

Judgment Debtor's Statement of Assets—A form listing the judgment debtor's assets and sources of income.

Judgment Execution—The formal or written evidence of the judgment which commands the officer to seize the goods and property of the judgment debtor to satisfy the judgment.

Judgment Proof—Refers to the status of an individual who does not have the financial resources or assets necessary to satisfy a judgment.

Lead Plaintiff—The class representative who is named in the lawsuit on behalf of the class; also referred to as a named plaintiff.

Legal Capacity—Referring to the legal capacity to sue, it is the requirement that a person bringing the lawsuit have a sound mind, be of lawful age, and be under no restraint or legal disability.

Levy—To seize property in order to satisfy a judgment.

Liability—Liability refers to one's obligation to do or refrain from doing something, such as the payment of a debt.

Lien—A claim against the property of another as security for a debt.

Malicious Abuse of Legal Process—Wilfully misapplying court process to obtain object not intended by law.

Mechanic's Lien—A claim created by law for the purpose of securing a priority of payment of the price of work performed and materials furnished.

Mediation—A process in which a neutral third person helps the parties in a dispute discuss their problem and work out their own mutually acceptable solution.

Mediator—A neutral third person who helps disputants arrive at their own settlement. The mediator doesn't decide the dispute.

Motion—A request to the court.

Multidistrict Litigation—The transfer of civil actions involving one or more common questions of fact, which are pending in several different federal district courts, to one district for coordinated and consolidated management and trial under a single judge.

Net Income—Gross income less deductions and exemptions proscribed by law.

Net Worth—The difference between one's assets and liabilities.

Nominal Damages—A trivial sum of money which is awarded as recognition that a legal injury was sustained, although slight.

Notary Public—A person whose most common function is to certify the signature of an individual.

Notice of Appeal—A request for a new trial of the a claim in a higher court.

Notice of Entry of Judgment—A form notifying the parties of the judge's decision in the lawsuit.

Notice of Motion to Vacate Judgment—A request that asks the court to cancel a judgment that was entered and to hold a new hearing.

Numerosity—In a class action, refers to the number of potential class members being so large that joinder of the claims would be impracticable.

Objection—A formal protest made by a party over testimony or evidence that the other side tries to introduce.

Order to Appear for Examination—A court order instructing the judgment debtor to appear in court at a specified date and time to answer questions about his or her property and sources of income.

Parties—The disputants.

Pecuniary—A term relating to monetary matters.

Perjury—A false statement made on purpose while under oath in a court proceeding.

Personal Jurisdiction—The power of a court over the person of a defendant.

Personal Service—Handing a copy of court papers directly to the person to be served.

Plaintiff—The person or entity who files the lawsuit.

Pro Tem Judge—Temporary judge.

Process—Court papers that notify a person that he or she is being sued.

Process Server—A person who serves court papers on a party to a suit.

Proof of Service—A form that must be completed by the person serving court papers on a party, stating that service was properly made.

Reformation—An equitable remedy which calls for the rewriting of a contract involving a mutual mistake or fraud.

Release—A document signed by one party, releasing claims he or she may have against another party, usually as part of a settlement agreement.

Repudiation—In contract law, refers to the declaration of one of the parties to the contract that he or she will not perform under the contract.

Request for Dismissal—A form filed with the court if a settlement or agreement is made between the parties before the case is heard.

Rescission—The cancellation of a contract which returns the parties to the positions they were in before the contract was made.

Response—Also referred to as an Answer, Defendant's statement as to why the claim is not true or is inaccurate as to amount.

Restitution—The act of restoring or giving the equivalent value to compensate for an injury, damage, or loss.

Satisfaction—The discharge and release of an obligation.

Service by Publication—When service of process is done by publishing a notice in a newspaper after a court determines that other means of service are impractical or have been unsuccessful.

Service of Process—The delivery of legal court documents, such as a complaint, to the defendant.

Settlement—An agreement by the parties to a dispute on a resolution of the claims, usually requiring some mutual action, such as payment of money in consideration of a release of claims.

Statute of Limitations—Any law which fixes the time within which parties must take judicial action to enforce rights or thereafter be barred from enforcing them.

Stay—A judicial order suspending some action until further court order lifting the stay.

Stipulation—An admission or agreement made by parties to a lawsuit concerning the pending matter.

Subpoena—A court issued document compelling the appearance of a witness before the court.

Subpoena Duces Tecum—A court issued document requiring a witness to produce certain documents in his or her possession or control.

Substitute Service—Service of process on a party by leaving the court papers with someone other than a party to the lawsuit.

Summons—The portion of the Complaint which informs the Defendant when and where to appear.

Tangible Property—Property which is capable of being possessed, whether real or personal.

Tax—A sum of money assessed upon one's income, property and purchases, for the purpose of supporting the government.

Tax Court—A federal administrative agency which acts as a court for the purposes of determining disputes between individuals and the Internal Revenue Service.

Tenancy at Will—The right to occupy property for an indefinite period of time.

Tenant—A person that rents property.

Tort—A private or civil wrong.

Tortfeasor—A person that commits or is found guilty of a tort.

Transcript—A written record of what was said at a trial.

Trial—The judicial procedure whereby disputes are determined based on the presentation of issues of law and fact. Issues of fact are decided by the trier of fact, either the judge or jury, and issues of law are decided by the judge.

Trial Court—The court of original jurisdiction over a particular matter.

Trial Date—The date that the Plaintiff and Defendant must appear in Court.

Unconscionable—Refers to a bargain so one-sided as to amount to an absence of meaningful choice on the part of one of the parties, together with terms which are unreasonably favorable to the other party.

Undue Influence—The exertion of improper influence upon another for the purpose of destroying that person's free will in carrying out a particular act, such as entering into a contract.

Usurious Contract—A contract that imposes interest at a rate which exceeds the legally permissible rate.

Usury—An excessive rate of interest above the maximum permissible rate established by the state legislature.

Venue—The particular court in which an action may properly be brought.

Vitiate—To make void.

Void—Having no legal force or binding effect.

Voidable—Capable of being rendered void and unenforceable.

Waive—To abandon or give up a claim or a right.

Writ of Execution—A document that directs the sheriff to enforce a judgment.

BIBLIOGRAPHY AND ADDITIONAL RESOURCES

Black's Law Dictionary, Fifth Edition. St. Paul, MN: West Publishing Company, 1979.

The Federal Judicial Center (Date Visited: October 2004) <http://www.fjc.gov/>

Federal Trade Commission (FTC) (Date Visited: October 2004) <http://www.ftc.gov/>

Findlaw (Date Visited: October 2004) <http://www.findlaw.com/>

The Legal Information Institute (Date Visited: October 2004) <http://www.law.cornell.edu/>

New York State Laws, New York State Assembly (Date Visited: October 2004) <http://assembly.state.ny.us/leg/>

Thomas: Legislative Information on the Internet (Date Visited: October 2004) <http://thomas.loc.gov/>

U.S. Food and Drug Administration (FDA) (Date Visited: October 2004) <http://www.fda.gov/>

U.S. Securities and Exchange Commission (SEC) (Date Visited: October 2004) <http://www.sec.gov/>